篮球规则

2020

中国篮球协会 审定

北京体育大学出版社

责任编辑：曾　莉
责任校对：吴海燕
版式设计：李　鹤

图书在版编目（CIP）数据

篮球规则. 2020 / 中国篮球协会审定. -- 北京：
北京体育大学出版社, 2020.12（2021.11重印）
　ISBN 978-7-5644-3392-5

　Ⅰ.①篮… Ⅱ.①中… Ⅲ.①篮球运动－竞赛规则
Ⅳ.①G841.4

中国版本图书馆CIP数据核字(2020)第210293号

| 篮球规则 2020 | LANQIU GUIZE 2020 | 中国篮球协会　审定 |

出版发行：北京体育大学出版社
地　　址：北京海淀区农大南路1号院2号楼2层办公B-212
邮　　编：100084
网　　址：http://cbs.bsu.edu.cn
发 行 部：010-62989320
邮 购 部：北京体育大学出版社读者服务部 010-62989432
印　　刷：河北盛世彩捷印刷有限公司
开　　本：880mm×1230mm　　1/32
成品尺寸：145mm×210mm
印　　张：8.25
字　　数：218千字
版　　次：2020年12月第1版
印　　次：2021年11月第3次印刷
定　　价：59.00元

本书如有印装质量问题，请与出版社联系调换

版权所有·侵权必究

编委会

主　任　姚　明
委　员　叶庆晖
翻　译　曾洪涛
审　定　马立军　陈梦熊　宁日辉
　　　　　温克明　周江安　靳　茁
　　　　　乔龙升

篮球规则2020
（英文版）

篮球规则2020
（彩色标示英文版）

篮球器材2020
（英文版）

出版说明

- 《篮球规则 2020》是中国篮球协会依照国际篮球联合会（简称"国际篮联"）发布的 *Official Basketball Rules 2020* 翻译和修订，2020年10月1日在世界范围内开始生效执行。今后所有正式国际篮球比赛和国内篮球比赛，以及各类篮球裁判员晋级考试，均按本规则执行。

- 《篮球规则 2020》的翻译和编订力求忠实于原文。如在理解和执行过程中出现争议，以国际篮联官方语言英文版为准。翻译和审校工作可能存在疏漏之处，欢迎广大读者提出意见和建议，以便我们及时修订和完善。

- 整本《篮球规则 2020》中所有提到的教练员、运动员、技术官员等都是男性，同样也适用于女性。必须理解到，这样写只是为了实用的缘故。

TABLE OF CONTENTS

PART ONE   OFFICIAL BASKETBALL RULES *2020*

RULE ONE — THE GAME
    Art. 1   Definitions   / 2

RULE TWO — PLAYING COURT AND EQUIPMENT
    Art. 2   Playing court   / 2
    Art. 3   Equipment   / 14

RULE THREE — TEAMS
    Art. 4   Teams   / 16
    Art. 5   Players: Injury and assistance   / 22
    Art. 6   Captain: Duties and powers   / 22
    Art. 7   Head coach and first assistant coach: Duties and powers   / 24

RULE FOUR — PLAYING REGULATIONS
    Art. 8   Playing time, tied score and overtime   / 28
    Art. 9   Beginning and end of a quarter, overtime or the game   / 28
    Art. 10   Status of the ball   / 30
    Art. 11   Location of a player and a referee   / 32
    Art. 12   Jump ball and alternating possession   / 34
    Art. 13   How the ball is played   / 38

目 录

第一部分　篮球规则 2020

第一章　比 赛
第1条　定　义 / 3

第二章　比赛场地和器材
第2条　比赛场地 / 3
第3条　器　材 / 15

第三章　球　队
第4条　球　队 / 17
第5条　队员：受伤和协助 / 23
第6条　队长：职责和权力 / 23
第7条　主教练和第一助理教练：职责和权力 / 25

第四章　比赛通则
第8条　比赛时间、比分相等和决胜期 / 29
第9条　比赛或节、决胜期的开始和结束 / 29
第10条　球的状态 / 31
第11条　队员和裁判员的位置 / 33
第12条　跳球和交替拥有 / 35
第13条　如何打球 / 39

- Art. 14 Control of the ball / 38
- Art. 15 Player in the act of shooting / 40
- Art. 16 Goal: When made and its value / 42
- Art. 17 Throw-in / 42
- Art. 18 Time-out / 48
- Art. 19 Substitution / 52
- Art. 20 Game lost by forfeit / 56
- Art. 21 Game lost by default / 56

RULE FIVE — VIOLATIONS

- Art. 22 Violations / 58
- Art. 23 Player out-of-bounds and ball out-of-bounds / 58
- Art. 24 Dribbling / 60
- Art. 25 Travelling / 62
- Art. 26 3 seconds / 64
- Art. 27 Closely guarded player / 64
- Art. 28 8 seconds / 66
- Art. 29 24 seconds / 68
- Art. 30 Ball returned to the backcourt / 72
- Art. 31 Goaltending and Interference / 74

RULE SIX — FOULS

- Art. 32 Fouls / 78
- Art. 33 Contact: General principles / 78
- Art. 34 Personal foul / 92
- Art. 35 Double foul / 94
- Art. 36 Technical foul / 96
- Art. 37 Unsportsmanlike foul / 100
- Art. 38 Disqualifying foul / 102
- Art. 39 Fighting / 106

第14条　控制球 / 39
第15条　队员正在做投篮动作 / 41
第16条　球中篮和它的得分值 / 43
第17条　掷球入界 / 43
第18条　暂　停 / 49
第19条　替　换 / 53
第20条　比赛因弃权告负 / 57
第21条　比赛因缺少队员告负 / 57

第五章　违　例

第22条　违　例 / 59
第23条　队员出界和球出界 / 59
第24条　运　球 / 61
第25条　带球走 / 63
第26条　3秒钟 / 65
第27条　被严密防守的队员 / 65
第28条　8秒钟 / 67
第29条　24秒钟 / 69
第30条　球回后场 / 73
第31条　干涉得分和干扰得分 / 75

第六章　犯　规

第32条　犯　规 / 79
第33条　身体接触：一般原则 / 79
第34条　侵人犯规 / 93
第35条　双方犯规 / 95
第36条　技术犯规 / 97
第37条　违反体育运动精神的犯规 / 101
第38条　取消比赛资格的犯规 / 103
第39条　打　架 / 107

RULE SEVEN — GENERAL PROVISIONS

Art. 40 5 fouls by a player / 110
Art. 41 Team fouls: Penalty / 110
Art. 42 Special situations / 110
Art. 43 Free throws / 114
Art. 44 Correctable errors / 118

RULE EIGHT — REFEREES, TABLE OFFICIALS, COMMISSIONER: DUTIES AND POWERS POWERS

Art. 45 Referees, table officials and commissioner / 124
Art. 46 Crew chief: Duties and powers / 124
Art. 47 Referees : Duties and powers / 126
Art. 48 Scorer and assistant scorer: Duties / 130
Art. 49 Timer: Duties / 132
Art. 50 Shot clock operator: Duties / 134

A — REFEREES' SIGNALS / 140
B — THE SCORESHEET / 156
C — PROTEST PROCEDURE / 180
D — CLASSIFICATION OF TEAMS / 184
E — MEDIA TIME-OUTS / 208
F — INSTANT REPLAY SYSTEM / 210

第七章 一般规定

第40条 队员5次犯规 / 111

第41条 全队犯规：处罚 / 111

第42条 特殊情况 / 111

第43条 罚　球 / 115

第44条 可纠正的失误 / 119

第八章 裁判员、记录台人员和技术代表：职责和权力

第45条 裁判员、记录台人员和技术代表 / 125

第46条 主裁判员：职责和权力 / 125

第47条 裁判员：职责和权力 / 127

第48条 记录员和助理记录员：职责 / 131

第49条 计时员：职责 / 133

第50条 进攻计时员：职责 / 135

A —— 裁判员的手势 / 141

B —— 记录表 / 157

C —— 申诉程序 / 181

D —— 球队的名次排列 / 185

E —— 媒体暂停 / 209

F —— 即时回放系统 / 211

第二部分　篮球器材 *2020*

前　言 / 218
1　篮球架 / 219
2　篮球 / 226
3　记录屏/视频显示屏 / 227
4　比赛计时钟 / 230
5　进攻计时钟 / 230
6　信号 / 232
7　队员犯规标示牌 / 232
8　全队犯规标示牌 / 232
9　交替拥有指示器 / 233
10　比赛地板 / 233
11　比赛场地 / 235
12　照明 / 236
13　哨音计时控制系统 / 241
14　口哨 / 244
15　广告板 / 242
16　观众区域 / 245
17　参考 / 247

第一部分

Official Basketball Rules 2020
篮球规则 2020

RULE ONE — THE GAME

Art. 1 Definitions

1.1 Basketball game

Basketball is played by 2 teams of 5 players each. The aim of each team is to score in the opponents' basket and to prevent the other team from scoring.

The game is controlled by the referees, table officials and a commissioner, if present.

1.2 Basket: opponents'/own

The basket that is attacked by a team is the opponents' basket and the basket which is defended by a team is its own basket.

1.3 Winner of a game

The team that has scored the greater number of game points at the end of playing time shall be the winner.

RULE TWO — PLAYING COURT AND EQUIPMENT

Art. 2 Playing court

2.1 Playing court

The playing court shall have a flat, hard surface free from obstructions (Diagram 1) with dimensions of 28 m in length by 15 m in width measured from the inner edge of the boundary line.

2.2 Backcourt

A team's backcourt consists of its team's own basket, the inbounds part of the backboard and that part of the playing court limited by the endline behind its own basket, the sidelines and the centre line.

篮球规则 2020

第一章　比　赛

第 1 条　定　义

1.1　篮球比赛
　　篮球比赛由 2 队参加，每队出场 5 名队员。每队的目标是进攻对方球篮得分，并阻止对方队得分。
　　比赛由裁判员、记录台人员和技术代表（如到场）管控。

1.2　球篮：对方/本方
　　被某队进攻的球篮是对方的球篮，由某队防守的球篮是该队的本方球篮。

1.3　比赛的胜者
　　比赛时间结束时比赛得分较多的队，是比赛的胜者。

第二章　比赛场地和器材

第 2 条　比赛场地

2.1　比赛场地
　　比赛场地应是一块平坦、无障碍物的硬质地面（图1）。其尺寸是长28米、宽15米，从界线的内沿丈量。

2.2　后　场
　　某队的后场由该队本方的球篮、篮板的界内部分，以及由该队本方球篮后面的端线、两条边线和中线所界定的比赛场地部分组成。

OFFICIAL BASKETBALL RULES *2020*

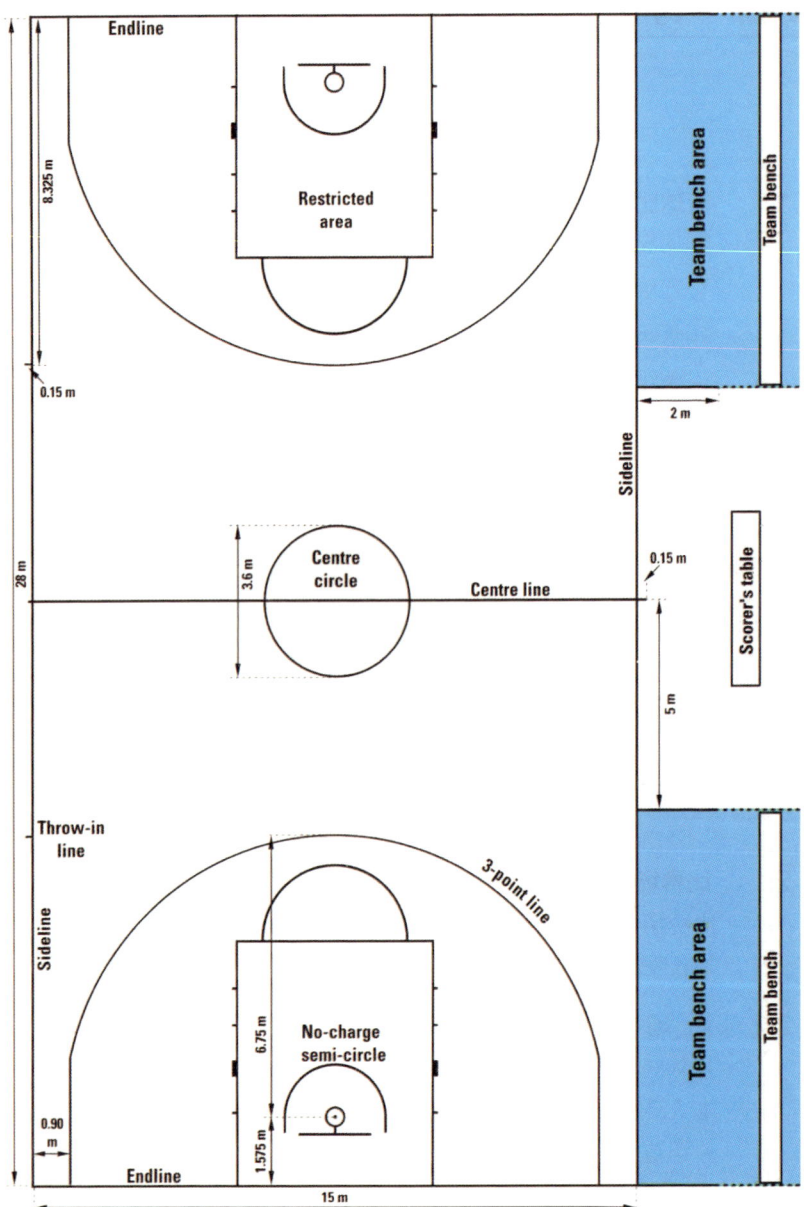

Diagram 1   Full size playing court

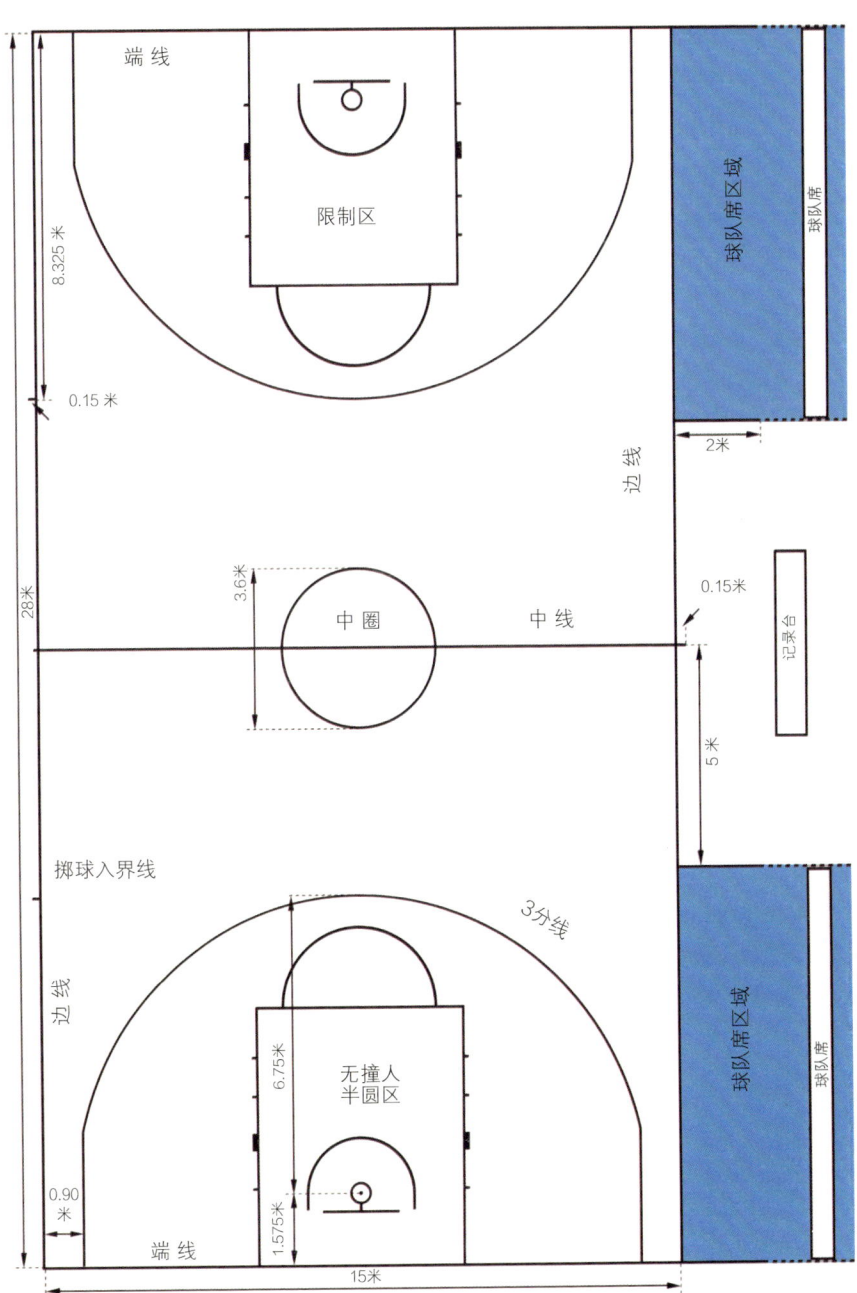

图1　比赛场地的全部尺寸

2.3 Frontcourt

A team's frontcourt consists of the opponents' basket, the inbounds part of the backboard and that part of the playing court limited by the endline behind the opponents' basket, the sidelines and the inner edge of the centre line nearest to the opponents' basket.

2.4 Lines

All lines shall be of the same colour and drawn in white or other contrasting colour, 5 cm in width and clearly visible.

2.4.1 Boundary line

The playing court shall be limited by the boundary line, consisting of the endlines and the sidelines. These lines are not part of the playing court.

Any obstruction including seated head coach, first assistant coach, substitutes, excluded players and accompanying delegation members shall be at least 2 m from the playing court.

2.4.2 Centre line, centre circle and free-throw semi-circles

The centre line shall be marked parallel to the endlines from the mid-point of the sidelines. It shall extend 0.15 m beyond each sideline. The centre line is part of the backcourt.

The centre circle shall be marked in the centre of the playing court and have a radius of 1.80 m measured to the outer edge of the circumference.

The free-throw semi-circles shall be marked on the playing court with a radius of 1.80 m measured to the outer edge of the circumference and with their centres at the mid-point of the free-throw lines (Diagram 2).

2.4.3 Free-throw lines, restricted areas and free-throw rebound places

The free-throw line shall be drawn parallel to each endline. It shall have its furthest edge 5.80 m from the inner edge of the endline and shall be 3.60 m long. Its mid-point shall lie on the imaginary line joining the mid-point of the 2 endlines.

The restricted areas shall be the rectangular areas marked on the playing court limited by the endlines, the extended free-throw lines and the lines which originate at the endlines, their outer edges being 2.45 m from the mid-point of the endlines and terminating at the outer edge of the extended free-throw lines. These lines, excluding the endlines, are part of the restricted area.

2.3 前场

某队的前场由对方的球篮、篮板的界内部分，以及对方球篮后面的端线、两条边线和距离对方球篮最近的中线内沿所界定的比赛场地部分组成。

2.4 线

所有的线应颜色相同，且应用白色或其他能明显区分的颜色画出，宽5厘米并清晰可见。

2.4.1 界线

比赛场地由两条端线和两条边线组成的界线所限定。这些线不是比赛场地的部分。

任何障碍物包括在球队席就座的主教练、第一助理教练、替补队员、出局的队员和随队人员，距离比赛场地应至少2米。

2.4.2 中线、中圈和罚球半圆

中线应从两条边线的中点画出并平行于两条端线。它向每条边线外延伸0.15米。中线是后场的一部分。

中圈应画在比赛场地的中央，半径为1.80米（从圆周的外沿丈量）。

两个罚球半圆应画在比赛场地上，半径是1.80米（从圆周的外沿丈量），它的圆心在两条罚球线的中点上。（图2）

2.4.3 罚球线、限制区和抢篮板球分位区

罚球线应画成与每条端线平行。从端线内沿到它的最外沿应是5.80米，其长度是3.60米。它的中点应落在连接2条端线中点的假想线上。

限制区应是画在比赛场地上的一个长方形区域，它由端线、延长的罚球线和起自端线（外沿距离端线中点2.45米）终于延长的罚球线外沿的线所限定。除了端线外，这些线都是限制区的一部分。

OFFICIAL BASKETBALL RULES *2020*

Free-throw rebound places along the restricted areas, reserved for players during free throws, shall be marked as in Diagram 2.

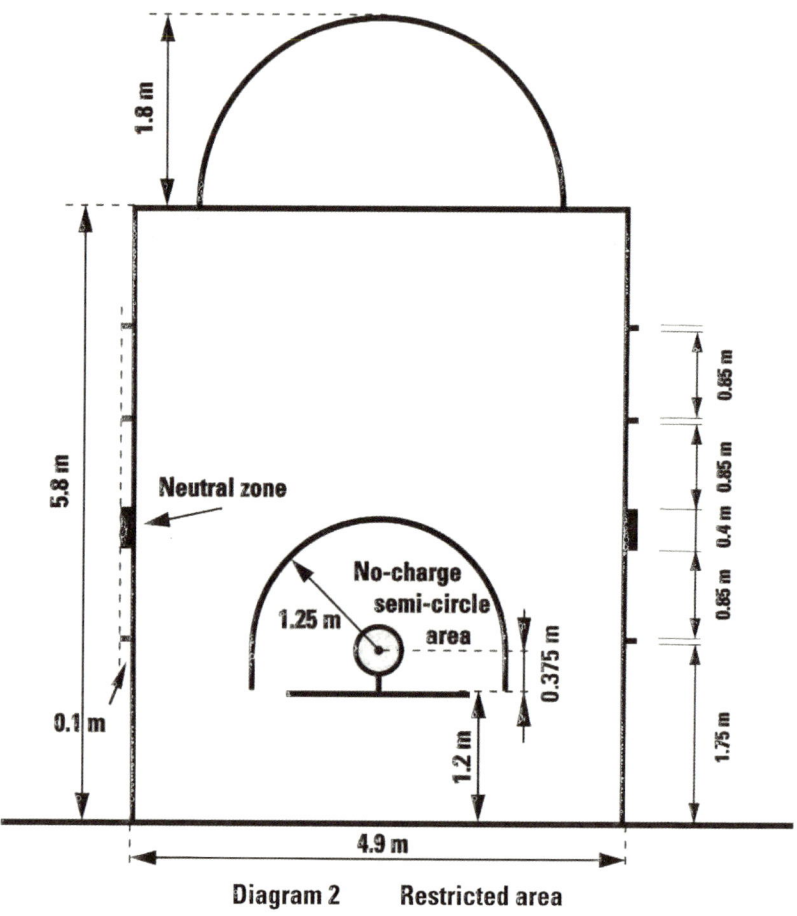

Diagram 2   Restricted area

篮球规则 *2020*

罚球时留给队员们的沿限制区两侧的抢篮板球分位区，应按图2标出。

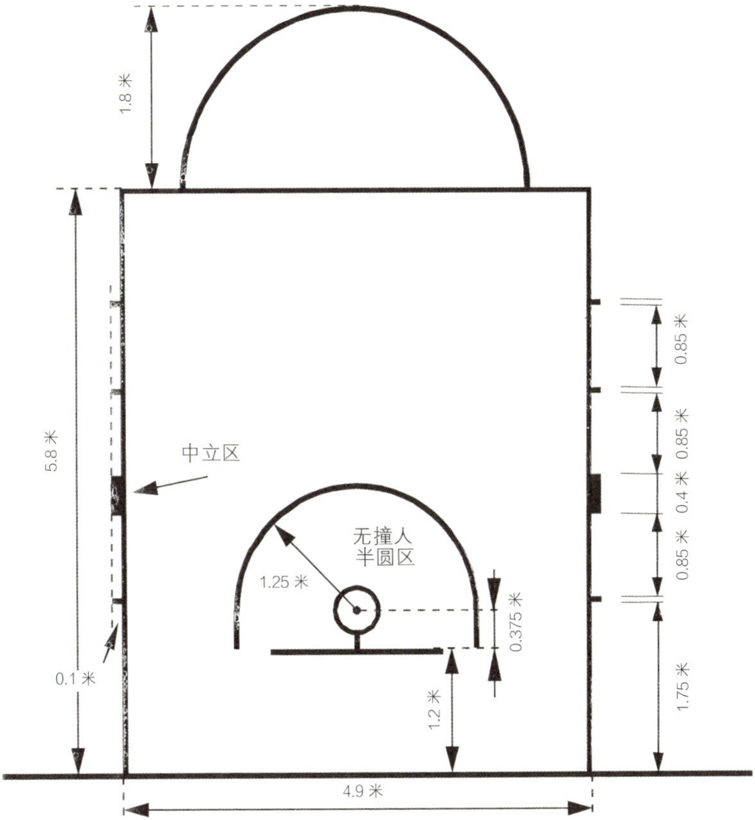

图2 限 制 区

2.4.4 3-point field goal area

The team's 3-point field goal area (Diagram 1 and Diagram 3) shall be the entire floor area of the playing court, except for the area near the opponents' basket, limited by and including:

- The 2 parallel lines extending from and perpendicular to the endline, with the outer edge 0.90 m from the inner edge of the sidelines.
- An arc of radius 6.75 m measured from the point on the floor beneath the exact centre of the opponents' basket to the outer edge of the arc. The distance of the point on the floor from the inner edge of the mid-point of the endline is 1.575 m. The arc is joined to the parallel lines.

The 3-point line is not part of the 3-point field goal area.

2.4.5 Team bench areas

The team bench areas shall be marked outside the playing court limited by 2 lines as in Diagram 1.

There must be 16 seats available in each team bench area for the head coach, the assistant coaches, the substitutes, the excluded players and the accompanying delegation members. Any other persons shall be at least 2 m behind the team bench.

2.4.6 Throw-in lines

The 2 lines of 0.15 m in length shall be marked outside the playing court at the sideline opposite the scorer's table, with the outer edge of the lines 8.325 m from the inner edge of the nearest endline.

2.4.7 No-charge semi-circle areas

The no-charge semi-circle areas shall be marked on the playing court, limited by:

- A semi-circle with the radius of 1.25 m measured from the point on the floor beneath the exact centre of the basket to the inner edge of the semi-circle. The semi-circle is joined to:
- The 2 parallel lines perpendicular to the endline, the inner edge 1.25 m from the point on the floor beneath the exact centre of the basket, 0.375 m in length and ending 1.20 m from the inner edge of the endline.

The no-charge semi-circle areas are completed by imaginary lines joining the ends of the parallel lines directly below the front edges of the backboards.

The no-charge semi-circle lines are part of the no-charge semi-circle areas.

2.4.4　3分投篮区域

某队的3分投篮区域（图1、图3）是除对方球篮附近被下述条件限制的区域之外的整个比赛场地的地面区域。

这些条件包括：

- 从端线引出的2条垂直于端线的平行线，其外沿距离边线的内沿0.90米。
- 以对方球篮中心正下方场地上的点为圆心，画一个半径（圆弧外沿）是6.75米的圆弧。此圆心距离端线中点的内沿是1.575米，且该圆弧与两平行线相交。

3分线不是3分投篮区域的一部分。

2.4.5　球队席区域

球队席区域应由2条线在场外画出。（图1）

球队席区域内必须有16个座位提供给双方球队席的主教练、助理教练、替补队员、出局的队员和随队人员。任何其他人员应在球队席后面至少2米处。

2.4.6　掷球入界线

2条0.15米长的掷球入界线应画在记录台对侧、比赛场地外的边线上，其外沿距离最近端线内沿是8.325米。

2.4.7　无撞人半圆区

无撞人半圆区应在场地上画出，其界线是：

- 以球篮中心正下方的场地上的点为圆心，半径（半圆内沿）为1.25米的半圆。
- 与端线垂直的2条平行线，内沿距球篮中心正下方的场地上的点距离是1.25米，其长度是0.375米，距离端线内沿1.2米。

无撞人半圆区由与篮板前沿平行的假想线和上述平行线末端连接封闭构成。

无撞人半圆区的界线是无撞人半圆区的一部分。

OFFICIAL BASKETBALL RULES *2020*

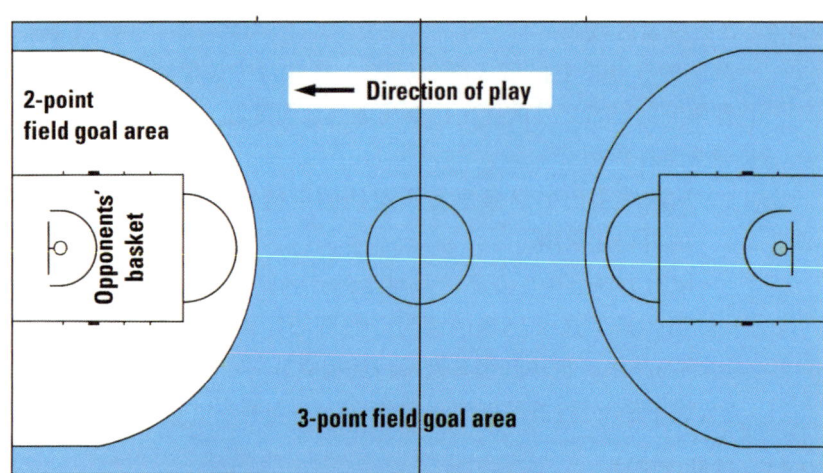

Diagram 3   2-point/3-point field goal area

2.5   Position of the scorer's table and substitution chairs (Diagram 4)

- 1 = Shot clock operator
- 2 = Timer
- x = Substitution chairs
- 3 = Commissioner, if present
- 4 = Scorer
- 5 = Assistant scorer

The scorer's table and its chairs must be placed on a platform. The announcer and/or statisticians (if present) can be seated at the side of and/or behind the scorer's table.

Diagram 4   Scorer's table and substitution chairs

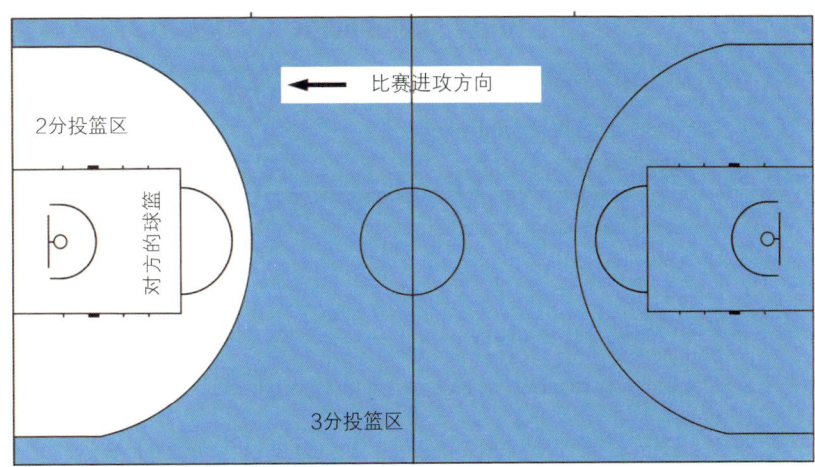

图3 2分和3分投篮区

2.5 记录台和替换椅子的位置（图4）

1=进攻计时员　　3=技术代表（如到场）
2=计时员　　　　4=记录员
X=替换椅子　　　5=助理记录员

记录台和它的椅子必须设在一个平台上。比赛解说员和（或）统计员（如到场）可坐在记录台的一侧和（或）后面。

图4 记录台和替换椅子

Art. 3 Equipment

The following equipment shall be required:

- Backstop units, consisting of:
  - Backboards.
  - Baskets comprising (pressure release) rings and nets.
  - Backboard support structures including padding.
- Basketballs.
- Game clock.
- Scoreboard.
- Shot clock.
- Stopwatch or suitable (visible) device (not the game clock) for timing time-outs.
- 2 separate, distinctly different and loud signals, one of each for the
  - shot clock operator,
  - timer.
- Scoresheet.
- Player foul markers.
- Team foul markers.
- Alternating possession arrow.
- Playing floor.
- Playing court.
- Adequate lighting.

For a more detailed description of basketball equipment, see the Appendix on Basketball Equipment.

第3条　器　材

下列器材是必需的：
- 挡件，包括：
    - ——篮板。
    - ——含有抗压篮圈和篮网的球篮。
    - ——篮板支撑构架（包括包扎物）。
- 篮球。
- 比赛计时钟。
- 记录屏。
- 进攻计时钟。
- 供暂停计时用的计秒表或适宜的（可见的）装置（不是比赛计时钟）。
- 2个独立的、显然不同的、非常响亮的声响信号，分别提供给：
    - ——进攻计时员。
    - ——计时员。
- 记录表。
- 队员犯规标志牌。
- 全队犯规标志牌。
- 交替拥有指示器。
- 比赛地板。
- 比赛场地。
- 足够的照明。

对篮球器材更详细的描述见本书"第二部分：篮球器材 *2020*"。

RULE THREE — TEAMS

Art. 4   Teams

4.1   Definition

4.1.1   A team member is eligible to play when he has been authorised to play for a team according to the regulations, including regulations governing age limits, of the organising body of the competition.

4.1.2   A team member is entitled to play when his name has been entered on the scoresheet before the beginning of the game and as long as he has neither been disqualified nor committed 5 fouls.

4.1.3   During playing time, a team member is:
- A player when he is on the playing court and is entitled to play.
- A substitute when he is not on the playing court but he is entitled to play.
- An excluded player when he has committed 5 fouls and is no longer entitled to play.

4.1.4   During an interval of play, all team members entitled to play are considered as players.

4.2   Rule

4.2.1   Each team shall consist of:
- No more than 12 team members entitled to play, including a captain.
- A head coach.
- A maximum of 8 accompanying delegation members, including a maximum of 2 assistant coaches who may sit on the team bench. In case a team has assistant coaches, the first assistant coach shall be entered on the scoresheet.

4.2.2   During playing time 5 team members from each team shall be on the playing court and may be substituted.

4.2.3   A substitute becomes a player and a player becomes a substitute when:
- The referee beckons the substitute to enter the playing court.
- During a time-out or an interval of play, a substitute requests the substitution to the timer.

第三章 球 队

第 4 条 球 队

4.1 定 义

4.1.1 当一名球队成员按照竞赛组织部门的规程（包括年龄限制）已被批准为某队参赛时，他是合格参赛的球队成员。

4.1.2 当一名球队成员的姓名在比赛开始前已被登记在记录表上，并且他既没有被取消比赛资格，又没有发生5次犯规，是有资格参赛的球队成员。

4.1.3 在比赛时间内，一名球队成员：
- 当他在比赛场地上，并且有资格参赛时，是一名队员。
- 当他未在比赛场地上，但他有资格参赛时，是一名替补队员。
- 当他已发生5次犯规，并且不再有资格参赛时，是一名出局的队员。

4.1.4 在比赛休息期间，所有有资格参赛的球队成员，都被认为是队员。

4.2 规 定

4.2.1 每个队应按下列要求组成：
- 不超过12名有资格参赛的球队成员，包括一名队长。
- 一名主教练。
- 最多 8 名随队人员（包含最多 2 名助理教练）可坐在球队席。如果球队有多名助理教练，第一助理教练应登记在记录表上。

4.2.2 在比赛时间内，每队应有 5 名队员在场上并可被替换。

4.2.3 一名替补队员成为队员和一名队员成为替补队员：
- 当裁判员招呼替补队员进入比赛场地时。
- 在暂停或比赛休息期间，一名替补队员向计时员请求替换时。

OFFICIAL BASKETBALL RULES *2020*

4.3 Uniforms

4.3.1 The uniform of all team members shall consist of:
- Shirts of the same dominant colour front and back as the shorts. If shirts have sleeves they must end above the elbow. Long sleeved shirts are not permitted. All players must tuck their shirts into their playing shorts. 'All-in-ones' are permitted.
- T-shirts, regardless of the style, are not permitted to be worn under the shirts.
- Shorts of the same dominant colour front and back as the shirts. The shorts must end above the knee.
- Socks of the same dominant colour for all team members. Socks need to be visible.

4.3.2 Each team member shall wear a shirt numbered on the front and back with plain numbers, of a colour contrasting with the colour of the shirt.
The numbers shall be clearly visible and:
- Those on the back shall be at least 20 cm high.
- Those on the front shall be at least 10 cm high.
- The numbers shall be at least 2 cm wide.
- Teams may only use numbers 0 and 00 and from 1 to 99.
- Players on the same team shall not wear the same number.
- Any advertising or logo shall be at least 5 cm away from the numbers.

4.3.3 Teams must have a minimum of 2 sets of shirts and:
- The first team named in the schedule (home team) shall wear light-coloured shirts (preferably white).
- The second team named in the schedule (visiting team) shall wear dark-coloured shirts.
- However, if the 2 teams agree, they may interchange the colours of the shirts.

4.4 Other equipment

4.4.1 All equipment used by players must be appropriate for the game. Any equipment that is designed to increase a player's height or reach or in any other way give an unfair advantage is not permitted.

4.4.2 Players shall not wear equipment (objects) that may cause injury to other players.
- The following are **not permitted**:
  — Finger, hand, wrist, elbow or forearm guards, helmets, casts or braces

4.3 服 装

4.3.1 所有球员的服装应符合下述要求:
- 背心和短裤一样,前后的主要颜色相同。如果背心带有袖子,袖子不能超过肘,不允许穿着长袖背心。所有队员必须把背心塞进比赛短裤内。允许穿着连体的服装。
- 无论什么类型的T恤,都不允许穿在背心里面。
- 短裤和背心一样,前后的主色与背心相同,但短裤必须高于膝盖。
- 所有球员穿着与主色相同的短袜,袜子必须是可见的。

4.3.2 每一球员应穿前后有号码的背心,其清楚的单色号码的颜色与背心的颜色有明显的区别。号码应清晰可见,并且:
- 后背的号码应至少高20厘米。
- 前胸的号码应至少高10厘米。
- 号码应至少宽2厘米。
- 球队仅可以使用0、00和1~99的号码。
- 同队队员不应佩戴相同的号码。
- 任何广告或标志离号码应至少5厘米。

4.3.3 球队必须至少有2套背心,并且:
- 竞赛日程表中队名列前的队(主队)应穿浅色背心(最好是白色)。
- 竞赛日程表中队名列后的队(客队)应穿深色背心。
- 但是,如果两队同意,他们可以互换背心的颜色。

4.4 其他装备

4.4.1 队员使用的所有装备必须合乎比赛要求。任何被设计成增加队员高度或延伸范围的,或用任何其他方法得到不正当利益的装备是不允许的。

4.4.2 队员不应佩戴可能使其他队员受伤的装备(物品)。
- 下列物品**不允许**:
—— 手指、手、手腕、肘或前臂部位的护具、头盔、模件或

made of leather, plastic, pliable (soft) plastic, metal or any other hard substance, even if covered with soft padding.
— Objects that could cut or cause abrasions (fingernails must be closely cut).
— Hair accessories and jewellery.

- The following are **permitted**:
  — Shoulder, upper arm, thigh or lower leg protective equipment if sufficiently padded.
  — Arm and leg compression sleeves.
  — Headgear. It shall not cover any part of the face entirely or partially (eyes, nose, lips etc.) and shall not be dangerous to the player wearing it and/or to other players. The headgear shall not have opening/closing elements around the face and/or neck and shall not have any parts extruding from its surface.
  — Knee braces.
  — Protector for an injured nose, even if made of a hard material.
  — Non-coloured transparent mouth guard.
  — Spectacles, if they do not pose a danger to other players.
  — Wristbands and headbands, maximum of 10 cm wide textile material.
  — Taping of arms, shoulders, legs etc.
  — Ankle braces.

All players on the team must have all their arm and leg compression sleeves, headgear, wristbands, headbands and tapings of the same solid colour.

4.4.3 During the game a player may wear shoes of any colour combination, but the left and right shoe must match. No flashing lights, reflective material or other adornments are permitted.

4.4.4 During the game a player may not display any commercial, promotional or charitable name, mark, logo or other identification including, but not limited to, on his body, in his hair or otherwise.

4.4.5 Any other equipment not specifically mentioned in this article must be approved by the FIBA Technical Commission.

保护套，它们由皮革、塑料、软塑料、金属或任何其他坚硬的物质制造，即使表面有软的包扎。
—— 能割破或引起擦伤的物品（指甲必须剪短）。
—— 头发饰物和珠宝饰物。

- 下列物品**是允许**的：
—— 肩、上臂、大腿或小腿部位的保护装备，如果其被充分地包裹了。
—— 弹力护臂和护腿。
—— 头饰。黑色、白色或者与上衣主色相同的头饰，但同队所有队员必须颜色一致。头饰不允许完全或部分地遮住脸部的任何部位（如眼、鼻、嘴唇等），并且不允许对佩戴它的队员和/或其他队员造成危险。头饰不允许在头部和/或颈部有结合口，也不允许在其表面任何部位有突出物。
—— 膝关节保护架。
—— 伤鼻保护器，即使是用硬质材料制成。
—— 无色透明的牙套。
—— 不会对其他队员造成危险的眼镜。
—— 腕带和头带，最宽10厘米。
—— 用于手臂、肩部、腿部等处的弹力贴。
—— 护踝。

球队所有队员的弹力护臂和护腿、头饰、腕带、头带及弹力贴必须是相同且单一的颜色。

4.4.3　球鞋可以使用任何颜色组合，但是左右两只鞋必须一致。闪烁的光源、反光材料或其他装饰都是不允许的。

4.4.4　比赛中，任何商业广告、促销产品或慈善团体的名称、标记、徽标或其他标识，包括上面提到的但不限于这些，都不允许显示在队员的肢体上、头发中或其他部位上。

4.4.5　本条中没有明确提到的任何其他装备，必须被国际篮联技术委员会批准。

Art. 5 Players: Injury and assistance

5.1 In the event of injury to a player(s), the referees may stop the game.

5.2 If the ball is live when an injury occurs, the referee shall not blow his whistle until the team in control of the ball has shot for a field goal, lost control of the ball, withheld the ball from play or the ball has become dead. If it is necessary to protect an injured player, the referees may stop the game immediately.

5.3 If the injured player cannot continue to play immediately (within approximately 15 seconds) or if he receives treatment or if a player receives any assistance from his own head coach, assistant coaches, team members and/or accompanying delegation members, he must be substituted unless the team is reduced to fewer than 5 players on the playing court.

5.4 Head coach, assistant coaches, substitutes, excluded players and accompanying delegation members may enter the playing court, only with the permission of a referee, to attend to an injured player before he is substituted.

5.5 A doctor may enter the playing court, without the permission of a referee if, in the doctor's judgement, the injured player requires immediate medical treatment.

5.6 During the game, any player who is bleeding or has an open wound must be substituted. He may return to the playing court only after the bleeding has stopped and the affected area or open wound has been completely and securely covered.

5.7 If the injured player or any player who is bleeding or has an open wound, recovers during a time-out taken by either team, before the timer's signal for the substitution, that player may continue to play.

5.8 Players who have been designated by the head coach to begin the game or who receive treatment between free throws may be substituted in the event of an injury. In this case, the opponents are also entitled to substitute the same number of players, if they so wish.

Art. 6 Captain: Duties and powers

6.1 The captain (**CAP**) is a player designated by his head coach to represent his team on the playing court. He may communicate in a courteous manner with the referees during the game to obtain information only when the ball is dead and the game clock is stopped.

第 5 条　队员：受伤和协助

5.1　如果队员受伤，裁判员可以停止比赛。

5.2　如果球是活球时发生了受伤情况，裁判员应等到控制球队投篮、失去控制球、持球停止进攻或球成死球时才可以鸣哨。但是，当有必要去保护受伤队员时，裁判员可以立即停止比赛。

5.3　如果受伤队员不能立即（大约15秒）继续比赛，或者接受了治疗，或者接受了任何本队的主教练、助理教练、球队成员和/或随队人员的协助，他必须被替换，除非该队能够上场的队员少于5名。

5.4　主教练、助理教练、替补队员、出局的队员和随队人员，只有经裁判员允许方可进入比赛场地，在受伤队员被替换前照料他。

5.5　如果医生判断受伤队员需要即时治疗，医生不经裁判员允许可进入比赛场地。

5.6　比赛期间，正在流血或有伤口的队员必须被替换。该队员只有在流血已经停止，并且受伤部位或伤口已被全面安全地包扎后，才可返回比赛场地。

5.7　如果在计时员发出替换信号之前，任一队获得了暂停，在此期间，受伤队员或任何一名正在流血或有伤口的队员恢复了，该队员可以继续比赛。

5.8　因为受伤，已经被主教练指定为比赛开始时上场的队员，或罚球之间接受治疗的队员可以被替换。在这种情况下，如果对方也希望替换，他们有权替换相同数量的队员。

第 6 条　队长：职责和权力

6.1　队长（**CAP**）是一名由主教练指定的在比赛场地上代表他的球队的队员。在比赛期间，队长可与裁判员联系以获得信息，但是做此举要有礼貌，而且只能在球成死球和比赛计时钟停止时进行。

6.2 The captain shall inform the crew chief no later than 15 minutes following the end of the game, if his team is protesting against the result of the game and sign the scoresheet in the 'Captain's signature in case of protest' column.

Art. 7 Head coach and first assistant coach: Duties and powers

7.1 At least 40 minutes before the game is scheduled to begin, each head coach or his representative shall give the scorer a list with the names and corresponding numbers of the team members who are eligible to play in the game, as well as the name of the captain of the team, the head coach and the first assistant coach. All team members whose names are entered on the scoresheet are entitled to play, even if they arrive after the beginning of the game.

7.2 At least 10 minutes before the game is scheduled to begin, each head coach shall confirm his agreement with the names and corresponding numbers of his teammembers and the names of the head coach and first assistant coach by signing the scoresheet. At the same time, the head coach shall indicate the 5 players to begin the game. The head coach of team 'A' shall be the first to provide this information.

7.3 The head coaches, assistant coaches, substitutes, excluded players and accompanying delegation members are the only persons permitted to sit on the team bench and remain within their team bench area. During playing time all substitutes, excluded players and accompanying delegation members shall remain seated.

7.4 The head coach or the first assistant coach may go to the scorer's table during the game to obtain statistical information only when the ball becomes dead and the game clock is stopped.

7.5 The head coach may communicate in a courteous manner with the referees during the game to obtain information only when the ball is dead and the game clock is stopped.

7.6 Either the head coach or the first assistant coach, but only one of them at any given time, is permitted to remain standing during the game. They may address the players verbally during the game provided they remain within their team bench area. The first assistant coach shall not communicate with the referees.

7.7 If there is a first assistant coach, his name must be entered on the scoresheet before the beginning of the game (his signature is not necessary). He shall assume all duties and powers of the head coach if, for any reason, the head coach is unable to continue.

6.2 如果球队申诉比赛的结果，队长应在比赛结束后15分钟内立即通知主裁判员并在记录表上标有"球队申诉队长签名"栏内签名。

第 7 条 主教练和第一助理教练：职责和权力

7.1 至少在预定的比赛开始前40分钟，每位主教练或他的代表应将该场比赛中合格的参赛球队成员的姓名和相应的号码，以及球队的队长、主教练和第一助理教练的名单提交给记录员。所有在记录表上填入姓名的球队成员有权参加比赛，即使他们在比赛开始后才到达。

7.2 至少在预定的比赛开始前10分钟，每位主教练应以在记录表上签字来确认已填入的他们球队成员的姓名、相应号码，以及主教练和第一助理教练的姓名。同时，主教练应指明比赛首发的5名队员，主队（A队）主教练应首先提供这个名单。

7.3 只允许主教练、助理教练、替补队员、出局的队员、随队人员坐在球队席或停留在他们的球队席区域内。比赛期间，所有替补队员、出局的队员和随队人员必须保持坐着。

7.4 主教练或第一助理教练可在比赛期间去记录台以获得统计资料，但是只能在球成死球和比赛计时钟停止时。

7.5 主教练可以在比赛期间礼貌地与裁判员交流以获取信息，但是只能在球成死球和比赛计时钟停止时。

7.6 只允许主教练或者第一助理教练其中一人在比赛期间保持站立。在比赛期间，他们可与队员们讲话，只要他们停留在他们的球队席区域内。第一助理教练不得与裁判员交流。

7.7 如果有第一助理教练，他的名字必须在比赛开始前填入记录表内（不需要他签字）。如果主教练因任何原因不能继续工作，第一助理教练应承担主教练的所有职责并行使其所有权力。

7.8 If the captain leaves the playing court, the head coach shall inform a referee of the number of the player who shall act as captain on the playing court.

7.9 The captain shall act as player coach if there is no head coach, or if the headcoach is unable to continue and there is no first assistant coach entered on the scoresheet (or the latter is unable to continue). If the captain must leave the playing court, he may continue to act as head coach. If he must leave following a disqualifying foul, or if he is unable to act as head coach because of injury, his substitute as captain may replace him as head coach.

7.10 The head coach shall designate the free-throw shooter of his team in all cases where the free-throw shooter is not determined by the rules.

7.8 当队长离开比赛场地时，主教练应通知裁判员担任场上队长的队员号码。

7.9 如果没有主教练，或者主教练不能继续工作，并且记录表内没有登记第一助理教练（或第一助理教练不能继续工作），队长应担任队员兼主教练。如果队长必须离开比赛场地，他可以继续担任主教练。如果队长在取消比赛资格的犯规后必须离开，或如果他因为受伤不能担任主教练，替换他的队员替代他当主教练。

7.10 在规则没有限定罚球队员的所有情况中，主教练应指定本队的罚球队员。

RULE FOUR — PLAYING REGULATIONS

Art. 8 Playing time, tied score and overtime

8.1 The game shall consist of 4 quarters of 10 minutes each.

8.2 There shall be an interval of play of 20 minutes before the game is scheduled to begin.

8.3 There shall be the intervals of play of 2 minutes between the first and second quarter (first half), between the third and fourth quarter (second half) and before each overtime.

8.4 There shall be a half-time interval of play of 15 minutes.

8.5 An interval of play begins:
- 20 minutes before the game is scheduled to begin.
- When the game clock signal sounds for the end of the quarter or overtimes.

8.6 An interval of play ends:
- At the beginning of the first quarter when the ball leaves the hand(s) of the crew chief on the toss for the jump ball.
- At the beginning of all other quarters and overtimes when the ball is at the disposal of the player taking the throw-in.

8.7 If the score is tied at the end of the fourth quarter, the game shall continue with as many overtimes of 5 minutes duration each as necessary to break the tie.

If the aggregated score of both games for a 2-games home and away total points series competition system is tied at the end of the second game, this game shall continue with as many overtimes of 5 minutes duration each as necessary to break the tie.

8.8 If a foul is committed during an interval of play, any eventual free throw(s) shall be administered before the beginning of the following quarter or overtime.

Art. 9 Beginning and end of a quarter, overtime or the game

9.1 The first quarter begins when the ball leaves the hand(s) of the crew chief on the toss for the jump ball in the centre circle.

9.2 All other quarters or overtimes begin when the ball is at the disposal of the player taking the throw-in.

第四章 比赛通则

第 8 条 比赛时间、比分相等和决胜期

8.1 比赛应由4节组成，每节10分钟。

8.2 在预定的比赛开始时间之前，应有20分钟的比赛休息期间。

8.3 在第1节和第2节（上半时）之间，第3节和第4节（下半时）之间，以及每一决胜期之前，应有2分钟的比赛休息期间。

8.4 两个半时之间的比赛休息期间应是15分钟。

8.5 一次比赛休息期间开始于：
- 预定的比赛开始时间之前20分钟。
- 结束一节或决胜期的比赛计时钟信号响时。

8.6 一次比赛休息期间结束于：
- 第1节开始，在跳球抛球中，当球离开主裁判员的手时。
- 所有其他节和决胜期的开始，当掷球入界队员可处理球时。

8.7 如果在第4节比赛结束时比分相等，比赛有必要再继续若干个5分钟的决胜期来打破平局。
对于主客场总得分制的系列比赛，如果在第2场比赛的第4节比赛结束时，两队两场比赛得分的总和相等，比赛有必要再继续若干个5分钟的决胜期来打破平局。

8.8 如果一起犯规发生在比赛休息期间，在下一节或决胜期比赛开始之前应执行最后的罚球。

第 9 条 比赛或节、决胜期的开始和结束

9.1 在中圈跳球抛球中，当球离开主裁判员的手时第1节开始。

9.2 所有其他节和决胜期比赛，当掷球入界队员可处理球时，该节开始。

9.3 The game cannot begin if one of the teams is not on the playing court with 5 players ready to play.

9.4 For all games, the first team named in the schedule (home team) shall have the team bench and its own basket on the left side of the scorer's table, facing the playing court.

However, if the 2 teams agree, they may interchange the team benches and/or baskets.

9.5 Before the first and third quarter, teams are entitled to warm-up in the half of the playing court in which their opponents' basket is located.

9.6 Teams shall exchange baskets for the second half.

9.7 In all overtimes the teams shall continue to play towards the same baskets as in the fourth quarter.

9.8 A quarter, overtime or game shall end when the game clock signal sounds for the end of the quarter or overtime. When the backboard is equipped with red lighting around its perimeter, the lighting takes precedence over the game clock signal sound.

Art. 10 Status of the ball

10.1 The ball can be either live or dead.

10.2 The ball becomes live when:
- During the jump ball, the ball leaves the hand(s) of the crew chief on the toss.
- During a free throw, the ball is at the disposal of the free-throw shooter.
- During a throw-in, the ball is at the disposal of the player taking the throw-in.

10.3 The ball becomes **dead** when:
- Any field goal or free throw is made.
- A referee blows his whistle while the ball is live.
- It is apparent that the ball will not enter the basket on a free throw which is to be followed by:
  — Another free throw(s).
  — A further penalty (free throw(s) and/or possession).
- The game clock signal sounds for the end of the quarter or overtime.
- The shot clock signal sounds while a team is in control of the ball.

9.3 如果某一队在比赛场地上准备比赛的队员不足5名，比赛不能开始。

9.4 对所有的比赛，在竞赛日程表中队名列前的队（主队）应拥有记录台（面对比赛场地）左侧的球队席和本方球篮。
然而，如果两队同意，他们可互换球队席和/或球篮。

9.5 在第1节和第3节前，球队有权在对方的球篮所在的半场做赛前准备活动。

9.6 球队下半时应交换球篮。

9.7 在所有的决胜期中，球队应继续进攻与第4节比赛方向相同的球篮。

9.8 当结束比赛时间的比赛计时钟信号响时，一节、决胜期或比赛应结束。当篮板四周装有红色光带时，光带信号亮先于比赛计时钟信号响。

第10条 球的状态

10.1 球可以是活球或死球。

10.2 球成**活球**，当：
- 跳球中，球离开主裁判员抛球的手时。
- 罚球中，罚球队员可处理球时。
- 掷球入界中，掷球入界队员可处理球时。

10.3 球成**死球**，当：
- 任何投篮或罚球中篮时。
- 活球中，裁判员鸣哨时。
- 在一次罚球中球明显不会进入球篮，且该次罚球后接着有：
  —— 另一次或多次罚球时。
  —— 进一步的罚则（罚球和/或掷球入界）时。
- 比赛计时钟信号响以结束一节或决胜期时。
- 某队控制球，进攻计时钟信号响时。

- The ball in flight on a shot for a field goal is touched by a player from either team after:
  — A referee blows his whistle.
  — The game clock signal sounds for the end of the quarter or overtime.
  — The shot clock signal sounds.

10.4 The ball does not become dead and the goal counts if made when:

- The ball is in flight on a shot for a field goal and:
  — A referee blows his whistle.
  — The game clock signal sounds for the end of the quarter or overtime.
  — The shot clock signal sounds.
- The ball is in flight on a free throw and a referee blows his whistle for any rule infraction other than by the free-throw shooter.
- The ball is in the control of a player in the act of shooting for a field goal who finishes his shot with a continuous motion which started before a foul is charged on any opponents' player or on any person permitted to sit on the opponents' team bench.

  This provision does not apply, and the goal shall not count if:
  — After a referee blows his whistle and an entirely new act of shooting is made.
  — During the continuous motion of a player in the act of shooting the game clock signal sounds for the end of the quarter or overtime or the shot clock signal sounds.

Art. 11 Location of a player and a referee

11.1 The location of a player is determined by where he is touching the floor.

While he is airborne, he retains the same status he had when he last touched the floor. This includes the boundary line, the centre line, the 3-point line, the free-throw line, the lines delimiting the restricted area and the lines delimiting the no-charge semi-circle area.

11.2 The location of a referee is determined in the same manner as that of a player. When the ball touches a referee, it is the same as touching the floor at the referee's location.

- 投篮中飞行的球在下述情况后被任一队的队员触及时：
  —— 裁判员鸣哨。
  —— 比赛计时钟信号响以结束一节或决胜期。
  —— 进攻计时钟信号响。

10.4 球不成死球，如中篮计得分，当：
- 投篮的球在飞行中，并且：
  —— 裁判员鸣哨。
  —— 比赛计时钟信号响以结束一节或决胜期。
  —— 进攻计时钟信号响。
- 罚球的球在飞行中，并且裁判员因除罚球队员之外的任何规则违犯而鸣哨。
- 进攻队员正在做投篮动作并控制着球时，判罚了对方队任何队员或被允许坐在对方队球队席的任何人员的犯规，该投篮队员以连续动作完成了犯规发生前已开始的投篮。

如果：
  —— 在裁判员鸣哨后做了一个全新的投篮动作。
  —— 一名队员在做连续的投篮动作时，结束该节或决胜期的比赛计时钟信号响起或进攻计时钟信号响起。
此规定不适用，并且如中篮不计得分。

第 11 条 队员和裁判员的位置

11.1 一名队员的位置由他正接触着的地面所确定。
当队员跳起在空中时，他保持当他最后接触地面时所拥有的相同位置。这包括界线、中线、3分线、罚球线、标定限制区的各条线和标定无撞人半圆区的各条线。

11.2 一名裁判员位置的确定与一名队员位置的确定相同。当球触及裁判员时，如同触及裁判员所位于的地面一样。

Art. 12 Jump ball and alternating possession

12.1 Jump ball definition

12.1.1 **A jump ball** occurs when a referee tosses the ball between any 2 opponents.

12.1.2 **A held ball** occurs when one or more players from opposing teams have one or both hands firmly on the ball so that neither player can gain control without undue roughness.

12.2 Jump ball procedure

12.2.1 Each jumper shall stand with both feet inside the half of the centre circle nearest to his own basket with one foot close to the centre line.

12.2.2 Team-mates may not occupy adjacent positions around the circle if an opponent wishes to occupy one of those positions.

12.2.3 The referee shall then toss the ball vertically upwards between the 2 opponents, higher than either of them can reach by jumping.

12.2.4 The ball must be tapped with the hand(s) of at least one of the jumpers after it reaches its highest point.

12.2.5 Neither jumper shall leave his position until the ball has been legally tapped.

12.2.6 Neither jumper may catch the ball or tap it more than twice until it has touched one of the non-jumpers or the floor.

12.2.7 If the ball is not tapped by at least one of the jumpers, the jump ball shall be repeated.

12.2.8 No part of a non-jumper's body may be on or over the circle line (cylinder) before the ball has been tapped.

An infraction of Art. 12.2.1, 12.2.4, 12.2.5, 12.2.6, and 12.2.8 is a violation.

12.3 Jump ball situations

A jump ball situation occurs when:
- A held ball is called.
- The ball goes out-of-bounds and the referees are in doubt or disagree about which of the opponents last touched the ball.
- A double free-throw violation occurs during an unsuccessful last free throw.
- A live ball lodges between the ring and the backboard except:
  — Between free throws,

第 12 条 跳球和交替拥有

12.1 定 义

12.1.1 一名裁判员在任何两名互为对方的队员之间将球抛起，**一次跳球**发生。

12.1.2 当双方球队各有一名或多名队员有一手或两手紧握在球上，以至不采用粗野动作任一队员就不能获得控制球时，**一次争球**发生。

12.2 跳球程序

12.2.1 每一跳球队员的双脚应站立在靠近该队本方球篮的中圈半圆内，一脚靠近中线。

12.2.2 如果一名对方队员要求占据其中一个位置，同队队员不得围绕圆圈占据相邻的位置。

12.2.3 然后，裁判员应在两名互为对方的队员之间将球向上（垂直地）抛起，其高度超过任一队员跳起能达到的高度。

12.2.4 在球到达它的最高点后，球必须被至少一名跳球队员用手拍击。

12.2.5 在球被合法地拍击前，任一跳球队员都不应离开他的位置。

12.2.6 在球触及非跳球队员或地面前，任一跳球队员都不得抓住球或拍击球超过两次。

12.2.7 如果球未被至少一名跳球队员拍击，则应重新跳球。

12.2.8 在球被拍击前，非跳球队员的身体部分不得在圆圈上或圆圈（圆柱体）上方。

违反12.2.1、12.2.4、12.2.5、12.2.6和12.2.8是违例。

12.3 跳球情况

一次跳球情况发生，当：
- 宣判了一次争球时。
- 球出界，但是裁判员无法判定谁是最后触及球的队员或意见不一致时。
- 在最后一次不成功的罚球中，双方队员发生违例时。
- 一个活球夹在篮圈和篮板之间，除非

OFFICIAL BASKETBALL RULES *2020*

- — After the last free throw followed by a throw-in from the throw-in line in the team's frontcourt.
- The ball becomes dead when neither team has control of the ball nor is entitled to the ball.
- After the cancellation of equal penalties on both teams, if there are no other foul penalties remaining for administration and neither team had control of the ball nor was entitled to the ball before the first foul or violation.
- All quarters other than the first one and all overtimes are to begin.

12.4 Alternating possession definition

12.4.1 Alternating possession is a method of causing the ball to become live with a throw-in rather than a jump ball.

12.4.2 Alternating possession throw-in:
- **Begins** when the ball is at the disposal of the player taking the throw-in.
- **Ends** when:
  — The ball touches or is legally touched by any player on the playing court.
  — The team taking the throw-in commits a violation.
  — A live ball lodges between the ring and the backboard during a throw-in.

12.5 Alternating possession procedure

12.5.1 In all jump ball situations teams shall alternate possession of the ball for a throw-in from the place nearest to where the jump ball situation occurs, except directly behind the backboard.

12.5.2 The team that does not gain control of the live ball on the playing court after the jump ball shall be entitled to the first alternating possession.

12.5.3 The team entitled to the next alternating possession at the end of any quarter or overtime shall begin the next quarter or overtime with a throw-in from the centre line extended, opposite the scorer's table, unless there are further free throws and a possession penalty to be administered.

12.5.4 The team entitled to the alternating possession throw-in shall be indicated by the alternating possession arrow in the direction of the opponents' basket. The direction of the alternating possession arrow shall be reversed immediately when the alternating possession throw-in ends.

12.5.5 A violation by a team during its alternating possession throw-in causes that team to lose the alternating possession throw-in. The direction of the alternating possession arrow shall be reversed immediately, indicating

——罚球之间。

——最后一次罚球之后还有记录台对侧球队前场掷球入界。
- 任一队既没有控制球又没有球权，球成死球时。
- 在抵消了双方球队的相等罚则后，没有留下其他要执行的犯规罚则，以及在第一次犯规或违例之前，任一队既没有控制球也没有球权时。
- 除第 1 节外的其他节、以及决胜期开始时。

12.4 交替拥有定义

12.4.1 交替拥有是以掷球入界而不是以跳球来使球成活球的一种方法。

12.4.2 交替拥有掷球入界：

- **开始于：**

  掷球入界队员可处理球时。

- **结束于：**

  —— 球触及任一场上队员或被任一场上队员合法触及时。

  —— 掷球入界队发生违例时。

  —— 掷球入界中活球夹在篮圈和篮板之间时。

12.5 交替拥有程序

12.5.1 在所有跳球情况中，双方球队应交替拥有从最靠近发生跳球情况的地点掷球入界，正好在篮板后面的地点除外。

12.5.2 跳球后未在场上获得控制活球的球队应拥有第一次交替拥有球权。

12.5.3 在任一节结束时，拥有下一次交替拥有球权的队应从记录台对侧的中线延长线以掷球入界开始下一节或决胜期，除非有进一步的罚球和球权罚则要执行。

12.5.4 应由指向对方球篮的交替拥有箭头来指明拥有交替拥有掷球入界球权的球队。当交替拥有掷球入界结束时，交替拥有箭头的方向立即反转。

12.5.5 某队在它的交替拥有掷球入界中违例，使该队失掉交替拥有掷球入界的球权。交替拥有箭头应立即反转，指明违例队的对方在下

OFFICIAL BASKETBALL RULES *2020*

that the opponents of the violating team shall be entitled to the alternating possession throw-in at the next jump ball situation. The game shall then be resumed by awarding the ball to the opponents of the violating team for a throw-in from the place of the original throw-in.

12.5.6 A foul by either team:
- Before the beginning of a quarter other than the first one or an overtime, or
- During the alternating possession throw-in,

does not cause the team entitled to the throw-in to lose that alternating possession.

Art. 13 How the ball is played

13.1 Definition
During the game, the ball is played with the hand(s) only and may be passed, thrown, tapped, rolled or dribbled in any direction, subject to the restrictions of these rules.

13.2 Rule
A player shall not run with the ball, deliberately kick or block it with any part of the leg or strike it with the fist.

However, to accidentally come into contact with or touch the ball with any part of the leg is not a violation.

An infraction of Art. 13.2 is a violation.

Art. 14 Control of the ball

14.1 Definition

14.1.1 Team control **starts** when a player of that team is in control of a live ball by holding or dribbling it or has a live ball at his disposal.

14.1.2 Team control **continues** when:
- A player of that team is in control of a live ball.
- The ball is being passed between team-mates.

14.1.3 Team control **ends** when:
- An opponent gains control.
- The ball becomes dead.
- The ball has left the player's hand(s) on a shot for a field goal or for a free throw.

一次跳球情况中拥有交替拥有掷球入界的球权。于是将球判给违例队的对方从最初的掷球入界地点掷球入界继续比赛。

12.5.6　在：
- 除第 1 节外的其他节、以及决胜期开始前，或
- 交替拥有掷球入界中，

任一球队犯规不使掷球入界队失去交替拥有掷球入界的球权。

第 13 条　如何打球

13.1　定　义

在比赛中，球只能用手来打，并且球可向任何方向传、投、拍、滚或运，但受本规则的限制。

13.2　规　定

队员不能带球跑，故意踢或用腿的任何部分阻挡球或用拳击球。然而，球意外地接触到腿的任何部分，或腿的任何部分意外地触及球，不是违例。

违反13.2是违例。

第 14 条　控制球

14.1　定　义

14.1.1　球队控制球**开始于**该队一名队员正拿着或运着一个活球，或者可处理一个活球时。

14.1.2　当：
- 某队一名队员控制一个活球时。
- 球在同队队员之间传递时。

是球队**继续**控制球。

14.1.3　当：
- 一名对方队员获得控制球时。
- 球成死球时。
- 在投篮或罚球中，球已经离开队员的手时。

是球队控制球**结束**。

Art. 15 Player in the act of shooting

15.1 Definition

15.1.1 **A shot for a field goal or a free throw** is when the ball is held in a player's hand(s) and is then thrown into the air towards the opponents' basket.

A tap for a field goal is when the ball is directed with the hand(s) towards the opponents' basket.

A dunk for a field goal is when the ball is forced downwards into the opponents' basket with one or both hands.

A continuous movement on drives to the basket or other moving shots is an action of a player who catches the ball while he is progressing or upon completion of the dribble and then continues with the shooting motion, usually upwards.

15.1.2 The act of shooting on a shot:

- **Begins** when the player starts, in the judgement of a referee, to move the ball upwards towards the opponents' basket.

- **Ends** when the ball has left the player's hand(s), or if an entirely new act of shooting is made and, in case of an airborne shooter, both feet have returned to the floor.

15.1.3 The act of shooting in a continuous movement on drives to the basket or other moving shots:
- **Begins** when the ball has come to rest in the player's hand(s), upon completion of a dribble or a catch in the air and the player starts, in the judgment of the referee, the shooting motion preceding the release of the ball for a field goal.
- **Ends** when the ball has left the player's hand(s), or if an entirely new act of shooting is made and, in case of an airborne shooter, both feet have returned to the floor.

15.1.4 There is no relationship between the number of legal steps taken and the act of shooting.

15.1.5 During the act of shooting the player might have his arm(s) held by an opponent, thus preventing him from scoring. In this case it is not essential that the ball leaves the player's hand(s).

15.1.6 When a player is in the act of shooting and after being fouled he passes the ball off, he is no longer considered to have been in the act of shooting.

第 15 条 队员正在做投篮动作

15.1 定 义

15.1.1 **投（投篮或者罚篮）**：队员手中持球，然后朝对方球篮将球投或掷入空中。

拍投：用手直接把球打向对方球篮。
扣投：用一手或双手迫使球向下进入对方球篮。
投篮动作中的连续动作是队员接住球或运球结束后持球向着球篮的上篮或其他的移动投篮（通常是向上的）。

15.1.2 投篮动作（原地）
- **开始于**：根据裁判员的判断，当队员将球朝着对方球篮做向上的动作时。
- **结束于**：球已离开队员的手，或者做了一个全新的投篮动作时。如果是跳起在空中的投篮队员，他必须双脚落回地面。

15.1.3 突破上篮或其他运动中投篮的连续动作：
- **开始于**：根据裁判员的判断，当队员结束运球或在空中接到球后，球已在手中停留时，队员在球离手前开始做投篮连续动作。
- **结束于**：球已离开队员的手，或者做了一个全新的投篮动作时。如果是跳起在空中的投篮队员，他必须双脚落回地面。

15.1.4 在跑动的合法步数和投篮动作之间没有联系。

15.1.5 队员正在做投篮动作的过程中，他的手臂可能被对方队员抓住，以此来阻碍他得分。在这种情况下，球是否离开队员的手不是关键因素。

15.1.6 当一名队员正在做投篮动作，在被犯规后，他将球传了出去，他不再被认为是在做投篮动作。

Art. 16 Goal: When made and its value

16.1 Definition

16.1.1 A goal is made when a live ball enters the basket from above and remains within or passes through the basket entirely.

16.1.2 The ball is considered to be within the basket when the slightest part of the ball is within the basket and below the level of the ring.

16.2 Rule

16.2.1 A goal is credited to the team attacking the opponents' basket into which the ball has entered as follows:
- A goal released from a free throw counts 1 point.
- A goal released from the 2-point field goal area counts 2 points.
- A goal released from the 3-point field goal area counts 3 points.
- After the ball has touched the ring on a last free throw and is legally touched by any player before it enters the basket, the goal counts 2 points.

16.2.2 If a player **accidentally** scores a field goal in his team's basket, the goal counts 2 points and shall be entered on the scoresheet as having been scored by the captain of the opponents' team on the playing court.

16.2.3 If a player **deliberately** scores a field goal in his team's basket, it is a violation and the goal does not count.

16.2.4 If a player causes the entire ball to pass through the basket from below, it is a violation.

16.2.5 The game clock or the shot clock must show 0.3 (3 tenths of a second) or more for a player to gain control of the ball on a throw-in or on a rebound after the last free throw in order to attempt a shot for a field goal. If the game clock or the shot clock show 0.2 or 0.1 the only type of a valid field goal made is by tapping or directly dunking the ball, provided that the hand(s) of the player are no longer touching the ball when the game clock or the shot clock show 0.0.

Art. 17 Throw-in

17.1 Definition

17.1.1 A throw-in occurs when the ball is passed into the playing court by the out-of-bounds player taking the throw-in.

17.2 Procedure

17.2.1 A referee must hand or place the ball at the disposal of the player taking the throw-in. He may also toss or bounce pass the ball provided that:

第 16 条 球中篮和它的得分值

16.1 定 义

16.1.1 当活球从上方进入球篮并保持在球篮中或完全地穿过球篮是球中篮。

16.1.2 当有极少部分的球体在球篮中并在篮圈水平面以下时，就认为球在球篮中。

16.2 规 定

16.2.1 球已进入对方的球篮，对投篮的队按如下计得分：
- 一次罚球投中篮计1分。
- 从2分投篮区域投中篮计2分。
- 从3分投篮区域投中篮计3分。
- 在最后一次罚球中，球触及篮圈后，在球进入球篮之前被任一队员合法触及，中篮计2分。

16.2.2 如果队员**意外地**将球投入本方球篮，中篮计2分，并应在记录表上登记在对方队的场上队长名下。

16.2.3 如果队员**故意地**将球投入本方球篮，这是违例，中篮不计得分。

16.2.4 如果队员使球整体从下方穿过球篮，这是违例。

16.2.5 一名队员在掷球入界中获得控制球，或者在最后一次罚球后抢篮板球时，比赛计时钟或进攻计时钟显示0.3（3/10秒）或者更多，他才可以尝试投篮。如果比赛计时钟或进攻计时钟显示0.2 或者0.1，唯一的投篮方式就是拍球或者直接扣篮得分，只要在比赛计时钟或进攻计时钟显示0.0时，队员的手不再接触着球。

第 17 条 掷球入界

17.1 定 义

17.1.1 由界外掷球入界队员将球传入比赛场地内时，掷球入界发生。

17.2 程 序

17.2.1 裁判员必须将球递交给执行掷球入界的队员或将球置于他可处理

- The referee is no more than 4 m from the player taking the throw-in.
- The player taking the throw-in is at the correct place as designated by the referee.

17.2.2 The player shall take the throw-in from the place nearest to the infraction or where the game was stopped, except directly behind the backboard.

17.2.3 At the beginning of all quarters other than the first one and all overtimes, the throw-in shall be administered from the centre line extended, opposite the scorer's table.

The player taking the throw-in shall have one foot on either side of the centre line extended, opposite the scorer's table, and shall be entitled to pass the ball to a team-mate at any place on the playing court.

17.2.4 When the game clock shows 2:00 minutes or less in the fourth quarter or overtime, following a time-out taken by the team that is entitled to the possession of the ball from its backcourt, the head coach of that team has the right to decide whether the game shall be resumed with a throw-in from the throw-in line in the team's frontcourt or from the team's backcourt at the place nearest to where the game was stopped.

17.2.5 Following a personal foul committed by a player of the team in control of a live ball, or of the team entitled to the ball, the game shall be resumed with a throw-in from the place nearest to the infraction.

17.2.6 Following a technical foul, the game shall be resumed with a throw-in from the place nearest to where the ball was located when the technical foul was called, unless otherwise stated in these rules.

17.2.7 Following an unsportsmanlike or disqualifying foul, the game shall be resumed with a throw-in from the throw-in line at the team's frontcourt, unless otherwise stated in these rules.

17.2.8 Following a fight, the game shall be resumed as stated in **Art. 39**.

17.2.9 Whenever the ball enters the basket, but the field goal or the free throw is not valid, the game shall be resumed with a throw-in from the free-throw line extended.

17.2.10 Following a successful field goal or a successful last free throw:
- Any player of the non-scoring team shall take the throw-in from any place behind that team's endline. This is also applicable after a referee hands or places the ball at the disposal of the player taking the throw-in after a time-out or after any interruption of the game following a successful field goal or a successful last free throw.
- The player taking the throw-in may move laterally and/or backwards and the ball may be passed between team-mates behind the endline, but the

的地方。只要
- 裁判员距离执行掷球入界的队员不超过4米。
- 执行掷球入界的队员是在裁判员指定的正确地点。

裁判员也可将球抛或反弹给执行掷球入界的队员。

17.2.2　队员应从最靠近违犯或比赛被停止的地点执行掷球入界，正好在篮板后面的地点除外。

17.2.3　除了第1节之外，其他所有节和所有决胜期的开始，从记录台对侧的中线延长线执行掷球入界。

掷球入界的队员应在记录台对侧，双脚分别跨立在中线延长线的两边，并有权将球传给场上任何地点的同队队员。

17.2.4　在第4节和每一决胜期的比赛计时钟显示2:00分钟或更少时，在后场拥有球权的队暂停之后，该队主教练有权决定接下来的掷球入界，是在该队前场的掷球入界线处，还是在该队后场比赛停止时的地点执行。

17.2.5　控制活球队的队员或拥有球权队的队员发生侵人犯规后，比赛应从最靠近违犯的地点掷球入界重新开始。

17.2.6　技术犯规后，应从最靠近宣判技术犯规时距离球最近的地点掷球入界重新开始比赛，除非本规则另有规定。

17.2.7　违反体育运动精神或取消比赛资格的犯规后，应从该队前场的掷球入界线处执行掷球入界重新开始比赛，除非本规则另有规定。

17.2.8　一起打架之后的比赛应按照**第39条**所陈述重新开始。

17.2.9　每当球进入球篮，但该投篮或罚球无效，应从罚球线延长线掷球入界重新开始比赛。

17.2.10　投篮成功或最后一次罚球成功后：
- 非得分队的任一队员应从该队端线后的任一地点掷球入界。这也适用于投篮成功或最后一次罚球成功后的一次暂停或任一比赛的中断之后，在裁判员将球递交给执行掷球入界的队员或将球置于他可处理的地方后。
- 执行掷球入界的队员可横向移动和/或后移，并且球可在端

5-second count starts when the ball is at the disposal of the first player out-of-bounds.

17.3 Rule
17.3.1 The player taking the throw-in shall not:
- Take more than 5 seconds to release the ball.
- Step into the playing court while having the ball in his hand(s).
- Cause the ball to touch out-of-bounds, after it has been released on the throw-in.
- Touch the ball on the playing court before it has touched another player.
- Cause the ball to enter the basket directly.
- Move from the designated throw-in place behind the boundary line laterally in one or both directions, exceeding a total distance of 1 m before releasing the ball.
However, he is permitted to move directly backwards from the boundary line as far as circumstances allow.

17.3.2 During the throw-in other player(s) shall not:
- Have any part of their bodies over the boundary line before the ball has been thrown-in across the boundary line.
- Be closer than 1 m to the player taking the throw-in when the throw-in place has less than 2 m distance between the boundary line and any out-of-bounds obstructions.

17.3.3 When the game clock shows 2:00 minutes or less in the fourth quarter and in each overtime, and there is a throw-in, the referee shall use an illegal boundary line crossing signal as a warning while administering the throw-in.
If a defensive player:
- Moves any part of his body over the boundary line to interfere with a throw-in, or
- Is closer than 1 m to the player taking the throw-in when the throw-in place has less than 2 m distance,

it is a violation and shall lead to a technical foul.
An infraction of Art. 17.3 is a violation.

17.4 Penalty
The ball is awarded to the opponents for a throw-in from the place of the original throw-in.

线后的同队队员之间传递。但是，当界外第一位队员可处理球时，5秒计算开始。

17.3 规 定

17.3.1 执行掷球入界的队员不应：
- 超过5秒球才离手。
- 球在手中时步入比赛场地内。
- 掷球入界的球离手后，使球触及界外。
- 在球触及另一队员前，在场上触及球。
- 直接使球进入球篮。
- 在球离手前，从界外指定的掷球入界地点，在一个或两个方向上横向移动总距离超过1米。然而，只要情况许可，执行掷球入界的队员从界线后退多远都可以。

17.3.2 在掷球入界中其他队员不应：
- 在球被掷过界线前，将身体的任何部位越过界线。
- 当掷球入界地点的界线外任何障碍物和界线之间距离少于2米时，靠近执行掷球入界的队员在1米之内。

17.3.3 第4节或每个决胜期比赛计时钟显示2:00分钟或更少时，有一起掷球入界，在管理掷球入界过程中，裁判员应使用非法超过界线的手势进行警告。

如果一名防守队员：
- 将他身体的任何部分移动超过界限以干扰掷球入界，或
- 当掷球入界地点的距离少于2米时，靠近执行掷球入界的队员在1米之内。

这是一起导致技术犯规的违例。

违反17.3是违例。

17.4 罚 则

将球判给对方队员从原掷球入界的地点掷球入界。

Art. 18 Time-out

18.1 Definition
A time-out is an interruption of the game requested by the head coach or first assis-tant coach.

18.2 Rule

18.2.1 Each time-out shall last 1 minute.

18.2.2 A time-out may be granted during a time-out opportunity.

18.2.3 A time-out opportunity begins when:
- For both teams, the ball becomes dead, the game clock is stopped and the referee has ended his communication with the scorer's table.
- For both teams, the ball becomes dead following a successful last free throw.
- For the non-scoring team, a field goal is scored.

18.2.4 A time-out opportunity ends when the ball is at the disposal of a player for a throw-in or for a first free throw.

18.2.5 Each team may be granted:
- 2 time-outs during the first half.
- 3 time-outs during the second half with a maximum of 2 of these time-outs when the game clock shows 2:00 minutes or less in the fourth quarter.
- 1 time-out during each overtime.

18.2.6 Unused time-outs may not be carried over to the next half or overtime.

18.2.7 A time-out is charged on the team whose head coach first made a request unless the time-out is granted following a field goal scored by the opponents and without an infraction having been called.

18.2.8 A time-out shall not be permitted to the scoring team when the game clock shows 2:00 minutes or less in the fourth quarter and in each overtime and, following a successful field goal unless A referee has interrupted the game.

18.3 Procedure

18.3.1 Only a head coach or first assistant coach has the right to request a time-out. He shall establish visual contact with the scorer's table or he shall go to the scorer's table and ask clearly for a time-out, making the proper conventional sign with his hands.

第 18 条 暂 停

18.1 定 义
主教练或第一助理教练请求中断比赛是暂停。

18.2 规 定

18.2.1 每次暂停应持续 1 分钟。

18.2.2 在暂停机会期间可以准予暂停。

18.2.3 当：
- （对于双方队）球成死球，比赛计时钟停止，以及当裁判员已结束了与记录台的联系时。
- （对于双方队）在最后一次罚球成功后，球成死球时。
- 对于非得分队，投篮得分时。

一次暂停机会开始。

18.2.4 当队员在掷球入界或第一次的罚球可处理球时，一次暂停机会结束。

18.2.5 每队可准予：
- 上半时 2 次暂停。
- 下半时 3 次暂停，第 4 节当比赛计时钟显示2:00分钟或更少时最多 2 次暂停。
- 每一个决胜期一次暂停。

18.2.6 未用过的暂停不得遗留给下半时或决胜期。

18.2.7 除了对方队员投篮得分并且没有宣判违犯后准予的暂停外，应给首先提出暂停请求的主教练的队登记暂停。

18.2.8 在第 4 节或每一决胜期的比赛计时钟显示2:00分钟或更少时，在一次成功的投篮后，不允许得分队暂停，除非裁判员已中断了比赛。

18.3 程 序

18.3.1 只有主教练或第一助理教练有权请求暂停。他应与记录台建立目光联系或亲自到记录台处清楚地要求暂停，并用手做出正确的常规手势。

18.3.2 A time-out request may be cancelled only before the timer's signal has sounded for such a request.

18.3.3 The time-out period:
- **Begins** when the referee blows his whistle and gives the time-out signal.
- **Ends** when the referee blows his whistle and beckons the teams back on the playing court.

18.3.4 As soon as a time-out opportunity begins, the timer shall sound his signal to notify referees that a team has requested a time-out.

If a field goal is scored against a team which has requested a time-out, the timer shall immediately stop the game clock and sound his signal.

18.3.5 During the time-out and during an interval of play before the beginning of the second and fourth quarter or each overtime the players may leave the playing court and sit on the team bench and any person permitted to sit on the team bench may enter the playing court provided they remain within the vicinity of their team bench area.

18.3.6 If the request for the time-out is made by either team after the ball is at the disposal of the free-throw shooter for the first free throw, the time-out shall be granted if:
- The last free throw is successful.
- The last free throw, if not successful, is followed by a throw-in.
- A foul is called between free throws. In this case the free throw(s) shall be completed, and the time-out shall be permitted before the new foul penalty is administered, unless otherwise stated in these rules.
- A foul is called before the ball becomes live after the last free throw. In this case the time-out shall be permitted before the new foul penalty is administered.
- A violation is called before the ball becomes live after the last free throw. In this case the time-out shall be permitted before the throw-in is administered.

In the event of consecutive sets of free throws and/or possession of the ball resulting from more than 1 foul penalty, each set is to be treated separately.

18.3.2 一次暂停请求只可在计时员发出该次暂停请求的信号之前被取消。

18.3.3 **暂停时段**：
- 当裁判员鸣哨并给出暂停手势时**开始**。
- 当裁判员鸣哨并招呼球队回到比赛场地上时**结束**。

18.3.4 暂停机会一开始，计时员就应发出信号，通知裁判员某队已请求了暂停。

如果某队已请求了暂停，在对方队投篮得分时，计时员应立即停止比赛计时钟并发出信号。

18.3.5 在暂停期间，以及第 2 节和第 4 节或每一决胜期开始之前的比赛休息期间，队员们可以离开比赛场地并坐在球队席上，任何允许坐在球队席的人员可以进入比赛场地，只要他们留在他们的球队席区域附近。

18.3.6 如果第一次罚球，球置于罚球队员可处理之后，任一队请求了一次暂停，则在下列情况下暂停应被准予：
- 最后一次罚球成功。
- 最后一次罚球，如果不成功，随后还有掷球入界。
- 在多次罚球之间宣判了犯规。这种情况下，应完成多次罚球，在新的犯规罚则执行之前。除非本规则另有规定。
- 在最后一次罚球后，在球成活球前宣判了一次犯规。这种情况下，在执行新的犯规罚则之前。
- 在最后一次罚球后，在球成活球前宣判了一次违例。在这种情况下，在执行掷球入界之前。

如果1个以上的犯规罚则造成连续的罚球单元和／或球权，每个单元分别处理。

Art. 19 Substitution

19.1 Definition
A substitution is an interruption of the game requested by the substitute to become a player.

19.2 Rule

19.2.1 A team may substitute a player(s) during a substitution opportunity.

19.2.2 A substitution opportunity begins when:
- For both teams, the ball becomes dead, the game clock is stopped and the referee has ended his communication with the scorer's table.
- For both teams, the ball becomes dead following a successful last free throw.
- For the non-scoring team, a field goal is scored when the game clock shows 2:00 minutes or less in the fourth quarter and in each overtime.

19.2.3 A substitution opportunity ends when the ball is at the disposal of a player for a throw-in or a first free throw.

19.2.4 A player who has become a substitute and a substitute who has become a player cannot respectively re-enter the game or leave the game until the ball becomes dead again, after a clock-running phase of the game, unless:
- The team is reduced to fewer than 5 players on the playing court.
- The player entitled to the free-throws as the result of the correction of an error is on the team bench after having been legally substituted.

19.2.5 A substitution shall not be permitted to the scoring team when the game clock is stopped following a successful field goal when the game clock shows 2:00 minutes or less in the fourth quarter and in each overtime unless a referee has interrupted the game.

19.2.6 If the player receives any treatment or any assistance, he must be substituted unless the team is reduced to fewer than 5 players on the playing court.

19.3 Procedure

19.3.1 Only a substitute has the right to request a substitution. He (not the head coach or the first assistant coach) shall go to the scorer's table and ask clearly for a substitution, making the proper conventional sign with his hands, or sit on the substitution chair. He must be ready to play immediately.

第19条 替 换

19.1 定 义

替补队员请求中断比赛成为队员是一次替换。

19.2 规 定

19.2.1 在替换机会期间球队可以替换队员。

19.2.2 一次替换机会开始：
- （对于双方队）当球成死球，比赛计时钟停止，以及裁判员已结束了与记录台的联系时。
- （对于双方队）在最后一次罚球成功后，球成为死球时。
- （对于非得分队）在第4节或每一决胜期的比赛计时钟显示2:00分钟或更少，投篮得分时。

19.2.3 一次替换机会结束于掷球入界的队员可处理球时，或第一次的罚球可处理球时。

19.2.4 队员已成为替补队员和替补队员已成为队员，分别不能重新进入比赛或离开比赛，直到一个比赛的计时钟运行片段之后球再次成死球为止。除非：
- 某队能够上场的队员少于5名。
- 作为纠正失误的结果，拥有罚球权的队员已被合法地替换后坐在球队席上。

19.2.5 在第4节或每个决胜期的比赛计时钟显示2:00分钟或更少时，一次成功的投篮后比赛计时钟停止时，不允许得分队替换，除非裁判员已中断了比赛。

19.2.6 如果队员接受了任何治疗或任何协助，他必须被替换，除非该队能够上场的队员少于5名。

19.3 程 序

19.3.1 只有替补队员有权请求替换。他（不是主教练或第一助理教练）应到记录台清楚地要求替换，用双手做出常规替换手势或者坐在替换的椅子上。他必须立即做好比赛的准备。

19.3.2 A substitution request may be cancelled only before the timer's signal has sounded for such a request.

19.3.3 As soon as a substitution opportunity begins, the timer shall sound his signal to notify the referees that a request for a substitution has been made.

19.3.4 The substitute shall remain outside the boundary line until the referee blows his whistle, gives the substitution signal and beckons him to enter the playing court.

19.3.5 The player being substituted is permitted to go directly to his team bench without reporting either to the timer or the referee.

19.3.6 Substitutions shall be completed as quickly as possible. A player who has committed 5 fouls or has been disqualified must be substituted immediately(taking no more than 30 seconds). If, in the judgement of a referee, there is a delay of the game, a time-out shall be charged on the offending team. If the team has no time-out remaining, a technical foul for delaying the game may be charged on the head coach, entered as 'B'.

19.3.7 If a substitution is requested during a time-out or during an interval of play other than the half-time interval, the substitute must report to the timer before entering the game.

19.3.8 If the free-throw shooter must be substituted because he:
- Is injured, or
- Has committed 5 fouls, or
- Has been disqualified,

the free throw(s) must be attempted by his substitute who may not be substituted again until he has played in the next clock-running phase of the game.

19.3.9 If the request for a substitution is made by either team after the ball is at the disposal of the free-throw shooter for the first free throw, the substitution shall be granted if:
- The last free throw is successful.
- The last free throw, if not successful, is followed by a throw-in.
- A foul is called between free throws. In this case the free throw(s) shall be completed, and the substitution shall be permitted before the new foul penalty is administered, unless otherwise stated in these rules.
- A foul is called before the ball becomes live after the last free throw. In this case the substitution shall be permitted before the new foul penalty is administered.
- A violation is called before the ball becomes live after the last free throw. In this case the substitution shall be permitted before the throw-in is administered.

19.3.2　一次替换请求可以被撤销，但只可在计时员发出该次替换请求的信号之前。

19.3.3　替换机会一开始，计时员就应发出信号通知裁判员替换请求已提出。

19.3.4　替补队员应停留在界线外，直到裁判员鸣哨、给出替换手势和招呼他进入比赛场地。

19.3.5　已被替换的队员不必向裁判员或计时员报告，允许他直接去他的球队席。

19.3.6　替换应尽可能快地完成。已发生第5次犯规或已被取消比赛资格的队员必须立即被替换（不超过30秒）。根据裁判员的判断，如果有不必要的延误，应给违犯的队登记一次暂停。如果该队没有剩余的暂停，可登记主教练一次技术犯规（B）。

19.3.7　如果在一次暂停或非半时的比赛休息期间中请求替换，该替换队员必须在比赛前向计时员报告。

19.3.8　如果罚球队员因为：
- 受伤了，或
- 已发生第5次犯规，或
- 已被取消比赛资格，

他必须被替换。罚球必须由替换他的替补队员执行，并且该替补队员在比赛的下一个计时钟运行片段前，不能再次被替换。

19.3.9　第一次罚球，球置于罚球队员可处理球之后，如果任一队请求替换，则在下列情况下替换应被准予：
- 最后一次的罚球成功。
- 最后一次罚球，如果不成功，随后还有掷球入界。
- 在多次罚球之间宣判了犯规。这种情况下，多次罚球应完成，在新的犯规罚则执行之前允许替换。除非本规则另有规定。
- 在最后一次的罚球后，在球成活球前宣判了一次犯规。这种情况下，在执行新的犯规罚则之前允许替换。
- 在最后一次的罚球后，在球成活球前宣判了一次违例。这种情况下，在执行掷球入界之前允许替换。

In the event of consecutive sets of free throws and/or possession of the ball resulting from more than 1 foul penalty, each set is to be treated separately.

Art. 20 Game lost by forfeit

20.1 Rule

A team shall lose the game by forfeit if:
- The team is not present or is unable to field 5 players ready to play 15 minutes after the game is scheduled to begin.
- Its actions prevent the game from being played.
- It refuses to play after being instructed to do so by the crew chief.

20.2 Penalty

20.2.1 The game is awarded to the opponents and the score shall be 20 to 0. Furthermore, the forfeiting team shall receive 0 classification point.

20.2.2 For a 2-games (home and away) total points series (aggregate score) and for Play-Offs (best of 3), the team that forfeits in the first, second, or third game shall lose the series or Play-Offs by 'forfeit'. This does not apply for Play-Offs (best of 5 and best of 7).

20.2.3 If in a tournament the team forfeits for the second time, the team shall be disqualified from the tournament and the results of all games played by this team shall be nullified.

Art. 21 Game lost by default

21.1 Rule

A team shall lose a game by default if, during the game, the team has fewer than 2 players on the playing court ready to play.

21.2. Penalty

21.2.1 If the team to which the game is awarded is ahead, the score shall stand as at the time when the game was stopped. If the team to which the game is awarded is not ahead, the score shall be 2 to 0 in its favour. The defaulting team shall receive 1 classification point.

21.2.2 For a 2-games (home and away) total point series (aggregate score), the team that defaults in the first or in the second game shall lose the series by 'default'.

如果1个以上的犯规罚则带来连续的罚球单元和／或球权，每个单元分别处理。

第 20 条 比赛因弃权告负

20.1 规 定

如果球队：
- 在比赛预定的开始时间15分钟后不到场或不能使5名队员入场准备比赛。
- 它的行为阻碍比赛继续进行。
- 在主裁判员通知比赛后拒绝比赛。

那么，该队由于弃权使比赛告负。

20.2 罚 则

20.2.1 判给对方队获胜，且比分为20:0。此外，弃权的队在名次排列中得0分。

20.2.2 对于两场比赛（主和客）总分定胜负的一组比赛和季后赛（3战定胜负），在第1场、第2场或第3场比赛中弃权的队应使该组比赛或季后赛因"弃权"告负。这不适用于季后赛（5战定胜负和 7战定胜负）。

20.2.3 如果在一次联赛中，一个球队弃权两次，该队应被取消比赛资格，并且该队在所有比赛的结果都视为无效。

第 21 条 比赛因缺少队员告负

21.1 规 定

在比赛中，如果某队在比赛场地上准备比赛的队员少于2名，该队因缺少队员使比赛告负。

21.2 罚 则

21.2.1 如判获胜的队领先，则在比赛停止时的比分应有效。如判获胜的队不领先，则比分应记录为2:0，对该队有利。此外，缺少队员的队在名次排列中应得 1 分。

21.2.2 对于两场比赛（主和客）总分定胜负的一组比赛，在第1场或第2场比赛中缺少队员的队应使该组比赛因"缺少队员"告负。

RULE FIVE — VIOLATIONS

Art. 22 Violations

22.1 Definition
A violation is an infraction of the rules.

22.2 Penalty
The ball shall be awarded to the opponents for a throw-in from the place nearest to the infraction, except directly behind the backboard, unless otherwise stated in these rules.

Art. 23 Player out-of-bounds and ball out-of-bounds

23.1 Definition

23.1.1 A **player** is out-of-bounds when any part of his body is in contact with the floor, or any object other than a player above, on or outside the boundary line.

23.1.2 The **ball** is out-of-bounds when it touches:
- A player or any other person who is out-of-bounds.
- The floor or any object above, on or outside the boundary line.
- The backboard supports, the back of the backboards or any object above the playing court.

23.2 Rule

23.2.1 The ball is caused to go out-of-bounds by the last player to touch or be touched by the ball before it goes out-of-bounds, even if the ball then goes out-of-bounds by touching something other than a player.

23.2.2 If the ball is out-of-bounds because of touching or being touched by a player who is on or outside the boundary line, this player causes the ball to go out-of-bounds.

23.2.3 If a player(s) move(s) to out-of-bounds or to his backcourt **during** a held ball, a jump ball situation occurs.

第五章 违 例

第 22 条 违 例

22.1 定 义
违例是违犯规则。

22.2 罚 则
将球判给对方队员从最靠近发生违例的地点掷球入界,但正好在篮板后面的地点除外,除非本规则另有规定。

第 23 条 队员出界和球出界

23.1 定 义
23.1.1 当**队员**身体的任何部分接触界线上方、界线上或界线外的除队员以外的地面或任何物体时,即是队员出界。

23.1.2 当**球**触及了:
- 在界外的队员或任何其他人员时。
- 界线上方、界线上或界线外的地面或任何物体时。
- 篮板支撑架、篮板背面或比赛场地上方的任何物体时。

是**球**出界。

23.2 规 定
23.2.1 在球出界,以及球触及了除队员以外的其他物体而出界之前,最后触及球或被球触及的队员是使球出界的队员。

23.2.2 如果球出界是由于触及了界线上或界线外的队员或被他所触及,是该队员使球出界。

23.2.3 在争球**期间**,如果队员移动到界外或他的后场,一次跳球情况发生。

Art. 24 Dribbling

24.1 Definition

24.1.1 A dribble is the movement of a live ball caused by a player in control of that ball who throws, taps, rolls or bounces the ball on the floor.

24.1.2 **A dribble starts** when a player, having gained control of a live ball on the playing court throws, taps, rolls or bounces it on the floor and touches it again before it touches another player.

A dribble ends when the player touches the ball with both hands simultaneously or permits the ball to come to rest in one or both hands.

During a dribble the ball may be thrown into the air provided the ball touches the floor or another player before the player who threw it touches it again with his hand.

There is no limit to the number of steps a player may take when the ball is not in contact with his hand.

24.1.3 A player who accidentally loses and then regains control of a live ball on the playing court is considered to be fumbling the ball.

24.1.4 The following are not dribbles:
- Successive shots for a field goal.
- Fumbling the ball at the beginning or at the end of a dribble.
- Attempts to gain control of the ball by tapping it from the vicinity of other players.
- Tapping the ball from the control of another player.
- Deflecting a pass and gaining control of the ball.
- Tossing the ball from hand to hand and allowing it to come to rest in one or both hands before touching the floor, provided that no travelling violation is committed.
- Throwing the ball against the backboard and regaining the control of the ball.

24.2 Rule

A player shall not dribble for a second time after his first dribble has ended unless between the 2 dribbles he has lost control of a live ball on the playing court because of:
- A shot for a field goal.
- A touch of the ball by an opponent.
- A pass or fumble that has touched or been touched by another player.

第 24 条 运 球

24.1 定 义

24.1.1 运球是指一名队员控制一个活球的一系列动作：在地面上掷、拍、滚、运或弹在地面上。

24.1.2 当在场上已获得控制活球的队员将球在地面上掷、拍、滚、运或弹在地面上，并在球触及另一队员之前再次触及球，为**运球开始**。当队员双手同时触及球或允许球在一手或双手中停留时**运球结束**。

在运球的时候球可被掷向空中，只要掷球的队员用手再次触及球之前球触及地面或另一队员。

当球不与队员的手接触时，队员可行进的步数不受限制。

24.1.3 队员意外地失掉并随后在场上恢复控制活球，被认为是漏接球。

24.1.4 下列情况不是运球：
- 连续的投篮。
- 一次运球的开始或结束时漏接球。
- 从其他队员的附近用拍击球来试图获得控制球。
- 拍击另一队员控制的球。
- 拦截传球并获得控制球。
- 只要不发生带球走违例，将球在两手之间抛接并在球触及地面前，允许球在一手或者两手中停留。
- 将球掷向篮板并再次获得控制球。

24.2 规 定

队员第一次运球结束后不得再次运球，除非在两次运球之间由于下述原因他已在场上失去了控制活球：
- 投篮。
- 球被对方队员触及。
- 传球或漏接，然后球触及了另一队员或被另一队员触及。

Art. 25 Travelling

25.1 Definition

25.1.1 Travelling is the illegal movement of one foot or both feet beyond the limits outlined in this article, in any direction, while holding a live ball on the playing court.

25.1.2 A pivot is the legal movement in which a player who is holding a live ball on the playing court steps once or more than once in any direction with the same foot, while the other foot, called the pivot foot, is kept at its point of contact with the floor.

25.2 Rule

25.2.1 Establishing a pivot foot by a player who catches a live ball on the playing court:

- A player who catches the ball while standing with both feet on the floor:
  — The moment one foot is lifted, the other foot becomes the pivot foot.
  — To start a dribble, the pivot foot may not be lifted before the ball is released from the hand(s).
  — To pass or shoot for a field goal, the player may jump off a pivot foot, but neither foot may be returned to the floor before the ball is released from the hand(s).

- A player who catches the ball while he is progressing, or upon completion of a dribble, may take two steps in coming to a stop, passing or shooting the ball:
  — If, after receiving the ball, a player shall release the ball to start his dribble before his second step.
  — The first step occurs when one foot or both feet touch the floor after gaining control of the ball.
  — The second step occurs after the first step when the other foot touches the floor or both feet touch the floor simultaneously.
  — If the player who comes to a stop on his first step has both feet on the floor or they touch the floor simultaneously, he may pivot using either foot as his pivot foot. If he then jumps with both feet, no foot may return to the floor before the ball is released from the hand(s).
  — If a player lands with one foot he may only pivot using that foot.

第 25 条 带球走

25.1 定 义

25.1.1 当队员在场上持着一个活球，其一脚或双脚超出本条款所述的限制，向任一方向非法的运动是**带球走**。

25.1.2 在场上正持着一个活球的队员用一脚（称为"中枢脚"）始终接触着该脚与地面接触的那个点，而另一只脚向任一方向踏出一次或多次的合法运动是**旋转**。

25.2 规 定

25.2.1 **对在场上接住活球的队员确立中枢脚：**

- 一名队员接住球时，双脚站在地面上：
  —— 一只脚抬起的瞬间，另一只脚成为中枢脚。
  —— 开始运球时，在球离手前中枢脚不得离开地面。
  —— 队员可以跳起中枢脚传球或投篮，但在球离手前，任意一只脚不得落回地面。

- 一名队员在移动中或在结束运球时拿球，他可以移动2步完成停步、传球或者投篮：
  —— 如果接到球的队员开始运球，他应在第2步（脚接触地面）之前球离手。
  —— 队员获得控制球之后，一只脚接触地面或双脚同时接触地面时，就视为是第1步。
  —— 在队员确立了第1步后，当他的另一只脚接触地面或双脚同时接触地面时，就视为是第2步。
  —— 如果队员在第1步就完成了停步，此时他双脚站在地面上时，或是两脚同时接触地面时，他可以用他的任一只脚作为中枢脚进行旋转。如果随后他双脚跳起，那么在他球离手之前，任一只脚都不得落回地面。
  —— 如果队员是脚分先后落地完成（合法）停步时，他仅可以用那只先着地的脚作为中枢脚进行旋转。

— If a player jumps off one foot on the first step, he may land with both feet simultaneously for the second step. In this situation, the player may not pivot with either foot. If one foot or both feet then leave the floor, no foot may return to the floor before the ball is released from the hand(s).

— If both feet are off the floor and the player lands on both feet simultaneously, the moment one foot is lifted the other foot becomes the pivot foot.

— A player may not touch the floor consecutively with the same foot or both feet after ending his dribble or gaining control of the ball.

25.2.2 A player falling, lying or sitting on the floor:
- It is legal when a player falls and slides on the floor while holding the ball or, while lying or sitting on the floor, gains control of the ball.
- It is a violation if the player then rolls or attempts to stand up while holding the ball.

Art. 26 3 seconds

26.1 Rule

26.1.1 A player shall **not** remain in the opponents' restricted area for more than 3 consecutive seconds while his team is in control of a live ball in the frontcourt and the game clock is running.

26.1.2 Allowances must be made for a player who:
- Makes an attempt to leave the restricted area.
- Is in the restricted area when he or his team-mate is in the act of shooting and the ball is leaving or has just left the player's hand(s) on the shot for a field goal.
- Dribbles in the restricted area to shoot for a field goal after having been there for less than 3 consecutive seconds.

26.1.3 To establish himself outside the restricted area, the player must place both feet on the floor outside the restricted area.

Art. 27 Closely guarded player

27.1 Definition

A player who is holding a live ball on the playing court is closely guarded when an opponent is in an active legal guarding position at a distance of no more than 1 m.

——如果队员第1步是一只脚落地，随即又跳起该脚，他可以双脚同时落地作为他的第2步。在这种情况下，该队员不可以再用任何一只脚为中枢脚进行旋转。如果随后他的一脚或双脚离开地面，那么，在球离手前哪一只脚都不得落回地面。

——如果队员双脚离开地面后又双脚同时落地作为第1步时，那么，在一只脚抬离地面的瞬间，另一只脚就成为中枢脚。

——队员结束运球或获得控制球后，他不得用同一只脚或双脚连续地接触地面行进。

25.2.2 一名跌倒、躺在或坐在地面上的队员：
- 当一名队员持着球跌倒并在地面上滑行，或躺在地面上或坐在地面上时获得了控制球，这是合法的。
- 如果随后该队员持球滚动或持着球尝试站起来，这是违例。

第 26 条 3 秒钟

26.1 规 定

26.1.1 某队在前场控制活球并且比赛计时钟正在运行时，该队的队员**不得**在对方队的限制区内停留超过持续的3秒。

26.1.2 队员在下列情况中应被默许：
- 他试图离开限制区。
- 他在限制区内，当他或他的同队队员正在做投篮动作并且球正离开或恰已离开投篮队员的手时。
- 他在限制区内已接近3秒时运球投篮。

26.1.3 为证实队员自身位于限制区外，他必须将双脚置于限制区外的地面上。

第 27 条 被严密防守的队员

27.1 定 义

一名队员在场上正持着一个活球，一名对方队员在距离他不超过1米处，并采取积极的、合法防守的动作时，该持球队员是被

27.2 Rule

A closely guarded player must pass, shoot or dribble the ball within 5 seconds.

Art. 28 8 seconds

28.1 Rule

28.1.1 Whenever:
- A player in the backcourt gains control of a live ball, or
- On a throw-in, the ball touches or is legally touched by any player in the back-court and the team of that player taking the throw-in remains in control of the ball in its backcourt, that team must cause the ball to go into its frontcourt within 8 seconds.

28.1.2 The team has caused the ball to go into its frontcourt whenever:
- The ball, not in control of any player, touches the frontcourt.
- The ball touches or is legally touched by an offensive player who has both feet completely in contact with his frontcourt.
- The ball touches or is legally touched by a defensive player who has part of his body in contact with his backcourt.
- The ball touches a referee who has part of his body in contact with the frontcourt of the team in control of the ball.
- During a dribble from the backcourt to the frontcourt, the ball and both feet of the dribbler are completely in contact with the frontcourt.

28.1.3 The 8-second period shall continue with any time remaining when the same team that previously had control of the ball is awarded a throw-in in the backcourt, as a result of:
- A ball having gone out-of-bounds.
- A player of the same team having been injured.
- A technical foul committed by that team.
- A jump ball situation.
- A double foul.
- A cancellation of equal penalties on both teams.

严密防守的队员。

27.2 规 定
一名被严密防守的队员必须在 5 秒内传球、投球或运球。

第 28 条 8 秒钟

28.1 规 定
28.1.1 每当：
- 一名在后场的队员获得控制活球时，或
- 在掷球入界中，球触及后场的任何队员或者被后场的任何队员合法触及，掷球入界队员所在队仍拥有在后场的球权。

该队必须在 8 秒内使球进入该队的前场。

28.1.2 每当：
- 没有被任何队员控制，球触及前场时。
- 球触及或者被双脚完全在他前场的进攻队员合法触及时。
- 球触及或者被有部分身体在他后场的防守队员合法触及时。
- 球触及有部分身体在控制球队前场的裁判员时。
- 运球队员在后场往前场运球的过程中，球和双脚完全进入前场时。

就是球队使球进入该队的前场。

28.1.3 当先前已控制球的同一队由于下列情况的结果被判在后场掷球入界时，8 秒应从剩余时间处连续计算：
- 球出界。
- 一名同队队员受伤。
- 该队被判技术犯规。
- 一次跳球情况。
- 一次双方犯规。
- 双方球队的相等罚则抵消。

67

Art. 29 24 seconds

29.1 Rule
29.1.1 Whenever:
- A player gains control of a **live** ball on the **playing court,**
- On a throw-in, the ball touches or is legally touched by any player on the playing court and the team of that player taking the throw-in remains in control of the ball,

that team must attempt a shot for a field goal within 24 seconds.

To constitute a shot for a field goal within 24 seconds:
- The ball must leave the player's hand(s) before the shot clock signal sounds, and
- After the ball has left the player's hand(s), the ball must touch the ring or enter the basket.

29.1.2 When **a shot for a field goal is attempted near the end of the 24-second period** and the shot clock signal sounds while the ball is in the air:
- If the ball enters the basket, no violation has occurred, the signal shall be disregarded and the goal shall count.
- If the ball touches the ring but does not enter the basket, no violation has occurred, the signal shall be disregarded and the game shall continue.
- If the ball misses the ring, a violation has occurred. However, if the opponents gain an immediate and clear control of the ball, the signal shall be disregarded and the game shall continue.

When the backboard is equipped with yellow lighting along its perimeter at the top, the lighting takes precedence over the shot clock signal sound.

All restrictions related to goaltending and interference shall **apply**.

29.2 Procedure
29.2.1 The shot clock shall be reset whenever the game is stopped by a referee:
- For a foul or violation (not for the ball having gone out-of-bounds) by the team not in control of the ball,
- For any valid reason by the team not in control of the ball,
- For any valid reason not connected with either team.

In these situations, the possession of the ball shall be awarded to the same team that previously had control of the ball. If the throw-in is then administered in that team's:
- Backcourt, the shot clock shall be reset to 24 seconds.
- Frontcourt, the shot clock shall be reset as follows:

第 29 条 24 秒钟

29.1 规 定

29.1.1 每当：

- 一名队员**在场上**获得控制**活球**时。
- 在掷球入界中，球接触场上的任何队员或被场上的任何队员合法触及，并且掷球入界队员的球队仍然控制球时。

该队必须在24秒内尝试投篮。

一次24秒内投篮的构成：

- 在进攻计时钟的信号发出前，球必须离开队员的手，而且
- 球离开了队员的手后，必须触及篮圈或进入球篮。

29.1.2 在临近24秒结束时尝试了一次投篮，并且球在空中时进攻计时钟信号响：

- 如果球进入球篮，没有违例发生，信号应被忽略并且计中篮得分。
- 如果球触及篮圈但未进入球篮，没有违例发生，信号应被忽略并且比赛应继续。
- 如果球未碰篮圈，一次违例发生。然而，如果对方队员立即和清晰地获得了控制球，信号应被忽略并且比赛应继续。

当篮板上沿装有黄色光带时，光带信号亮先于进攻计时钟信号响。关系到干涉得分和干扰得分的**所有限制应适用**。

29.2 程 序

29.2.1 每当裁判员停止了比赛，进攻计时钟应复位：

- 因为不控制球的球队犯规或者违例（不是因为球出界）。
- 因为任何不控制球的球队有关的正当原因。
- 因为任何与双方球队都无关的正当原因。

在这些情况中，球权应判给先前控制球的球队。如果掷球入界在其：

- 后场执行，进攻计时钟应复位到24秒。
- 前场执行，进攻计时钟应按照下述原则复位：

- If 14 seconds or more are displayed on the shot clock at the time when the game was stopped, the shot clock shall not be reset, but shall continue from the time it was stopped.
- If 13 seconds or less are displayed on the shot clock at the time when the game was stopped, the shot clock shall be reset to 14 seconds.

However, if the game is stopped by a referee for any valid reason not connected with either team and, in the judgement of a referee, the reset of the shot clock would place the opponents at a disadvantage, the shot clock shall continue from the time it was stopped.

29.2.2 The shot clock shall be reset whenever a throw-in is awarded to the opponents' team after the game is stopped by a referee for a foul or violation (including for the ball having gone out-of-bounds) committed **by the team in control of the ball.**

The shot clock shall also be reset if the new offensive team is awarded a throw-in according to the alternating possession procedure.

If the throw-in is then administered in that team's:
- Backcourt, the shot clock shall be reset to a new 24 seconds.
- Frontcourt, the shot clock shall be reset to 14 seconds.

29.2.3 Whenever the game is stopped by a referee for a technical foul committed by the team in control of the ball, the game shall be resumed with a throw-in from the place nearest to where the game was stopped. The shot clock shall not be reset but shall continue from the time it was stopped.

29.2.4 When the game clock shows 2:00 minutes or less in the fourth quarter or overtime, following a time-out taken by the team that is entitled to the possession of the ball from its backcourt, the head coach of that team has the right to decide whether the game shall be resumed with a throw-in from the throw-in line in the team's frontcourt or from the team's backcourt at the place nearest to where the game was stopped.

After the time-out, the throw-in shall be administered as follows:
- If as a result of the ball having gone out-of-bounds and if from the team's:
  - Backcourt, the shot clock shall continue from the time it was stopped.
  - Frontcourt: If the shot clock shows 13 seconds or less it shall continue from the time it was stopped. If the shot clock shows 14 seconds or more, it shall be reset to 14 seconds.
- If as a result of a foul or violation (not for the ball having gone out-of-bounds) and if from the team's:
  - Backcourt, the shot clock shall be reset to 24 seconds.
  - Frontcourt, the shot clock shall be reset to 14 seconds.
- If the time-out is taken by the team which has a new control of the ball, and if from the team's:

— 当比赛停止时，如果进攻计时钟显示为14秒或者多于14秒，进攻计时钟不复位，从被停止的时间处连续计算。

— 当比赛停止时，如果进攻计时钟显示为13秒或者少于13秒，进攻计时钟应复位到14秒。

然而，如果比赛因为与双方球队都无关的正当原因而被裁判员停止，根据裁判员的判断，进攻计时钟复位将置对方于不利，进攻计时钟应从停止的时间连续计算。

29.2.2 每当在裁判员因为**控制球队**的犯规或者违例（包括球出界）停止比赛后，判给对方队一次掷球入界时，进攻计时钟应复位。

如果根据交替拥有程序新的进攻方拥有掷球入界权，进攻计时钟也应复位。

如果掷球入界在该队的：
- 后场，进攻计时钟应复位到新的24秒。
- 前场，进攻计时钟应复位到14秒。

29.2.3 无论何时比赛因裁判员判罚控制球队技术犯规被停止，应在最靠近比赛停止时的地点掷球入界重新开始。进攻计时钟不复位并从被停止的时间处连续计算。

29.2.4 当第4节或决胜期比赛计时钟显示2:00分钟或更少时，随后在后场拥有球权的队申请了一次暂停，该队主教练有权决定在记录台对侧的前场掷球入界线处或后场距离比赛停止最近的地点掷球入界重新开始比赛。

暂停结束后，应按如下原则执行掷球入界：
- 如果作为球出界的结果并且在该队的：
  — 后场，进攻计时钟应从时间被停止时连续计算。
  — 前场：如果进攻计时钟显示13秒或更少，应从时间被停止处连续计算。如果进攻计时钟显示14秒或更多，则应复位进攻计时钟为14秒。
- 如果作为一次犯规或违例的结果（非球出界）并且在该队的：
  — 后场，应复位进攻计时钟为24秒。
  — 前场，应复位进攻计时钟为14秒。
- 如果新的控制球队请求了暂停，并且在该队的：

- Backcourt, the shot clock shall be reset to 24 seconds.
- Frontcourt, the shot clock shall be reset to 14 seconds.

29.2.5 When the team is awarded a throw-in from the throw-in line in the team's frontcourt as part of the penalty for an unsportsmanlike or disqualifying foul, the shot clock shall be reset to 14 seconds.

29.2.6 After the ball has touched the ring of the opponents' basket, the shot clock shall be reset to:
- 24 seconds, if the opponents' team gains control of the ball.
- 14 seconds, if the team which regains control of the ball is the same team that was in control of the ball before the ball touched the ring.

29.2.7 If the shot clock signal **sounds in error** while a team has control of the ball or neither team has control of the ball, the signal shall be disregarded, and the game shall continue.

However, if in the judgement of a referee, the team in control of the ball has been placed at a disadvantage, the game shall be stopped, the shot clock shall be corrected and possession of the ball shall be awarded to that team.

Art. 30 Ball returned to the backcourt

30.1 Definition

30.1.1 A team is in control of a live ball in its frontcourt when:
- A player of that team is touching his frontcourt with both feet while holding, catching or dribbling the ball in his frontcourt, or
- The ball is passed between the players of that team in its frontcourt.

30.1.2 A team in control of a live ball in the frontcourt has caused the ball to be illegally returned to its backcourt, if a player of that team is the last to touch the ball in his frontcourt and the ball is then first touched by a player of that team:
- Who has part of his body in contact with the backcourt, or
- After the ball has touched the backcourt of that team.

This restriction applies to all situations in a team's frontcourt, including throw-ins. However, it does not apply to a player who jumps from his frontcourt, establishes new team control while still airborne and then lands with the ball in his team's backcourt.

30.2 Rule

A team which is in control of a live ball in its frontcourt may not cause the ball to be illegally returned to its backcourt.

—— 后场，应复位进攻计时钟为24秒。

—— 前场，应复位进攻计时钟为14秒。

29.2.5 当判罚了违反体育运动精神或取消比赛资格的犯规，作为罚则的一部分，在球队前场的掷球入界线处进行掷球入界时，进攻计时钟应复位到14秒。

29.2.6 在球已经触及对方球篮篮圈之后，进攻计时钟应复位到：
- 24秒，如果对方获得控制球。
- 14秒，如果球触及篮圈前的同一控制球队再次获得控制球。

29.2.7 如果某队已控制球或双方队都未控制球时，进攻计时钟**错误地发出信号**，此信号应被忽略并且比赛应继续。

然而，如果根据裁判员的判断，控制球队已被置于不利，应停止比赛，进攻计时钟应被纠正，并且把球权判给该队。

第30条 球回后场

30.1 定 义

30.1.1 某队在他的前场控制活球，当：
- 一名双脚触及前场的该队队员正持球、接住球或在他的前场运球，或
- 球在位于前场的该队队员之间传递。

30.1.2 在他的前场控制活球的球队使球非法地回到他的后场，如果该队一名队员在他的前场最后触及球，并且随后球被该队一名队员首先触及：
- 该队员有部分身体触及后场，或
- 在球已触及该队后场之后。

这个限制适用于在某队前场的所有情况，包括掷球入界。然而，它不适用于队员从他的前场跳起，仍在空中时建立新的球队控制球，然后持球落在该队的后场。

30.2 规 定

在前场控制活球的球队不得使球非法地回到他的后场。

73

30.3 Penalty

The ball shall be awarded to the opponents' team for a throw-in in its frontcourt from the place nearest to the infraction except directly behind the backboard.

Art. 31 Goaltending and Interference

31.1 Definition

31.1.1 A shot for a field goal or a free throw:

- **Begins** when the ball leaves the hand(s) of a player in the act of shooting.

- **Ends** when the ball:
    — Enters the basket directly from above and remains within the basket or passes through the basket entirely.
    — No longer has the possibility to enter the basket.
    — Touches the ring.
    — Touches the floor.
    — Becomes dead.

31.2 Rule

31.2.1 **Goaltending** occurs during a **shot for a field goal** when a player touches the ball while it is completely above the level of the ring and:
- It is on its downward flight to the basket, or
- After it has touched the backboard.

31.2.2 **Goaltending** occurs during a **shot for a free throw** when a player touches the ball while it is in flight to the basket and before it touches the ring.

31.2.3 The goaltending restrictions apply until:
- The ball no longer has the possibility to enter the basket.
- The ball has touched the ring.

31.2.4 **Interference** occurs when:

- After a shot for a field goal or the last free throw a player touches the basket or the backboard while the ball is in contact with the ring.

30.3 罚 则

球应判给对方球队在他的前场最靠近违犯的地点掷球入界，正好在篮板后面的地点除外。

第 31 条 干涉得分和干扰得分

31.1 定义

31.1.1 投篮或罚球：
- **开始于**：球离开正在做投篮动作的队员的手时。
- **结束于**：
  —— 球从上方直接进入球篮并且停留在球篮中或完全地穿过球篮时。
  —— 球不再有进入球篮的可能性时。
  —— 球触及篮圈时。
  —— 球触及地面时。
  —— 球成为死球时。

31.2 规定

31.2.1 **在一次投篮中**，当一名队员触及完全在篮圈水平面之上的球时，并且：
- 球是下落飞向球篮中，或
- 在球已碰击篮板后。

干涉得分发生。

31.2.2 在一次**罚球**中，当一名队员触及飞向球篮的、触及篮圈前的球时，**干涉得分**发生。

31.2.3 干涉得分限制适用于：
- 球不再有进入球篮的可能性前。
- 球触及篮圈前。

31.2.4 当：
- 在一次投篮或最后一次罚球中，当球与篮圈接触时，队员触及球篮或篮板。

- After a free throw followed by an additional free throw(s), a player touches the ball, the basket or the backboard while there is still a possibility that the ball will enter the basket.
- A player reaches through the basket from below and touches the ball.
- A defensive player touches the ball or the basket while the ball is within the basket, thus preventing the ball from passing through the basket.
- A player causes the basket to vibrate or grasps the basket in such a way that, in the judgement of a referee, the ball has been prevented from entering the basket or has been caused to enter the basket.
- A player grasps the basket and plays the ball.

31.2.5 When:
- A referee has blown his whistle while:
  — The ball was in the hands of a player in the act of shooting, or
  — The ball was in flight on a shot for a field goal or on a last free throw,
- The game clock signal has sounded for the end of the quarter or overtime, No player shall touch the ball after it has touched the ring while it still has the possibility to enter the basket.

All restrictions related to goaltending and interference shall **apply**.

31.3 Penalty

31.3.1 If the violation is committed by an **offensive player**, no points can be awarded. The ball shall be awarded to the opponents for a throw-in from the free-throw line extended, unless otherwise stated in these rules.

31.3.2 If the violation is committed by a **defensive player**, the offensive team is awarded:
- 1 point, if the ball was released for a free throw.
- 2 points, if the ball was released from the 2-point field goal area.
- 3 points, if the ball was released from the 3-point field goal area.

The awarding of the points is considered as if the ball had entered the basket.

31.3.3 If the goaltending is committed by a **defensive player** during a last free throw, 1 point shall be awarded to the offensive team, followed by a technical foul penalty charged on the defensive player.

- 在一次罚球（随后还有进一步的罚球）后，球有进入球篮的可能性时，一名队员触及球、球篮或篮板时。
- 队员从下方伸手穿过球篮并触及球时。
- 当球在球篮中，防守队员触及球或球篮，从而阻止球穿过球篮时。
- 队员使篮板颤动或者抓球篮，根据裁判员的判定，这种手段已妨碍球进入球篮或者使球进入球篮时。
- 队员抓球篮打球时。

干扰得分发生。

31.2.5 当：
- 一名裁判员鸣哨，此时：
  —— 球在一名正在做投篮动作的队员的手中，或
  —— 球正在一次投篮或最后一次的罚球飞行中，
- 结束一节或决胜期的比赛计时钟的信号响，在球已触及篮圈之后仍有进入球篮的可能性时，任何队员不得触及球。

涉及干涉得分和干扰得分的**所有限制应适用**。

31.3 罚 则

31.3.1 如果一名**进攻队员**发生违例，不判给得分。将球判给对方队员从罚球线延长线掷球入界，除非本规则另有规定。

31.3.2 如果一名**防守队员**发生违例，应判给进攻的队：
- 当球在罚球中出手时，得1分。
- 当球在2分投篮区域出手时，得2分。
- 当球在3分投篮区域出手时，得3分。

判给的得分就如同球进入球篮一样。

31.3.3 如果**防守队员**在最后一次罚球中发生干涉得分违例，应判给进攻队得1分，随后执行防守队员技术犯规的罚则。

RULE SIX — FOULS

Art. 32 Fouls

32.1 Definition

32.1.1 A foul is an infraction of the rules concerning illegal personal contact with an opponent and/or unsportsmanlike behaviour.

32.1.2 Any number of fouls may be called on a team. Irrespective of the penalty, each foul shall be charged, entered on the scoresheet on the offender and penalised according to these rules.

Art. 33 Contact: General principles

33.1 Cylinder principle

The cylinder principle is defined as the space within an imaginary cylinder occupied by a player on the floor. These dimensions, and the distance between his feet, shall vary according to the height and size of the player. It includes the space above the player and is limited to the boundaries of the cylinder of the defensive player or the offensive player without the ball which are:
- The front by the palms of the hands,
- The rear by the buttocks, and
- The sides by the outer edge of the arms and legs.

The hands and arms may be extended in front of the torso no further than the position of the feet and knees, with the arms bent at the elbows so that the forearms and hands are raised in the legal guarding position.

The defensive player may not enter the cylinder of the offensive player with the ball and cause an illegal contact when the offensive player is attempting a normal basketball play within his cylinder. The boundaries of the cylinder of the offensive player with the ball are:
- The front by the feet, bent knees and arms, holding the ball above the hips,
- The rear by the buttocks, and
- The sides by the outer edge of elbows and legs.

The offensive player with the ball must be allowed enough space for a normal basketball play within his cylinder. The normal basketball play includes starting a dribble, pivoting, shooting and passing.

第六章 犯规

第 32 条 犯规

32.1 定义

32.1.1 犯规是对规则的违犯，含有与对方队员的非法身体接触和／或违反体育运动精神的举止。

32.1.2 可宣判一个队任何数量的犯规，不管罚则是什么，都要登记犯规者的每一次犯规，记入记录表并且根据这些规则进行处罚。

第 33 条 身体接触：一般原则

33.1 圆柱体原则

圆柱体原则定义为一名站在地面上的队员占据一个假想的圆柱体的空间。双脚之间的尺寸和距离应根据他的身高和体型有所不同。它包括该队员上面的空间，防守队员或无球进攻队员的圆柱体边界限定如下：

- 前至手的双掌，
- 后至臀部，及
- 两侧至双臂和双腿的外侧。（图5）

双手和双臂可以在躯干前面伸展，但不超过双脚和双膝的位置，因此两前臂和双手在合法的防守位置中是举起的。

防守队员不可以进入一名持球进攻队员的圆柱体并在进攻队员在他的圆柱体内试图做一个正常的篮球动作时造成非法身体接触。持球进攻队员的圆柱体边界限制如下：

- 前至双脚、弯曲的膝盖和手臂，持球在臀部以上。
- 后至臀部，及
- 两侧至双肘和双腿的外侧。

持球进攻队员应被允许在其圆柱体内有足够的空间完成正常的篮球动作。正常的篮球动作包括开始运球、旋转、投篮或传球。

OFFICIAL BASKETBALL RULES *2020*

Diagram 5 Cylinder principle

The offensive player cannot spread his legs or arms outside of his cylinder and cause an illegal contact with the defensive player in order to gain an additional space.

33.2 Principle of verticality

During the game, each player has the right to occupy any position (cylinder) on the playing court not already occupied by an opponent.

This principle protects the space on the floor which he occupies and the space above him when he jumps vertically within that space.

As soon as the player leaves his vertical position (cylinder) and body contact occurs with an opponent who had already established his own vertical position (cylinder), the player who left his vertical position (cylinder) is responsible for the contact.

The defensive player must not be penalised for leaving the floor vertically (within his cylinder) or having his hands and arms extended above him within his own cylinder.

The offensive player, whether on the floor or airborne, shall not cause contact with the defensive player in a legal guarding position by:
- Using his arms to create more space for himself (pushing off).
- Spreading his legs or arms to cause contact during or immediately after a shot for a field goal.

图5　圆柱体原则

进攻队员不能伸展他的腿或者手臂超出圆柱体并造成与防守队员的一起非法身体接触以获得额外的空间。

33.2 垂直原则

在比赛中，每一队员都有权占据未被对方队员已经占据的任何场上位置（圆柱体）。

这个原则保护队员所占据的地面空间和当他在此空间内垂直跳起时的上方空间。

队员一旦离开他的垂直位置（圆柱体），并与已经建立了自己的垂直位置（圆柱体）的对方队员发生身体接触，则离开他的垂直位置（圆柱体）的队员须对此接触负责。

防守队员垂直地离开地面（在他的圆柱体内）或在他自己的圆柱体内把双手和双臂伸展在他的上方，则不必判罚。

无论是在地面上或在空中的进攻队员，不应用下列方式与处于合法防守位置的防守队员发生接触。

- 用他的手臂为自己创造额外的空间（推开障碍）。
- 在投篮中或紧接投篮后伸展他的双腿或双臂去造成接触。

81

33.3 Legal guarding position

A defensive player has established an initial legal guarding position when:
- He is facing his opponent, and
- He has both feet on the floor.

The legal guarding position extends vertically above him (cylinder) from the floor to the ceiling. He may raise his arms and hands above his head or jump vertically but he must maintain them in a vertical position inside the imaginary cylinder.

33.4 Guarding a player who controls the ball

When guarding a player who controls (holding or dribbling) the ball, **the elements of time and distance do not apply.**

The player with the ball must expect to be guarded and must be prepared to stop or change his direction whenever an opponent takes an initial legal guarding position in front of him, even if this is done within a fraction of a second.

The guarding (defensive) player must establish an initial legal guarding position without causing contact before taking his position.

Once the defensive player has established an initial legal guarding position, he may move to guard his opponent, but he may not extend his arms, shoulders, hips or legs to prevent the dribbler from passing by him.

When judging a charge/block situation involving a player with the ball, a referee shall use the following principles:
- The defensive player must establish an initial legal guarding position by facing the player with the ball and having both feet on the floor.
- The defensive player may remain stationary, jump vertically, move laterally or backwards in order to maintain the initial legal guarding position.
- When moving to maintain the initial legal guarding position, one foot or both feet may be off the floor for an instant, as long as the movement is lateral or backwards, but **not towards** the player with the ball.

33.3 合法的防守位置

当一名防守队员：
- 面对对手，并且
- 双脚着地时。

他就建立了最初的合法防守位置。

合法的防守位置从地面到天花板，垂直地伸展到他（圆柱体）的上方。他可将他的双臂和双手举过头或垂直跳起，但是他必须在假想的圆柱体内使手和臂保持垂直的姿势。

33.4 防守控制球的队员

当防守控制（正持着或运着）球的队员时，**时间和距离的因素不适用**。

每当对方队员在持球队员前面获得了一个最初的合法防守位置（甚至是一瞬间完成的），持球队员必须料到被防守并必须准备停步或改变他的方向。

防守队员建立一个最初的合法防守位置，必须在占据位置前没有造成接触。

一旦防守队员已建立了一个最初的合法防守位置，他可移动去防守其对手，但他不得伸展双臂、双肩、双髋或双腿，并通过这样做来造成接触以阻止从他身边通过的运球队员。

判断一起涉及持球队员撞人／阻挡情况时，裁判员应运用下列原则：
- 防守队员必须面对持球队员并双脚着地来建立一个最初的合法防守位置。
- 防守队员为保持最初的合法防守位置，可保持静立、垂直跳起、侧移或后移。
- 在保持最初的合法防守位置的移动中，一脚或双脚可以瞬间离地，只要该移动是侧向或向后的，而**不是朝向**持球队员前移的。

- Contact must occur on the torso, in which case the defensive player would be considered as having been at the place of contact first.
- Having established a legal guarding position, the defensive player may turn **within** his cylinder to avoid injury.

In any of the above situations, the contact shall be considered as having been caused by the player with the ball.

33.5 Guarding a player who does not control the ball

A player who does not control the ball is entitled to move freely on the playing court and take any position not already occupied by another player.

When guarding a player who does not control the ball, **the elements of time and distance shall apply.** A defensive player cannot take a position so near and/or so quickly in the path of a moving opponent that the latter does not have sufficient time or distance either to stop or change his direction.

The distance is directly proportional to the speed of the opponent, but never less than 1 normal step.

If a defensive player does not respect the elements of time and distance in taking his initial legal guarding position and contact with an opponent occurs, he is responsible for the contact.

Once a defensive player has established an initial legal guarding position, he may move to guard his opponent. He may not prevent him from passing by extending his arms, shoulders, hips or legs in his path. He may turn within his cylinder to avoid injury.

33.6 A player who is in the air

A player who has jumped into the air from a place on the playing court has the right to land again at the same place.

He has the right to land on another place on the playing court provided that the lan-ding place and the direct path between the take-off and landing place is not already occupied by an opponent(s) at the time of take-off.

If a player has taken off and landed but his momentum causes him to contact an oppo-nent who has taken a legal guarding position beyond the landing place, the jumper is responsible for the contact.

An opponent may not move into the path of a player after that player has jumped into the air.

- 接触必须发生在躯干上，在这样的情况下，防守队员将被认为是已经先占据了接触地点。
- 已建立了合法防守位置的防守队员可以在其圆柱体**之内**转身，以避免受伤。

在上述任何情况中，应认为该接触是由持球队员造成的。

33.5 防守不控制球的队员

不控制球的队员有权在球场上自由地移动，并占据任何未被另一队员已经占据的位置。

当防守不控制球的队员时，**时间和距离的因素应适用**。防守队员不能太靠近和/或太快地在移动的对方队员的路径中占据一个位置，以至于后者没有足够的时间或距离去停步或改变其方向。

此距离与对方队员的速度成正比，但绝不要少于正常的一步。

如果一名防守队员在获得最初的合法防守位置中不顾及时间和距离的因素，并与对方队员发生接触，则他对该接触负责。

一旦一名防守队员已经建立了一个最初的合法防守位置，他可移动去防守他的对手。他不得在对方队员的路径中伸展臂、肩、臀或腿去阻止该队员从他身边通过。他可以在他的圆柱体内转身来避免受伤。

33.6 腾空的队员

从球场某地点跳起在空中的队员有权再落回同一地点。

他有权落在场上的另一地点，只要在起跳时，该落地点上，以及起跳点和落地点之间的直接路径上，尚未被对方队员占据。

如果一名队员已跳起并落地，可是他的冲力使其接触了在落地地点之外已获得了一个合法防守位置的对方队员，则该跳起队员对此接触负责。

在队员已跳起在空中后，对方队员不得移动到他的下落路径上。

Moving under a player who is in the air and causing contact is usually an unsports-manlike foul and in certain circumstances may be a disqualifying foul.

33.7 Screening: Legal and illegal

Screening is an attempt to delay or prevent an opponent without the ball from reaching a desired position on the playing court.

Legal screening is when the player who is screening an opponent:
- **Was stationary** (inside his cylinder) when contact occurred.
- Had both feet on the floor when contact occurred.

Illegal screening is when the player who is screening an opponent:
- **Was moving** when contact occurred.
- Did not give sufficient distance in setting a screen outside the field of vision of a **stationary** opponent when contact occurred.
- Did not respect the elements of time and distance of an opponent in motion when contact occurred.

If the screen is set **within** the field of vision of a stationary opponent (front or lateral), the screener may establish the screen as close to him as he wishes, provided there is no contact.

If the screen is set **outside** the field of vision of a stationary opponent, the screener must permit the opponent to take 1 normal step towards the screen without making contact.

If the opponent is **in motion**, the elements of time and distance shall apply. The screener must leave enough space so that the player who is being screened is able to avoid the screen by stopping or changing direction.

The distance required is never less than 1 and never more than 2 normal steps.

A player who is legally screened is responsible for any contact with the player who has set the screen.

33.8 Charging

Charging is illegal personal contact, with or without the ball, by pushing or moving into an opponent's torso.

移动到腾空队员的身下并造成接触，通常是违反体育运动精神的犯规，某些情况下可能是取消比赛资格的犯规。

33.7 掩护：合法的和非法的

掩护是试图延误或阻止一名不持球的对方队员到达他希望到达的场上位置。

当正在掩护对手的队员：
- 发生接触时**是静止的**（在他的圆柱体内）。
- 发生接触时双脚着地。

是**合法的**掩护。

当正在掩护对手的队员：
- 发生接触时**正在移动**。
- 在**静止**对手的视野之外做掩护，发生接触时没有给出足够的距离。
- 发生接触时，对移动中的对手没有顾及时间和距离的因素。

是**非法的**掩护。

如果在静止对手的视野**之内**做掩护（前面的或侧面的），做掩护的队员可按自己的意愿靠近对手以建立掩护，只要没有接触。

如果在静止对手的视野**之外**做掩护，做掩护的队员必须允许对手向掩护迈出正常的1步而不发生接触。

如果对手**在移动中**，时间和距离的因素应适用。做掩护的队员必须留出足够的空间，以便被掩护的队员能通过停步或改变方向来避免掩护。

要求的距离是不得少于正常的1步，也不必多于正常的2步。

被合法掩护的队员与已经建立该掩护的队员的任何接触，由被合法掩护的队员负责。

33.8 撞　人

撞人是持球或不持球队员推开或顶动对方队员，在对方队员的躯干处发生的非法身体接触。

33.9 Blocking

Blocking is illegal personal contact which impedes the progress of an opponent with or without the ball.

A player who is attempting to screen is committing a blocking foul if contact occurs when he is moving and his opponent is stationary or retreating from him.

If a player disregards the ball, faces an opponent and shifts his position as the opponent shifts, he is primarily responsible for any contact that occurs, unless other factors are involved.

The expression 'unless other factors are involved' refers to deliberate pushing, charging or holding of the player who is being screened.

It is legal for a player to extend his arm(s) or elbow(s) outside of his cylinder in taking position on the floor but they must be moved inside his cylinder when an opponent attempts to pass by. If the arm(s) or elbow(s) are outside his cylinder and contact occurs, it is blocking or holding.

33.10 No-charge semi-circle areas

The no-charge semi-circle areas are drawn on the playing court for the purpose of designating a specific area for the interpretation of charge/block situations under the basket.

On any penetration play into the no-charge semi-circle area any contact caused by an airborne offensive player with a defensive player inside the no-charge semi-circle shall not be called as an offensive foul, unless the offensive player is illegally using his hands, arms, legs or body. This rule applies when:
- The offensive player is in control of the ball whilst airborne, and
- He attempts a shot for a field goal or passes the ball, and
- The defensive player has **one foot or both feet in contact with** the no-charge semi-circle area.

33.11 Contacting an opponent with the hand(s) and/or arm(s)

The touching of an opponent with the hand(s) is, in itself, not necessarily a foul.

The referees shall decide whether the player who caused the contact has gained an advantage. If contact caused by a player in any way restricts the freedom of movement of an opponent, such contact is a foul.

33.9 阻挡

阻挡是阻碍持球或不持球对方队员行进的非法身体接触。

如果试图做掩护的队员在移动中与静止或后退的对方队员发生接触，则判罚掩护队员一起阻挡犯规。

如果队员不顾球，面对着对方队员并随着对方队员的移动而移动他的位置，除非包含其他因素，该队员对所发生的任何接触负主要责任。

所谓"除非包含其他因素"，是指被掩护的队员故意推人、撞人或拉人。

队员在场上占据位置时，把手臂或肘伸在其圆柱体之外是合法的，但当对方队员试图通过时，手臂或肘必须被移到其圆柱体之内。如果手臂或肘是在他的圆柱体之外并发生接触，这是阻挡或拉人。

33.10 无撞人半圆区

球场上画出无撞人半圆区的目的是，指定一个特定的区域用于解释篮下的撞人／阻挡情况。

向无撞人半圆区的任何突破情况中，一名腾空的进攻队员造成的与防守队员在无撞人半圆区内的任何身体接触不应被宣判为进攻犯规，除非进攻队员非法地使用他的手、手臂或者身体。这一规则适用于：

- 进攻队员腾空并控制着球，并且
- 他试图投篮或者传球，并且
- 防守队员的**一脚或双脚触及**无撞人半圆区。

33.11 用手和／或手臂接触对方队员

用手触及对方队员，本身未必是犯规。

裁判员应判定引起接触的队员是否已经获得了不公正的利益。如果队员引起的接触在任何方面限制对方队员的移动自由，这样的接触是犯规。

Illegal use of the hand(s) or extended arm(s) occurs when the defensive player is in a guarding position and his hand(s) or arm(s) is placed upon and remains in contact with an opponent **with** or **without** the ball, to impede his progress.

To repeatedly touch or 'jab' an opponent with or without the ball is a foul, as it may lead to rough play.

It is a foul by an **offensive player with the ball** to:
- 'Hook' or wrap an arm or an elbow around a defensive player in order to obtain an advantage.
- 'Push off' to prevent the defensive player from playing or attempting to play the ball, or to create more space for himself.
- Use an extended forearm or hand, while dribbling, to prevent an opponent from gaining control of the ball.

It is a foul by an **offensive player without the ball** to 'push off' to:
- Get free to catch the ball.
- Prevent the defensive player from playing or attempting to play the ball.
- Create more space for him.

33.12 Post play

The principle of verticality (cylinder principle) applies also to post play.

The offensive player in the post position and the defensive player guarding him must respect each other's rights to a vertical position (cylinder).

It is a foul by an offensive or defensive player in the post position to shoulder or hip his opponent out of position or to interfere with his opponent's freedom of movement using extended arms, shoulders, hips, legs or other parts of the body.

33.13 Illegal guarding from the rear

Illegal guarding from the rear is personal contact with an opponent, by a defensive player, from behind. The fact that the defensive player is attempting to play the ball does not justify his contact with an opponent from the rear.

当防守队员处于防守位置，并且其手或手臂放置在**持球**或**不持球**的对方队员身上并保持接触以阻碍其行进，就发生了非法用手或非法伸展手臂。

反复地触及或"戳刺"**持球**或**不持球**的对方队员是犯规，因为这可能会导致粗暴的比赛。

当**持球进攻队员**：

- 为了获得不公正的利益，用手臂或肘"勾住"或缠绕防守队员。
- 为了阻止防守队员的防守或试图抢球，或为了在他和防守队员之间创造更大的空间而"推开"防守队员。
- 运球时，用伸展的前臂或手去阻止对方队员获得控制球。

这是持球进攻队员的犯规。

当**不持球的进攻队员**为了：

- 摆脱去接球。
- 阻止防守队员的防守或试图抢球。
- 为他创造更大的空间。

而"推开"防守队员，这是不持球进攻队员的犯规。

33.12 中锋位置的攻防

垂直原则（圆柱体原则）适用于中锋位置的攻防。

位于中锋位置的进攻队员和防守队员必须尊重彼此的垂直位置（圆柱体）的权利。

位于中锋位置的进攻队员或防守队员用肩或髋将对方队员挤出位置，或用伸展的肘、臂、膝或身体的其他部位去干扰对方队员的活动自由，是犯规。

33.13 背后非法防守

背后非法防守是防守队员从对方队员的背后与其发生的身体接触。防守队员正试图去抢球的事实，不证明从背后与对方队员发生接触是正当的。

33.14 Holding

Holding is illegal personal contact with an opponent that interferes with his freedom of movement. This contact (holding) can occur with any part of the body.

33.15 Pushing

Pushing is illegal personal contact with any part of the body where a player forcibly moves or attempts to move an opponent with or without the ball.

33.16 Fake being fouled

Fake is any action by a player to simulate that he has been fouled or to make theatrical exaggerated movements in order to create an opinion of being fouled and therefore gaining an advantage.

Art. 34 Personal foul

34.1 Definition

34.1.1 A personal foul is a player's illegal contact with an opponent, whether the ball is live or dead.

A player shall not hold, block, push, charge, trip or impede the progress of an opponent by extending his hand, arm, elbow, shoulder, hip, leg, knee or foot, nor by bending his body into an 'abnormal' position (outside his cylinder), nor shall he indulge in any rough or violent play.

34.2 Penalty

A personal foul shall be charged on the offender.

34.2.1 If the foul is committed on a player not in the act of shooting:
- The game shall be resumed with a throw-in by the non-offending team at the place nearest to the infraction.
- If the offending team is in the team foul penalty situation, then Art. 41 shall apply.

34.2.2 If the foul is committed on a player in the act of shooting, that player shall be awarded a number of free throws as follows:

- If the shot released from the field goal area is successful, the goal shall count and, in addition, 1 free throw.

- If the shot released from the 2-point field goal area is unsuccessful, 2 free throws.

33.14 拉人

拉人是干扰对方队员移动自由的非法身体接触。这种接触（拉人）可能发生在身体的任何部位。

33.15 推人

推人是队员用身体的任何部位强行移动或试图移动控制或未控制球的对方队员时发生的非法身体接触。

33.16 骗取犯规

一名队员采用任何手段假装被侵犯，或采取戏剧性的夸张动作来制造"被侵犯了"的假象并从中获利，是骗取犯规。

第34条 侵人犯规

34.1 定 义

34.1.1 侵人犯规是：无论在活球或死球的情况下，攻守双方队员发生的非法身体接触的犯规。

队员不应通过伸展手、臂、肘、肩、髋、腿、膝、脚或将身体弯曲成"不正常的姿势"（超出他的圆柱体）去拉、阻挡、推、撞、绊对方队员，或阻止对方队员行进；也不得放纵任何粗野或猛烈的动作去这样做。

34.2 罚 则

应登记犯规队员一次侵人犯规。

34.2.1 如果对没有做投篮动作的队员发生犯规：
- 由非犯规的队在最靠近违犯的地点掷球入界重新开始比赛。
- 如果犯规的队处于全队犯规处罚状态，则应运用第41条（全队犯规：处罚）的规定。

34.2.2 如果对正在做投篮动作的队员发生犯规，应按下列所述判给投篮队员若干罚球：
- 如果出手投篮成功：应计得分并追加一次罚球。
- 如果从2分投篮区域的出手投篮不成功：2次罚球。

- If the shot released from the 3-point field goal area is unsuccessful, 3 free throws.

- If the player is fouled as, or just before, the game clock signal sounds for the end of the quarter or overtime or as, or just before, the shot clock signal sounds, while the ball is still in the player's hand(s) and the field goal is successful, the goal shall not count and 2 or 3 free throws shall be awarded.

Art. 35 Double foul

35.1 Definition

35.1.1 A double foul is a situation in which 2 opponents commit personal or unsportsman-like/disqualifying fouls on each other at approximately the same time.

35.1.2 To consider 2 fouls as a double foul the following conditions must apply:
- Both fouls are player fouls.
- Both fouls involve physical contact.
- Both fouls are between the same 2 opponents fouling each other.
- Both fouls are either 2 personal or any combination of unsportsmanlike and disqualifying fouls.

35.2 Penalty

A personal or unsportsmanlike /disqualifying foul shall be charged on each offender. No free throws shall be awarded and the game shall be resumed as follows:

If at approximately the same time as the double foul:

- A valid field goal, or a last free throw is scored, the ball shall be awarded to the non-scoring team for a throw-in from any place behind that team's endline.

- A team had control of the ball or was entitled to the ball, the ball shall be awarded to this team for a throw-in from the place nearest to the infraction.

- Neither team had control of the ball nor was entitled to the ball, a jump ball situation occurs.

- 如果从3分投篮区域的出手投篮不成功：3次罚球。
- 在结束一节或决胜期的比赛计时钟信号响时或恰好响之前，或当进攻计时钟信号响时或恰好响之前，投篮队员被犯规了，此时球仍在该队员的手中，并且随后投篮成功：中篮不应计得分，应判给2次或3次罚球。

第35条 双方犯规

35.1 定 义

35.1.1 双方犯规是两名互为对方的队员大约同时相互发生侵人犯规或违反体育运动精神犯规/取消比赛资格犯规的情况。

35.1.2 如果将两个犯规视为一起双方犯规，下列条件是必须的：
- 两个犯规都是队员犯规。
- 两个犯规都包含身体接触。
- 两个犯规是比赛双方两个队员之间的相互犯规。
- 两个犯规是两个侵人犯规或任何违反体育运动精神的犯规和取消比赛资格的犯规的组合。

35.2 罚 则

应给每一犯规队员登记一次侵人犯规或违犯体育运动精神犯规/取消比赛资格犯规。不判给罚球，比赛应按下列所述重新开始：

在发生双方犯规的大约同一时间，如果：
- 投篮得分，或最后一次的罚球得分，应将球判给非得分队从该队端线后的任何地点掷球入界。
- 某队已控制球或拥有球权，应将球判给该队从最靠近违犯的地点掷球入界。
- 任一队都没有控制球也没有球权，一次跳球情况发生。

Art. 36 Technical foul

36.1 Rules of conduct

36.1.1 The proper conduct of the game demands the full and loyal cooperation of the players, head coaches, assistant coaches, substitutes, excluded players and accom-panying delegation members with the referees, table officials and commissioner, if present.

36.1.2 Each team shall do its best to secure victory, but this must be done in the spirit of sportsmanship and fair play.

36.1.3 Any deliberate or repeated non-cooperation or non-compliance with the spirit and intent of this rule shall be considered as a technical foul.

36.1.4 The referees may prevent technical fouls by giving warnings or even overlooking minor infractions which are obviously unintentional and have no direct effect upon the game, unless there is repetition of the same infraction after the warning.

36.1.5 If an infraction is recognised after the ball becomes live, the game shall be stopped and a technical foul charged. The penalty shall be administered as if the technical foul had occurred at the time it is charged. Whatever occurred during the interval between the infraction and the game being stopped shall remain valid.

36.2 Definition

36.2.1 A technical foul is a player non-contact foul of a behavioural nature including, but not limited to:
- Disregarding warnings given by referees.
- Disrespectfully dealing and/or communicating with the referees, the commissioner, the table officials, the opponents or persons permitted to sit on the team benches.
- Using language or gestures likely to offend or incite the spectators.
- Baiting and taunting an opponent.
- Obstructing the vision of an opponent by waving/placing his hand(s) near his eyes.
- Excessive swinging of elbows.
- Delaying the game by deliberately touching the ball after it passes through the basket or by preventing a throw-in or a free throw from being taken promptly.
- Fake being fouled.

第 36 条 技术犯规

36.1 行为规定

36.1.1 比赛的正当行为要求双方球队的队员、主教练、助理教练、替补队员、出局的队员和随队人员，与裁判员、记录台人员、技术代表（如到场）有完美和真诚的合作。

36.1.2 每支球队应尽最大的努力去获取胜利，但胜利的取得必须符合体育运动精神和公正竞赛的要求。

36.1.3 任何故意的或再三的不合作，或不遵守本规则的精神，应被认为是一次技术犯规。

36.1.4 裁判员可以通过警告或甚至宽容那些明显是无意的并不直接影响比赛的、轻微的违纪来预防技术犯规的发生，除非在警告后又重复出现同样的违犯。

36.1.5 如果在球成活球后发生了一起技术违犯，比赛应停止并登记一次技术犯规。应将技术犯规视同发生在它被登记的时候一样来执行罚则。在违犯与比赛停止之间的间隔内无论发生了什么都应保持有效。

36.2 定 义

36.2.1 技术犯规是没有身体接触的犯规，行为种类包括但不限于：
- 无视裁判员的警告。
- 与裁判员、技术代表、记录台人员、对方队或允许坐在球队席的人员讨论和/或交流中没有礼貌。
- 使用很可能冒犯或煽动观众的粗话或手势。
- 戏弄或嘲讽对方队员。
- 在对方队员眼睛附近挥手或手保持不动妨碍其视觉。
- 过分挥肘。
- 在球穿过球篮之后故意地触及球，阻碍迅速地掷球入界或罚球以延误比赛。
- 伪造被犯规。

- Hanging on the ring in such a way that the weight of the player is supported by the ring, unless a player grasps the ring momentarily following a dunk shot or, in the judgement of a referee, is trying to prevent injury to himself or to another player.
- Goaltending during the last free throw by a defensive player. The offensive team shall be awarded 1 point, followed by the technical foul penalty charged on the defensive player.

36.2.2 A technical foul by any person permitted to sit on the team bench is a foul for disrespectfully communicating with or touching the referees, the commissioner, the table officials or the opponents, or an infraction of a procedural or an administrative nature.

36.2.3 A player shall be disqualified for the remainder of the game when he is charged with 2 technical fouls, or 2 unsportsmanlike fouls, or with 1 unsportsmanlike foul and 1 technical foul.

36.2.4 A head coach shall be disqualified for the remainder of the game when:
- He is charged with 2 technical fouls ('C') as a result of his personal unsportsmanlike behaviour.
- He is charged with 3 technical fouls, either all of them ('B') or one of them ('C'), as a result of the unsportsmanlike behaviour of other persons permitted to sit on the team bench.

36.2.5 If a player or a head coach is disqualified under Art. 36.2.3 or Art. 36.2.4, that technical foul shall be the only foul to be penalised and no additional penalty for the disqualification shall be administered.

36.3 Penalty

36.3.1 If a technical foul is committed:
- By a player, a technical foul shall be charged on him as a player foul and shall count as one of the team fouls.
- By any person permitted to sit on the team bench, a technical foul shall be charged on the head coach and shall not count as one of the team fouls.

36.3.2 The opponents shall be awarded 1 free throw. The game shall be resumed as follows:
- The free throw shall be administered immediately. After the free throw, the throw-in shall be administered by the team which had control of the ball or was entitled to the ball when the technical foul was called, from the place nearest to where the ball was located when the game was stopped.

- 悬吊在篮圈上，致使队员的重量由篮圈支撑，除非扣篮后，队员瞬间抓住篮圈，或者根据裁判员的判断，他正试图防止自己受伤或另一名队员受伤。
- 在最后一次的罚球中防守队员干涉得分，应判给进攻队得1分，随后执行登记在该防守队员名下的技术犯规罚则。

36.2.2 球队席人员的技术犯规是与裁判员、技术代表、记录台人员或对方队员交流中没有礼貌或无礼地触碰他们的犯规；或是一次程序上的或管理性质的违犯。

36.2.3 当登记了一名队员2次技术犯规或2次违反体育运动精神的犯规，或一次技术犯规和一次违反体育运动精神的犯规时，应该取消他本场剩余比赛的资格。

36.2.4 当出现下述情况时，应取消主教练本场剩余比赛的资格：
- 由于自身违反体育运动精神行为的结果登记了2次技术犯规（"C"）时。
- 由于其他球队席人员的违反体育运动精神行为累积登记了3次技术犯规（3次全部登记为"B"，或者其中一次是"C"）。

36.2.5 如果一名队员或主教练在36.2.3或36.2.4的情况下被取消比赛资格，应只处罚技术犯规的罚则，不追加取消比赛资格的罚则。

36.3 罚 则

36.3.1 如果：
- 判罚队员技术犯规，应作为队员的犯规登记在该队员名下，并计入全队犯规中。
- 判罚球队席人员，应登记在主教练名下，并不计入全队犯规次数中。

36.3.2 应判给对方队员1次罚球，比赛应按下述重新开始：
- 应立即执行罚球。罚球后，由宣判技术犯规时，控制球队或拥有球权队在比赛停止时距离球最近的地点执行掷球入界。

- The free throw shall also be administered immediately, regardless whether the order of any other possible penalties for any other fouls has been determined or whether the administration of the penalties has been started. After the free throw for a technical foul, the game shall be resumed by the team which had control of the ball or was entitled to the ball when the technical foul was called, from the place where the game has been interrupted for the technical foul penalty.
- If a valid field goal, or a last free throw is scored, the game shall be resumed with a throw-in from any place behind the endline.
- If neither team had control of the ball nor was entitled to the ball, a jump ball situation occurs.
- With a jump ball in the centre circle at the beginning of the first quarter.

Art. 37 Unsportsmanlike foul

37.1 Definition

37.1.1 An unsportsmanlike foul is a player contact which, in the judgement of a referee is:
- Contact with an opponent and not legitimately attempting to directly play the ball within the spirit and intent of the rules.
- Excessive, hard contact caused by a player in an effort to play the ball or an opponent.
- An unnecessary contact caused by the defensive player in order to stop the progress of the offensive team in transition. This applies until the offensive player begins his act of shooting.
- An illegal contact caused by the player from behind or laterally on an opponent, who is progressing towards the opponent's basket and there are no other players between the progressing player, the ball and the basket. This applies until the offensive player begins his act of shooting.
- Contact by the defensive player on an opponent on the playing court when the game clock shows 2:00 minutes or less in the fourth quarter and in each overtime, when the ball is out-of-bounds for a throw-in and still in the hands of the referee or at the disposal of the player taking the throw-in.

37.1.2 The referee must interpret the unsportsmanlike fouls consistently throughout the game and to judge only the action.

- 也应立即执行罚球，不管是否有其他犯规带来的罚则的先后顺序，也不管这些罚则是否已经开始执行。技术犯规的罚球后，由宣判技术犯规时，控制球队或拥有球权队在最靠近比赛被技术犯规的罚则中断时的最近地点重新开始比赛。
- 如果一次有效得分或最后一次罚球得分，应在端线后任意地点掷球入界重新开始比赛。
- 如果既没有球队控制球，也没有球队拥有球权，这是一起跳球情况。
- 在中圈跳球开始第 1 节。

第 37 条 违反体育运动精神的犯规

37.1 定 义

37.1.1 违反体育运动精神的犯规是一起队员身体接触的犯规，并且根据裁判员判定，包含：
- 与对方发生身体接触并且不在本规则的精神和意图的范畴内努力比赛。
- 在尽力抢球或在与对方队员尽力争抢中，造成与对方队员过分的严重身体接触。
- 一起攻防转换中，防守队员为了中断进攻队的进攻，与进攻队员造成不必要的身体接触。该原则在进攻队员开始他的投篮动作之前均适用。
- 一起对方队员从正朝着对方球篮行进的队员身后或侧面与其造成的非法接触，并且在该行进队员、球和对方球篮之间没有其他队员。该原则在进攻队员开始他的投篮动作之前均适用。
- 在第 4 节和每一决胜期比赛计时钟显示2:00分钟或更少，当掷球入界的球在界外并且仍在裁判员手中，或掷球入界队员可处理时，防守队员在比赛场内对进攻队员造成身体接触。

37.1.2 在整场比赛中，裁判员对违反体育运动精神的犯规的解释必须一致，并且只能根据其所作所为来判定。

37.2 Penalty

37.2.1 An unsportsmanlike foul shall be charged on the offender.

37.2.2 Free throw(s) shall be awarded to the player who was fouled, followed by:
- A throw-in from the throw-in line in the team's frontcourt.
- A jump ball in the centre circle at the beginning of the first quarter.

The number of free throws shall be awarded as follows:
- If the foul is committed on a player not in the act of shooting: 2 free throws.
- If the foul is committed on a player in the act of shooting: the goal, if made, shall count and, in addition, 1 free throw.
- If the foul is committed on a player in the act of shooting and the goal is not made, 2 or 3 free throws.

37.2.3 A player shall be disqualified for the remainder of the game when he is charged with 2 unsportsmanlike fouls or 2 technical fouls, or with 1 technical foul and 1 unsportsmanlike foul.

37.2.4 If a player is disqualified under Art. 37.2.3, that unsportsmanlike foul shall be the only foul to be penalised and no additional penalty for the disqualification shall be administered.

Art. 38 Disqualifying foul

38.1 Definition

38.1.1 A disqualifying foul is any flagrant unsportsmanlike action by players, substitutes, head coaches, assistant coaches, excluded players and accompanying delegation members.

38.1.2 A head coach who has received a disqualifying foul shall be replaced by the first assistant coach as entered on the scoresheet. If no first assistant coach is entered on the scoresheet, he shall be replaced by the captain **(CAP)**.

38.2 Violence

38.2.1 Acts of violence may occur during the game, contrary to the spirit of sportsmanship and fair play. These should be stopped immediately by the referees and, if necessary, by public order enforcement officers.

37.2 罚　则

37.2.1　应给犯规队员登记一次违反体育运动精神的犯规。

37.2.2　应判给被犯规的队员执行罚球，以及随后：
- 在该队前场的掷球入界线处掷球入界。
- 在中圈跳球开始第 1 节。

应按下述原则判给若干罚球：
- 如果对没有做投篮动作的队员发生犯规：2 次罚球。
- 如果对正在做投篮动作的队员发生犯规：如果中篮应计得分并追加一次罚球。
- 如果对正在做投篮动作的队员发生犯规，并且球未中篮：2 次或 3 次罚球。

37.2.3　当登记了一名队员 2 次违反体育运动精神的犯规或 2 次技术犯规，或一次技术犯规和一次违反体育运动精神的犯规时，应该取消他本场剩余比赛的资格。

37.2.4　如果队员在 37.2.3 情况下被取消比赛资格，应只处罚该违反体育运动精神的犯规的罚则，不追加取消比赛资格的罚则。

第 38 条　取消比赛资格的犯规

38.1 定　义

38.1.1　队员、替补队员、主教练、助理教练、出局的队员和随队人员的任何恶劣的违反体育运动精神的行为是取消比赛资格的犯规。

38.1.2　已被取消比赛资格的主教练应由登记在记录表上的第一助理教练接替。如果记录表上没有登记第一助理教练，应由队长（**CAP**）接替。

38.2 暴力行为

38.2.1　比赛中可能发生与体育运动精神和公正竞赛相违背的暴力行为。裁判员应立即制止，如有必要，通过负责维持公共秩序的保安人员来制止。

38.2.2 Whenever acts of violence occur involving players on the playing court or in its vicinity, the referees shall take the necessary action to stop them.

38.2.3 Any of the above persons who are guilty of flagrant acts of aggression on opponents or referees shall be disqualified. The crew chief must report the incident to the organising body of the competition.

38.2.4 Public order enforcement officers may enter the playing court only if requested to do so by the referees. However, should spectators enter the playing court with the obvious intention of committing acts of violence, the public order enforcement officers must intervene immediately to protect the teams and referees.

38.2.5 All areas beyond the playing court or its vicinity, including entrances, exits, hallways, dressing rooms, etc., come under the jurisdiction of the organising body of the competition and the public order enforcement officers.

38.2.6 Physical actions by players or any person permitted to sit on the team bench, which could lead to damaging of game equipment, must not be permitted by the referees.

When behaviour of this nature is observed by the referees, the head coach of the offending team shall be given a warning.

Should the action(s) be repeated, a technical or even disqualifying foul shall immediately be called on the individual(s) involved.

38.3 Penalty

38.3.1 A disqualifying foul shall be charged on the offender.

38.3.2 Whenever the offender is disqualified according to the respective articles of these rules, he shall go to and remain in his team's dressing room for the duration of the game or, if he so wishes, he shall leave the building.

38.3.3 Free throw(s) shall be awarded:
- To any opponent, as designated by his head coach in case of a non-contact foul.
- To the player who was fouled in the case of a contact foul.

Followed by:
- A throw-in from the throw-in line in the team's frontcourt.
- A jump ball in the centre circle at the beginning of the first quarter.

38.2.2 无论何时，队员在比赛场地上或其附近与球队席人员之间发生暴力行为，裁判员应采取必要的措施去制止他们。

38.2.3 任何上述的人员公然地挑衅对方队员或裁判员，应被取消比赛资格。主裁判员必须将此事件报告给竞赛的组织部门。

38.2.4 保安人员可以进入比赛场地，只要裁判员要求这样做。然而，如果带有明显采用暴力行为意图的观众进入球场，保安人员必须立即干预以保护球队和裁判员。

38.2.5 球场之外或附近的所有区域，包括入口、出口、过道、休息室等，由竞赛组织部门和负责维持公共秩序的保安人员管辖。

38.2.6 裁判员绝不允许队员以及坐在球队席的任何人员出现可能导致比赛器材损坏的粗野行为。

当裁判员观察到这类行为时，应立即给违犯队的主教练一次警告。

如果重复该行为，应立即宣判有关的违犯者一次技术犯规甚至取消比赛资格的犯规。

38.3 罚 则

38.3.1 应给犯规者登记一次取消比赛资格的犯规。

38.3.2 每当犯规者依据这些规则的各个条款被取消比赛资格，他应去该队的休息室，并在比赛期间留在那里，或者如果他愿意，也可以选择离开体育馆。

38.3.3 罚球应判给：
- 如果是一起非身体接触犯规：由对方主教练指定的任一本队队员。
- 如果是一起身体接触犯规：被犯规的队员。

以及随后：
- 在该队前场的掷球入界线处掷球入界。
- 第1节开始在中圈跳球。

38.3.4. The number of free throws shall be awarded as follows:
- If the foul is a non-contact foul: 2 free throws.
- If the foul is committed on a player not in the act of shooting: 2 free throws.
- If the foul is committed on a player in the act of shooting: the goal, if made, shall count and in addition 1 free throw.
- If the foul is committed on a player in the act of shooting and the goal is not made: 2 or 3 free throws.
- If the foul is a disqualification of a head coach: 2 free throws.
- If the foul is a disqualification of a first assistant coach, substitute, excluded player or an accompanying delegation member, this foul is charged on the head coach as a technical foul: 2 free throws.

In addition, if a disqualification of a first assistant coach, substitute, excluded player or an accompanying delegation member after leaving the team bench area is for their active participation during any fight:
— For each single disqualifying foul of a first assistant coach, substitute and excluded player: 2 free throws. All disqualifying fouls shall be charged on each offender.
— For each single disqualifying foul of any accompanying delegation member: 2 free throws. All disqualifying fouls shall be charged on the head coach.

All free-throw penalties shall be executed, unless there are equal penalties on the opponent's team to be cancelled.

Art. 39 Fighting

39.1 Definition

Fighting is physical interaction between 2 or more opponents (players, substitutes, head coaches, assistant coaches, excluded players and accompanying delegation members).

This article only applies to the substitutes, head coaches, assistant coaches, excluded players and accompanying delegation members who leave the confines of the team bench area during a fight or during any situation which may lead to a fight.

39.2 Rule

39.2.1 Substitutes, excluded players or accompanying delegation members who leave

38.3.4 罚球的次数应按如下规定：
- 如果是一起没有身体接触的犯规：2次罚球。
- 如果对没有做投篮动作的队员发生犯规：2次罚球。
- 如果对正在做投篮动作的队员发生犯规：如果中篮应计得分并追加一次罚球。
- 如果对正在做投篮动作的队员发生犯规，并且球未中篮：2次或3次罚球。
- 如果是主教练的取消比赛资格的犯规：2次罚球。
- 如果是第一助理教练、替补队员、出局的队员或随队人员的取消比赛资格的犯规，应登记主教练一次技术犯规：2次罚球。

  另外，如果在打架期间，第一助理教练、替补队员、出局的队员或随队人员因离开球队席区域参加打架而判取消比赛资格的犯规：
  —— 第一助理教练、替补队员和出局的队员的每一个单一的取消比赛资格的犯规：2次罚球。所有取消比赛资格的犯规都应登记在他们个人身上。
  —— 随队人员的每一个单一的取消比赛资格的犯规：2次罚球。所有取消比赛资格的犯规都应登记在主教练身上。

应执行所有的罚球罚则，除非对方队有相同的罚则进行抵消。

第39条 打架

39.1 定义

打架是2名或多名互为对方队的人员（队员和替补队员、主教练、助理教练、出局的队员和随队人员）之间的肢体冲突。

本条款仅适用于在打架中或在可能导致打架的任何情况中离开球队席区域界限的替补队员、主教练、助理教练、出局的队员和随队人员。

39.2 规定

39.2.1 在打架中或在可能导致打架的任何情况中，离开球队席区域的替

the team bench area during a fight, or during any situation which may lead to a fight, shall be disqualified.

39.2.2 Only a head coach and/or first assistant coach are permitted to leave the team bench area during a fight, or during any situation which may lead to a fight, to assist the referees to maintain or to restore order. In this situation, they shall not be disqualified.

39.2.3 If a head coach and/or first assistant coach leave the team bench area and neither assist nor attempt to assist the referees to maintain or to restore order, they shall be disqualified.

39.3 Penalty

39.3.1 Irrespective of the number of persons disqualified for leaving the team bench area, a single technical foul ('B') shall be charged on the head coach.

39.3.2 If persons of both teams are disqualified under this article and there are no other foul penalties remaining for administration, the game shall be resumed as follows.

If at approximately the same time when the game was stopped because of the fighting:
- A valid field goal or a last free throw is scored, the ball shall be awarded to the non-scoring team for a throw-in from any place behind that team's endline.
- A team had control of the ball or was entitled to the ball, the ball shall be awarded to that team for a throw-in from the place nearest to where the ball was located when the fight has begun.
- Neither team has control of the ball nor was entitled to the ball, a jump ball situation occurs.

39.3.3 All disqualifying fouls shall be entered on the scoresheet as described in B.8.3 and shall not count as team fouls.

39.3.4 All possible foul penalties on players on the playing court involved in a fight or any situation which leads to a fight, shall be dealt with in accordance with **Art. 42**.

39.3.5 All possible disqualification foul penalties on first assistant coach, substitute, excluded player or an accompanying delegation member involved actively in a fight or any situation which leads to a fight, shall be penalised in accordance with **Art. 38.3.4**, sixth bullet.

补队员、出局的队员和随队人员，应被取消比赛资格。

39.2.2 在打架中或在可能导致打架的任何情况中，为了协助裁判员维持或恢复秩序，只允许主教练和／或第一助理教练离开球队席区域，协助裁判员维持或恢复秩序。在这种情况中，他们不应被取消比赛资格。

39.2.3 如果主教练和／或第一助理教练离开球队席区域，并不协助或试图协助裁判员维持或恢复秩序，他们应被取消比赛资格。

39.3 罚则

39.3.1 不论由于离开球队席区域而被取消比赛资格的球队席人员的数量有多少，应登记主教练一次单一的技术犯规（"B"）。

39.3.2 如果双方球队的球队席成员在本条规定下被取消比赛资格并且没有留下其他要执行的犯规罚则，比赛应按下面所述重新开始：

由于打架而停止比赛，大约在同一时间，如果：
- 投篮得分或者最后一次的罚球得分，应将球判给非得分队从该队端线后的任何地点掷球入界。
- 某队已控制球或拥有球权，应将球判给该队从打架开始时距离球最近的地点执行掷球入界。
- 任一队都没有控制球也没有球权，一次跳球情况发生。

39.3.3 所有的取消比赛资格的犯规，应按照 B.8.3 所描述的登入记录表，并不计入全队犯规次数中。

39.3.4 所有涉及在场上打架的队员或在打架之前发生的任何情况的可能存在的犯规罚则，应按**第42条**（特殊情况）处理。

39.3.5 所有涉及参与打架或任何可能导致打架的情况的第一助理教练、替补队员、出局的队员或随队人员的可能的取消比赛资格的犯规罚则应根据**第38.3.4条**第 6 小点执行。

RULE SEVEN — GENERAL PROVISIONS

Art. 40 5 fouls by a player

40.1 A player who has committed 5 fouls shall be informed by a referee and must leave the game immediately. He shall be substituted within 30 seconds.

40.2 A foul by a player who has previously committed 5 fouls is considered as an excluded player's foul and it is charged and entered on the scoresheet on the head coach ('B').

Art. 41 Team fouls: Penalty

41.1 Definition

41.1.1 A team foul is a personal, technical, unsportsmanlike or disqualifying foul committed by a player. A team is in the team foul penalty situation after it has committed 4 team fouls in a quarter.

41.1.2 All team fouls committed in an interval of play shall be considered as being committed in the following quarter or overtime.

41.1.3 All team fouls committed in each overtime shall be considered as being committed in the fourth quarter.

41.2 Rule

41.2.1 When a team is in the team foul penalty situation, all following player personal fouls committed on a player not in the act of shooting shall be penalised by 2 free throws, instead of a throw-in. The player on whom the foul was committed shall attempt the free throws.

41.2.2 If a personal foul is committed by a player of the team in control of the live ball, or of the team entitled to the ball, such a foul shall be penalised by a throw-in for the opponents.

Art. 42 Special situations

42.1 Definition
In the same stopped-clock period which follows an infraction, special situations may arise when additional infraction(s) are committed.

第七章 一般规定

第 40 条 队员 5 次犯规

40.1 一名队员已发生了 5 次犯规时，裁判员应通知其本人，他必须立即离开比赛，并且必须在 30 秒内被替换。

40.2 已发生了 5 次犯规队员的再次犯规，是出局队员的犯规，应在记录表上的主教练名下登记 "B"。

第 41 条 全队犯规：处罚

41.1 定 义

41.1.1 全队犯规是指该队队员被判罚的侵人犯规、技术犯规、违反体育运动精神的犯规或取消比赛资格的犯规。在一节中某队全队犯规已发生了 4 次时，该队处于全队犯规处罚状态。

41.1.2 在比赛休息期间发生的所有全队犯规，应被认为是随后一节或决胜期比赛中的犯规。

41.1.3 在决胜期内发生的所有全队犯规应被认为是发生在第 4 节内的。

41.2 规 定

41.2.1 当某队处于全队犯规处罚状态时，所有随后发生的对未做投篮动作的队员的侵人犯规应被判 2 次罚球，代替掷球入界。由被犯规的队员执行罚球。

41.2.2 如果控制活球队的队员或拥有球权队的队员发生了一次侵人犯规，这样的犯规应判对方队员掷球入界。

第 42 条 特殊情况

42.1 定 义

在一次违犯后的同一个停止比赛计时钟期间又发生了一次或多次违犯时，可能出现特殊情况。

42.2 Procedure

42.2.1 All fouls shall be charged and all penalties identified.

42.2.2 The order in which all infractions occurred shall be determined.

42.2.3 All equal penalties on the teams and all double foul penalties shall be cancelled in the order in which they were called. Once the penalties have been entered on the scoresheet and cancelled they are considered as never having occurred.

42.2.4 If a technical foul is called, that penalty shall be administered first, regardless whether the order of the penalties has been determined or whether the administration of the penalties has been started.

If the technical foul is called on the head coach for a disqualification of a first assistant coach, substitute, excluded player and accompanying delegation member, that penalty shall not be administered first. It shall be administered in the order in which all fouls and violations have occurred, unless they were cancelled.

42.2.5 The right to possession of the ball as part of the last penalty to be administered shall cancel any prior rights to possession of the ball.

42.2.6 Once the ball has become live on the first free throw or on a throw-in penalty, that penalty can no longer be used for cancelling any remaining penalties.

42.2.7 All remaining penalties shall be administered in the order in which they were called.

42.2.8 If, after the cancellation of equal penalties on both teams, there are no other penalties remaining for administration, the game shall be resumed as follows.
If at approximately the same time as the first infraction:
- A valid field goal or a last free throw is scored, the ball shall be awarded to the non-scoring team for a throw-in from any place behind that team's endline.
- A team had control of the ball or was entitled to the ball, the ball shall be awarded to this team for a throw-in from the place nearest to the first infraction.
- Neither team had control of the ball nor was entitled to the ball, a jump ball situation occurs.

42.2 程 序

42.2.1 应登记所有的犯规，并确认所有的罚则。

42.2.2 应确定所有犯规发生的次序。

42.2.3 双方球队所有相等的罚则和所有双方犯规的罚则应按照它们宣判的顺序被抵消。一旦罚则已被登入记录表和抵消，就认为它们从未发生过。

42.2.4 如果宣判了技术犯规，无论判罚的顺序或罚则是否已经开始执行，应先执行技术犯规的罚则。

如果因为第一助理教练、替补队员、出局的队员或随队人员的取消比赛资格的犯规登记在主教练名下的技术犯规，罚则不应首先执行。所有的犯规和违例应按发生的顺序去执行罚则，除非罚则相互抵消。

42.2.5 作为最后要执行罚则一部分的球权，应当取消任何先前的球权。

42.2.6 在第一次罚球中，或在掷球入界中，一旦球已成为活球，那么该罚则就不能再用来抵消另一罚则。

42.2.7 所有剩余的罚则应按它们被宣判的次序执行。

42.2.8 如果双方球队抵消了相等的罚则后，没有留下其他要执行的罚则，比赛应按下述原则重新开始：

第一次违犯发生的大约同一时间，如果：

- 投篮或最后一次罚球得分，应将球判给非得分队从该队端线后的任何地点掷球入界。
- 某队已控制球或拥有球权，应将球判给该队从最靠近第一次违犯的地点掷球入界。
- 任一队都没有控制球也没有球权，一次跳球情况发生。

Art. 43 Free throws

43.1 Definition

43.1.1 A free throw is an opportunity given to a player to score 1 point, uncontested, from a position behind the free-throw line and inside the semi-circle.

43.1.2 A set of free throws is defined as all free throws and possible following possession of the ball resulting from a single foul penalty.

43.2 Rule

43.2.1 When a personal, an unsportsmanlike or a disqualifying contact foul is called, the free throw(s) shall be awarded as follows:
- The player on whom the foul was committed shall attempt the free throw(s).
- If there is a request for him to be substituted, he must attempt the free throw(s) before leaving the game.
- If he must leave the game due to injury, having committed 5 fouls or having been disqualified, his substitute shall attempt the free throw(s). If no substitute is available, any teammate as designated by his head coach shall attempt the free throw(s).

43.2.2 When a technical or a disqualifying non-contact foul is called, any member of the opponents' team as designated by his head coach shall attempt the free throw(s).

43.2.3 The free-throw shooter shall:
- Take a position behind the free-throw line and inside the semi-circle.
- Use any method to shoot a free throw in such a way that the ball enters the basket from above or the ball touches the ring.
- Release the ball within 5 seconds after it is placed at his disposal by the referee.
- Not touch the free-throw line or enter the restricted area until the ball has entered the basket or has touched the ring.
- Not fake a free throw.

43.2.4 The players in the free-throw rebound places shall be entitled to occupy alternating positions in these spaces, which are considered to be 1 m in depth (Diagram 6).
During the free throws these players shall not:
- Occupy free-throw rebound places to which they are not entitled.

第43条 罚 球

43.1 定 义

43.1.1 一次罚球是给予一名队员从罚球线后的半圆内的位置上，在无争抢的情况下得1分的机会。

43.1.2 由一次单一的犯规罚则带来的所有罚球和随后可能的球权被定义为一个罚球单元。

43.2 规 定

43.2.1 当宣判了一起侵人犯规、违反体育运动精神的犯规或有身体接触的取消比赛资格的犯规，应按下述原则判给罚球：
- 被侵犯的队员应执行全部罚球。
- 如果请求替换被侵犯的队员，他必须在离开比赛前执行完该罚则的全部罚球。
- 如果被侵犯的队员因受伤、第5次犯规或取消比赛资格而必须离开比赛，替换他的替补队员应执行罚球。如果没有替补队员，应由他的主教练指定任意一名同队队员执行罚球。

43.2.2 当宣判了一起技术犯规或非身体接触的取消比赛资格的犯规时，由对方队的主教练指定他球队中的任一队员执行罚球。

43.2.3 罚球队员：
- 应在罚球线后并在半圆内占据一个位置。
- 可用任何方式罚篮，并且以这样的方式使球从上方进入球篮或球触及篮圈。
- 在裁判员将球置于他可处理后，在5秒内应罚篮出手。
- 不应触及罚球线或进入限制区，直到球已进入球篮或已触及篮圈。
- 不应做假动作罚球。

43.2.4 在分位区的队员们有权占据这些空间的交错位置，这些分位区的深度应被看作是1米深。（图6）

在罚球中，这些队员们不应该：
- 占据他们无权占据的分位区。

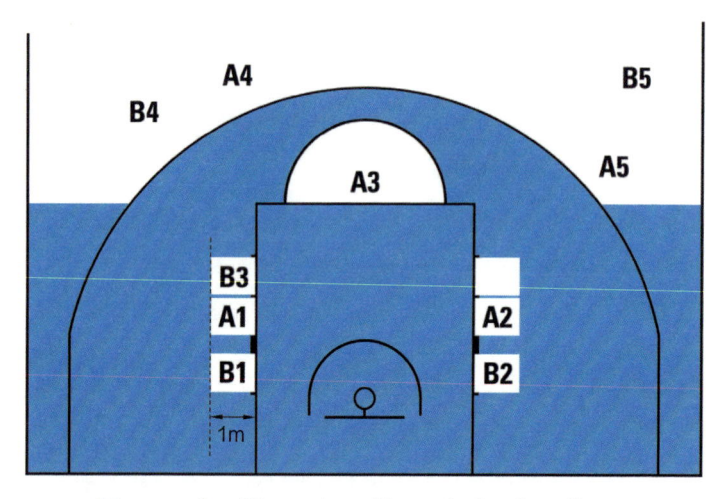

Diagram 6   Players' positions during free throws

- Enter the restricted area, the neutral zone or leave the free-throw rebound place until the ball has left the hand(s) of the free-throw shooter.
- Distract the free-throw shooter by their actions.

43.2.5 Players not in the free-throw rebound places shall remain behind the free-throw line extended and behind the 3-point field goal line until the free throw ends.

43.2.6 During a free throw(s) to be followed by another set(s) of free throws or by a throw-in, all players shall remain behind the free-throw line extended and behind the 3-point field goal line.

An infraction of Art. 43.2.3, 43.2.4, 43.2.5 and 43.2.6 is a violation.

43.3   Penalty

43.3.1 If a **free throw is successful** and the violation(s) is committed by the free-throw shooter, the point shall not count.

The ball shall be awarded to the opponents for a throw-in from the free-throw line extended, unless there is a further free throw(s) or possession penalty to be administered.

43.3.2 If a **free throw is successful** and the violation(s) is committed by any player(s) other than
the free-throw shooter:
- The point shall count.

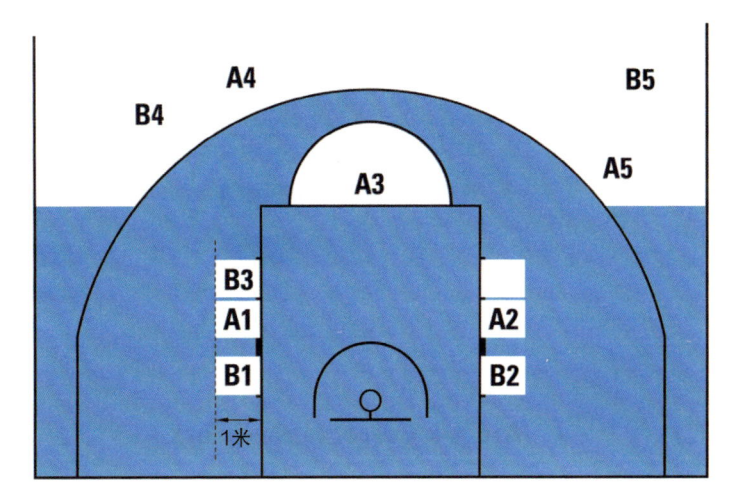

图6 在罚球中队员的位置

- 在球离开罚球队员的手前进入限制区、中立区或离开他的分位区。
- 用他的行为扰乱罚球队员。

43.2.5 不在分位区内的队员们应留在罚球线的延长线和3分投篮线后面，直到罚球结束。

43.2.6 在罚球后接着有另一罚球单元或一次掷球入界，所有队员应在罚球线延长线和3分投篮线后面。

违反43.2.3、43.2.4、43.2.5和43.2.6是违例。

43.3 罚 则

43.3.1 如果**罚球成功**并且罚球队员违例，中篮应不计得分。

应将球判给对方队员在罚球线延长线掷球入界，除非还要执行后续的罚球或者球权。

43.3.2 如果**罚球成功**并且除罚球队员外的任一队员发生了违例：
- 中篮应计得分。

OFFICIAL BASKETBALL RULES *2020*

- The violation(s) shall be disregarded.

In case of the last free throw, the ball shall be awarded to the opponents for a throw-in from any place behind that team's endline.

43.3.3 If a **free throw is not successful** and the violation is committed by:
- A **free-throw shooter** or his **teammate** on the last free throw, the ball shall be awarded to the opponents for a throw-in from the free-throw line extended unless that team is entitled to further possession.
- An **opponent** of the free-throw shooter, a substitute free throw shall be awarded to the free-throw shooter.
- **Both teams,** on the last free throw, a jump ball situation occurs.

Art. 44 Correctable errors

44.1 Definition

Referees may correct an error if a rule is inadvertently disregarded in the following situations only:
- Awarding an unmerited free throw(s).
- Failing to award a merited free throw(s).
- Erroneous awarding or cancelling of a point(s).
- Permitting the wrong player to attempt a free throw(s).

44.2 General procedure

44.2.1 To be correctable the above-mentioned errors must be recognized by the referees, commissioner, if present, or table officials before the ball becomes live following the first dead ball after the game clock has started following the error.

44.2.2 A referee may stop the game immediately upon recognition of a correctable error, as long as neither team is placed at a disadvantage.

44.2.3 Any fouls committed, points scored, time used and additional activity which may have occurred after the error has occurred and before its recognition, shall remain valid.

44.2.4 After the correction of the error the game shall be resumed from the place it was stopped to correct the error, unless otherwise stated in these rules. The ball shall be awarded to the team entitled to the ball at the time the game was stopped for the correction of the error.

- 违例应不究。

如果是最后一次的罚球，应将球判给对方队员从端线的任何地点掷球入界。

43.3.3 如果**罚球不成功**并且发生违例：
- **罚球队员**或他的**同队队员**在最后一次罚球中违例，应将球判给对方队员从罚球线延长线掷球入界，除非该队有进一步的球权。
- 罚球队员的**对方队员违例**，应判给罚球队员再罚球一次。
- **双方球队**在最后一次罚球中都违例，一次跳球情况发生。

第 44 条 可纠正的失误

44.1 定 义

如果仅在下述情况中某条规则被无意地忽视了，裁判员可纠正该失误：
- 判给不应得的罚球。
- 没有判给应得的罚球。
- 不正确地判给得分或取消得分。
- 允许不该罚球的队员执行罚球。

44.2 一般程序

44.2.1 要纠正上述提到的失误，它们必须在失误后且开动了比赛计时钟之后的第一次死球后、球成活球之前被裁判员、技术代表（如到场）或记录台人员发现。

44.2.2 发现了一起可纠正的失误时，裁判员可立即停止比赛，只要不把任一队置于不利。

44.2.3 在失误发生了之后到失误被发现之前，可能发生的任何犯规、得分、用去的时间和附加的活动，应保持有效。

44.2.4 在失误纠正之后，除非规则另有规定，比赛应在纠正失误停止比赛的地点重新开始，应将球判给在纠正失误停止比赛时拥有球权的球队。

44.2.5 Once an error that is still correctable has been recognised, and:
- The player involved in the correction of the error is on the team bench after being legally substituted, he must re-enter the playing court to participate in the correction of the error, at which point he becomes a player.

  Upon completion of the correction, he may remain in the game unless a legal substitution has been requested again, in which case the player may leave the playing court.
- The player was substituted due to his injury or assistance, having committed 5 fouls or having been disqualified, his substitute must participate in the correction of the error.

44.2.6 Correctable errors cannot be corrected after the crew chief has signed the scoresheet.

44.2.7 An error in scorekeeping, timekeeping or shot clock operations involving the score, number of fouls, number of time-outs, game clock and shot clock time consumed or omitted, may be corrected by the referees at any time before the crew chief has signed the scoresheet.

44.3 Special procedure

44.3.1 Awarding an unmerited free throw(s).

The free throw(s) attempted as a result of the error shall be cancelled and the game shall be resumed as follows:
- If the game clock has not started, the ball shall be awarded for a throw-in from the free-throw line extended to the team whose free throws had been cancelled.
- If the game clock has started and:
  — The team in control of the ball or entitled to the ball at the time the error is recognised is the same team that was in control of the ball at the time the error occurred, or
  — Neither team is in control of the ball at the time the error is recognised, the ball shall be awarded to the team entitled to the ball at the time the error occurred.
- If the game clock has started and, at the time the error is recognised, the team in control of the ball or entitled to the ball is the opponent of the team that was in control of the ball at the time of the error, a jump ball situation occurs.
- If the game clock has started and, at the time the error is recognised, a foul penalty involving a free throw(s) has been awarded, the free throw(s)

44.2.5 一旦一个可纠正的失误被发现了，并且：
- 如果涉及纠正失误的队员已被合法替换后坐在球队席上，他必须重新进入比赛场地参加该失误的纠正，此时他成为一名队员。

  在完成纠正后，他可以继续留在比赛中，除非已再次请求了一次合法的替换，在此情况下他才可以离开比赛场地。
- 如果该队员因为受伤或接受协助、5次犯规或者已被取消比赛资格而被替换，替换他的队员必须参加该失误的纠正。

44.2.6 主裁判员已在记录表上签字后，可纠正的失误不能被纠正。

44.2.7 主裁判员在记录表上签字前，记录台人员在记录、比赛计时钟和进攻计时钟操作中的任何失误，包括比分、犯规次数、暂停次数、消耗或遗漏的比赛时间和进攻时间，裁判员可在任何时间改正。

44.3 特殊程序

44.3.1 判给不应得的罚球。

由于失误而执行的罚球应被取消，并且比赛应按下述原则重新开始：

- 如果失误之后比赛计时钟没有开动，应将球判给罚球被取消的队从罚球线延长线掷球入界。
- 如果失误之后比赛计时钟已开动，并且：
  —— 在失误被发现时控制球（或拥有球权）的队与该失误发生时控制球的队是同一队，或
  —— 在失误被发现时没有球队控制球，
  应将球判给在失误发生时拥有球权的队。
- 如果比赛计时钟已开动，并且在该失误被发现时，控制球（或拥有球权）的队是在失误发生时控制球的队的对方球队，一次跳球情况发生。
- 如果比赛计时钟已开动，并且该失误被发现时，判了一个包含罚球的犯规罚则，应该执行罚球。然后，将球判给在该失误发

shall be administered and the ball shall be awarded for a throw-in to the team that was in control of the ball at the time the error occurred.

44.3.2 Failing to award a merited free throw(s).
- If there has been no change in possession of the ball after the error occurred, the game shall be resumed after correction of the error as after any normal last free throw.
- If the same team scores after having been erroneously awarded possession of the ball for a throw-in, the error shall be disregarded.

44.3.3 Permitting the wrong player to attempt a free throw(s).
The free throw(s) attempted, and the possession of the ball if part of the penalty, shall be cancelled and the ball shall be awarded to the opponents for a throw-in from the free-throw line extended, unless the game has continued and was stopped for the correction of the error or penalties for further infractions are to be administered, in which case the game shall be resumed from the place it was stopped to correct the error.

生时控制球的队掷球入界。

44.3.2 没有判给应得的罚球。
- 如果在该失误发生后球权没有改变，在失误纠正后应如同任何正常的最后一次罚球后一样地重新开始比赛。
- 如果在错误地判给了掷球入界的球权之后，该队得分了，则失误应不究。

44.3.3 允许错误的球员执行了罚球。
该执行的罚球应被取消，如有作为罚则的一部分的球权，也应被取消，并将球判给对方从罚球线的延长线掷球入界，除非比赛已经继续进行并且为了纠正失误而被停止，或者还有另外的违犯罚则要执行。在这样的情况下，比赛应在纠正失误停止比赛的地点重新开始。

RULE EIGHT — REFEREES, TABLE OFFICIALS, COMMISSIONER: DUTIES AND POWERS POWERS

Art. 45 Referees, table officials and commissioner

45.1 The **referees** shall be a crew chief and 1 or 2 umpire(s). They shall be assisted by the table officials and by a commissioner, if present.

45.2 The **table officials** shall be a scorer, an assistant scorer, a timer and a shot clock operator.

45.3 The **commissioner** shall sit between the scorer and the timer. His primary duty during the game is to supervise the work of the table officials and to assist the crew chief and umpire(s) in the smooth functioning of the game.

45.4 The referees of a given game should not be connected in any way with either team on the playing court.

45.5 The referees, the table officials and the commissioner shall conduct the game in accordance with these rules and have no authority to change them.

45.6 The referees' uniform shall consist of an referees' shirt, long black trousers, black socks and black basketball shoes.

45.7 The referees and table officials shall be uniformly dressed.

Art. 46 Crew chief: Duties and powers

The crew chief shall:

46.1 Inspect and approve all equipment to be used during the game.

46.2 Designate the official game clock, shot clock, stopwatch and recognise the table officials.

46.3 Select a game ball from at least 2 used balls provided by the home team. Should neither of these balls be suitable as the game ball, he may select the best quality ball available.

46.4 Not permit any player to wear objects that may cause injury to other players.

46.5 Administer a jump ball at the beginning of the first quarter and an alternating possession throw-in at the beginning of all other quarters and overtimes.

第八章 裁判员、记录台人员和技术代表：职责和权力

第 45 条 裁判员、记录台人员和技术代表

45.1 **裁判员**应是1名主裁判员和1名或2名副裁判员。他们由记录台人员和技术代表（如在场）协助。

45.2 **记录台人员**应是1名记录员、1名助理记录员、1名计时员和1名进攻计时员。

45.3 **技术代表**应坐在记录员和计时员之间。比赛中他的主要职责是监督记录台人员的工作，并协助主裁判员和副裁判员使比赛顺利进行。

45.4 担任1场比赛的裁判员不应与场上任一队有任何方式的联系。

45.5 裁判员、记录台人员和技术代表应按照这些规则来指导比赛并无权改变这些规则。

45.6 裁判员的服装应由裁判衫、黑色长裤、黑色袜子和黑色篮球鞋组成。

45.7 裁判员和记录台人员应分别着装一致。

第 46 条 主裁判员：职责和权力

主裁判员应：

46.1 检查和批准在比赛中使用的所有器材。

46.2 指定正式的比赛计时钟、进攻计时钟、秒表，并确认记录台人员。

46.3 从主队提供的至少2个用过的球中挑选比赛球。如果2个球中没有一个适宜作为比赛球，他可在提供的球中挑选最好的。

46.4 不允许任何队员佩戴可能对其他队员造成伤害的物品。

46.5 在第1节开始时执行跳球，在所有其他节和决胜期开始时管理掷球入界。

46.6 Have the power to stop a game when conditions warrant it.

46.7 Have the power to determine that a team shall forfeit the game.

46.8 Carefully examine the scoresheet at the end of playing time or at any time he feels is necessary.

46.9 Approve and sign the scoresheet at the end of playing time, **terminating** the referees' administration and **connection** with the game. The referees' **power** shall **begin** when they arrive on the playing court 20 minutes before the game is scheduled to begin, and **end** when the game clock signal sounds for the end of the game as approved by the referees.

46.10 Enter on the reverse side of the scoresheet, in the dressing room before signing the scoresheet:
- Any forfeit or disqualifying foul,
- Any unsportsmanlike behaviour by team members, head coaches, assistant coaches and accompanying delegation members that occurs prior to the 20 minutes before the game is scheduled to begin, or between the end of the game and the approval and signing of the scoresheet.

In such a case, the crew chief (or commissioner, if present) must send a detailed report to the organising body of the competition.

46.11 Make the final decision whenever necessary or when the referees disagree. To make a final decision he may consult the umpire(s), the commissioner, if present, and/or the table officials.

46.12 For games where the Instant Replay System is used please refer to Appendix F.

46.13 After being notified by the timer, shall blow his whistle before the first and third quarter when 3 minutes and 1.5 minutes remain until the beginning of the quarter. The crew chief shall also blow his whistle before the second and fourth quarter and each overtime when 30 seconds remain until the beginning of the quarter and overtime.

46.14 Have the power to make decisions on any point not specifically covered by these rules.

Art. 47 Referees : Duties and powers

47.1 The referees shall have the power to make decisions on infractions of the rules committed either within or outside the boundary line including the scorer's table, the team benches and the areas immediately behind the lines.

篮球规则 2020

46.6 当情况需要时有权停止比赛。

46.7 有权判定某队弃权。

46.8 在比赛时间结束时，或在任何他认为有必要的时候，仔细地审查记录表。

46.9 在比赛时间结束时核准记录表并在上面签字，**终止**裁判员对比赛的管理，以及裁判员和比赛的**联系**。裁判员的**权力**应从预定的比赛开始时间前20分钟到达比赛场地时**开始**，当结束比赛的计时钟信号响并被裁判员认可时，裁判员的权力**结束**。

46.10 在记录表上签字之前，在更衣室里，在记录表的背面记录：
- 任何弃权或取消比赛资格犯规。
- 任何队员、主教练、助理教练和随队人员在早于预定比赛开始前20分钟或者在比赛时间结束和核准记录表并签字之间发生了违反体育运动精神的行为。

  在这种情况下，主裁判员（或到场的技术代表）必须向竞赛的组织部门送交详细的报告。

46.11 每当有必要或裁判员的意见不一致时做出最终的决定。为做出最终的决定，他可与副裁判员、技术代表（如到场）和／或记录台人员商量。

46.12 在比赛中使用即时回放的情况请参照附录F。

46.13 计时员提醒时间后，距离第1节和第3节开始还有3分钟和1.5分钟时，主裁判员应鸣哨。同样，距离第2节和第4节，以及每一决胜期开始还有30秒时应鸣哨。

46.14 有权对本规则中未明确规定的任何事项做出决定。

第 47 条 裁判员：职责和权力

47.1 裁判员有权对不论发生在界线内或界线外（包括记录台、球队席及紧靠线后的区域）所发生的对规则的违犯做出宣判。

127

47.2 The referees shall blow their whistles when an infraction of the rules occurs, a quarter or overtime ends or the referees find it necessary to stop the game. The referees shall not blow their whistles after a successful field goal, a successful free throw or when the ball becomes live.

47.3 When deciding on a personal contact or violation, the referees shall, in each instance, have regard to and weigh up the following fundamental principles:
- The spirit and intent of the rules and the need to uphold the integrity of the game.
- Consistency in application of the concept of 'advantage/disadvantage'. The referees should not seek to interrupt the flow of the game unnecessarily in order to penalise incidental personal contact which does not give the player responsible an advantage nor place his opponent at a disadvantage.
- Consistency in the application of common sense to each game, bearing in mind the abilities of the players concerned and their attitude and conduct during the game.
- Consistency in the maintenance of a balance between game control and game flow, having a 'feeling' for what the participants are trying to do and calling what is right for the game.

47.4 Should a protest be filed by one of the teams, the crew chief (or commissioner, if present) shall, upon receipt of the protest reasons, report in writing the incident to the organising body of the competition.

47.5 If a referee is injured or for any other reason cannot continue to perform his duties within 5 minutes of the incident, the game shall be resumed. The remaining referee(s) shall officiate for the remainder of the game alone unless there is the possibility of replacing the injured referee with a qualified substitute referee. After consulting with the commissioner, if present, the remaining referee(s) shall decide upon the possible replacement.

47.6 For all international games, if verbal communication is necessary to make a decision clear, it shall be conducted in the English language.

47.7 **Each referee has the power to make decisions within the limits of his duties, but he has no authority to disregard or question decisions made by the other referee.**

47.8 **The implementation and interpretation of the Official Basketball Rules by the referees, regardless if an explicit decision was made or not, is final and cannot be contested or disregarded, except in cases where a protest is allowed (see Annex C).**

47.2 当发生一起违犯规则、一节或决胜期结束，或裁判员发现有必要停止比赛时，裁判员应鸣哨。在一次成功的投篮、一次成功的罚球之后或当球成活球时，裁判员不应鸣哨。

47.3 当判定身体接触或违例时，裁判员应在每一个实例中遵循和权衡下列基本原则：
- 规则的精神和意图，以及坚持比赛完整的需要。
- 运用"有利／无利"概念中的一致性，裁判员不应企图靠不必要的打断比赛的流畅来处罚附带的身体接触，况且这样的接触没有让有责任的队员获利，也未置对方队员于不利。
- 在每场比赛中运用常识的一致性，要记住有关队员的能力，以及他们在比赛中的态度和行为。
- 在比赛控制和比赛流畅之间保持平衡的一致性，对于参与者们正想做什么，以及宣判什么对比赛是正确的，要有一种"感觉"。

47.4 如果其中一支球队提出申诉，主裁判员（或到场的技术代表）在收到队伍提交的申诉原因后，应将该起申诉的事件情况书面报告给竞赛的组织部门。

47.5 如果一位裁判员受伤或因任何其他原因，在事故发生的5分钟内还不能继续执行职责，比赛应继续。剩余的裁判员应一直独立地执裁到比赛结束，除非有符合资格的替补裁判员替换他的可能性。在与技术代表（如到场）商议之后，剩余的裁判员将决定该可能的更换。

47.6 对所有的国际比赛，如果有必要用口语使宣判清楚，则应使用英语。

47.7 **每位裁判员有权在他的职责范围内做出宣判，但他无权漠视或质问另一（两）位裁判员做出的宣判。**

47.8 **不论是否作出明确的决定，裁判员对国际篮联篮球规则的执行和解释是最终的，不能被争辩或漠视，除非是已被允许申诉的情况（参见C——申诉程序）。**

Art. 48 Scorer and assistant scorer: Duties

48.1 The **scorer** shall be provided with a scoresheet and shall keep a record of:
- Teams, by entering the names and numbers of the players who are to begin the game and of all substitutes who enter the game. When there is an infraction of the rules regarding the 5 players to begin the game, substitutions or numbers of players, he shall notify the nearest referee as soon as possible.
- Running summary of points scored, by entering the field goals and the free throws made.
- Fouls charged on each player. The scorer must notify a referee immediately when 5 fouls are charged on any player. He shall enter the fouls charged on each head coach and must notify a referee immediately when a head coach should be disqualified. Similarly, he must notify a referee immediately that a player should be disqualified, if he has committed 2 technical fouls, or 2 unsportsmanlike fouls, or 1 technical and 1 unsportsmanlike foul.
- Time-outs. He must notify the referees of the time-out opportunity when a team has requested a time-out and notify the head coach through a referee when the head coach has no more time-out(s) left in a half or overtime.
- The next alternating possession, by operating the alternating possession arrow. The scorer shall reverse the direction of the alternating possession arrow immediately after the end of the first half as the teams shall exchange baskets for the second half.

48.2 The **assistant scorer** shall operate the scoreboard and assist the scorer and timer. In case of any discrepancy between the scoreboard and the scoresheet which cannot be resolved, the scoresheet shall take precedence and the scoreboard shall be corrected accordingly.

48.3 If a scorekeeping error is recognised on the scoresheet:
- During the game, the timer must wait for the first dead ball before sounding his signal.
- After the end of the playing time and before the scoresheet has been signed by the crew chief, the error shall be corrected, even if this correction influences the final result of the game.
- After the scoresheet has been signed by the crew chief, the error may no longer be corrected. The crew chief or the commissioner, if present, shall send a detailed report to the organising body of the competition.

第48条 记录员和助理记录员：职责

48.1 应给**记录员**提供记录表，他应：

- 登记比赛开始时上场的队员和所有参加比赛的替补队员的姓名和号码。当涉及比赛开始时上场的5名队员、替换或队员的号码违反规则时，他应尽快通知最靠近的裁判员。
- 在累积分表上登记投篮和罚球得分。
- 把每名球员的犯规登记在其名下。当登记任一队员第5次犯规时，记录员必须立即通知裁判员。他应把每一主教练的犯规登记在其名下，当主教练被取消比赛资格时，他必须立即通知裁判员。同样，当某队员已发生2次技术犯规、2次违反体育运动精神的犯规或一次技术犯规和一次违反体育运动精神的犯规并应被取消比赛资格时，他必须立即通知裁判员。
- 登记暂停。当某队已提出暂停请求，在出现暂停机会时通知裁判员。当主教练在该半时或决胜期中不再有剩余暂停时，他应通过裁判员通知该主教练。
- 操作交替拥有箭号来指明下一次交替拥有。上半时结束后，由于球队在下半时将交换球篮，记录员应立即反转交替拥有箭头的方向。

48.2 **助理记录员**应操纵记录屏、协助记录员和计时员。如果记录屏和记录表之间的任何差异不能被解决，应以记录表为准，并将记录屏做相应的改正。

48.3 如果发现记录表上的记录错误：

- 在比赛中，计时员必须等到第一次死球时才发出信号。
- 在比赛时间结束之后，和在主裁判员签字之前，该错误应被改正，即使这个改正影响比赛的最终结果。
- 在主裁判员已在记录表上签字之后，该错误不再可能被改正。主裁判员或技术代表（如到场）必须向竞赛的组织部门送交详细的报告。

Art. 49 Timer: Duties

49.1 The timer shall be provided with a game clock and a stopwatch and shall:
- Measure playing time, time-outs and intervals of play.
- Ensure that the game clock signal sounds very loudly and automatically at the end of a quarter or overtime.
- Use any means possible to notify the referees immediately if his signal fails to sound or is not heard.
- Indicate the number of fouls committed by each player by raising, in a manner visible to both head coaches, the marker with the number of fouls committed by that player.
- Position the team foul marker on the scorer's table, at the end nearest to the bench of the team in the team foul penalty situation, when the ball becomes live after the fourth team foul in a quarter.
- Effect substitutions.
- Sound his signal only when the ball becomes dead and before the ball becomes live again. The sound of his signal does not stop the game clock or the game nor cause the ball to become dead.

49.2 The timer shall measure **playing time** as follows:

- Starting the game clock when:
  — During a jump ball, the ball is legally tapped by a jumper.
  — After an unsuccessful last free throw and the ball continues to be live, the ball touches or is touched by any player on the playing court.
  — During a throw-in, the ball touches or is legally touched by any player on the playing court.
- Stopping the game clock when:
  — Time expires at the end of a quarter and overtime, if not stopped automatically by the game clock itself.
  — A referee blows his whistle while the ball is live.
  — A field goal is scored against a team which has requested a time-out.
  — A field goal is scored when the game clock shows 2:00 minutes or less in the fourth quarter and in each overtime.
  — The shot clock signal sounds while a team is in control of the ball.

第49条 计时员：职责

49.1 应给计时员提供一块比赛计时钟和一块计秒表，计时员应该：
- 计量比赛时间、暂停和比赛休息期间。
- 保证一节或决胜期比赛时间结束时自动发出非常响亮的信号。
- 如果信号失灵或未被听到，应立即使用任何可能的办法通知裁判员。
- 每一队员发生犯规时，举示队员犯规次数牌，使双方主教练能清楚看到该队员的犯规次数。
- 在每一节全队犯规累计已达4次，球队处于全队处罚状态，球成为活球时将全队犯规指示器放置在记录台最靠近该队球队席的一端。
- 发出替换信号。
- 只有在球成为死球，并且球再次成为活球之前发出信号。计时员的信号不停止比赛计时钟或比赛，也不使球成为死球。

49.2 计时员应按下列所述计量**比赛时间**：
- 当：
  ——跳球中，球被跳球队员合法地拍击时。
  ——最后一次罚球不成功，并且球继续是活球，球触及任一场上队员或被他触及时。
  ——掷球入界中，球触及任一场上队员或被他合法触及时。
  开动比赛计时钟。

- 当：
  ——在一节或决胜期比赛结束的时间终了，但比赛计时钟没有自动停止时。
  ——活球中裁判员鸣哨时。
  ——某队已请求暂停，对方队投篮得分时。
  ——在第4节和每一决胜期比赛计时钟显示2:00分钟或更少投篮得分时。
  ——某队控制球，进攻计时钟响起信号时。
  停止比赛计时钟。

OFFICIAL BASKETBALL RULES *2020*

49.3 The timer shall measure a **time-out** as follows:
- Starting the stopwatch immediately when the official blows his whistle and gives the time-out signal.
- Sounding his signal when 50 seconds of the time-out have elapsed.
- Sounding his signal when the time-out has ended.

49.4 The timer shall measure an **interval of play** as follows:
- Starting the stopwatch immediately when the referee blows his whistle and gives the time-out signal.
- Notifying the referees before the first and third quarter when 3 minutes and 1.5 minutes remain until the beginning of the quarter.
- Sounding his signal before the second and fourth quarter and each overtime when 30 seconds remain until the beginning of the quarter or overtime.
- Sounding his signal and simultaneously stopping the stopwatch immediately when an interval of play has ended.

Art. 50 Shot clock operator: Duties

The shot clock operator shall be provided with a shot clock which shall be:

50.1 **Started or restarted** when:
- On the playing court a team gains control of a live ball. After that, the mere touching of the ball by an opponent does not start a new shot clock period if the same team remains in control of the ball.
- On a throw-in, the ball touches or is legally touched by any player on the playing court.

50.2 **Stopped, but not reset,** with the remaining time visible, when the same team that previously had control of the ball is awarded a throw-in as the result of:
- A ball having gone out-of-bounds.
- A player of the same team having been injured.
- A technical foul committed by that team.
- A jump ball situation (not when the ball lodges between the ring and the backboard).
- A double foul.
- A cancellation of equal penalties on both teams.

Stopped, but also not reset, with the remaining time visible, when the same team that previously had control of the ball is awarded a frontcourt throw-in and 14 or more seconds are displayed on the shot clock as a result of a foul or violation.

134

49.3 计时员应按下列所述计量**暂停**：
- 裁判员鸣哨并给出暂停手势，立即开动秒表。
- 当暂停已走过50秒时发出他的信号。
- 当暂停已结束时发出他的信号。

49.4 计时员应按下列所述计量**比赛休息时间**：
- 先前的一节或决胜期已结束，立即开动秒表。
- 在第1节和第3节之前，距该节开始剩余3分钟、1分30秒时通知裁判员。
- 在第2节和第4节和每一决胜期之前，距该节或决胜期开始剩余30秒时发出他的信号。
- 当比赛休息时间结束时，发出他的信号并同时立即停止秒表。

第 50 条 进攻计时员：职责

应给进攻计时员提供一个进攻计时钟，并按下述要求操作：

50.1 **开动**或**重新**开动进攻计时钟，当：
- 某队在场上控制活球时。此后对方队员仅仅是触及球，而原控制球队依然控制球时，则不开始一个新的进攻时间周期。
- 在掷球入界中，球触及或者被场上任何队员合法触及时。

50.2 **停止但不复位**进攻计时钟，且剩余时间可见，当判给原控制球队掷球入界，因为：
- 球出界。
- 一名同队队员受伤。
- 该队被判技术犯规。
- 一次跳球情况（球夹在篮圈和篮板之间时除外）。
- 一次双方犯规。
- 判给双方球队的相等罚则相互抵消。

停止但不复位进攻计时钟，且剩余时间可见，当判给原控制球队掷球入界，作为犯规或违例的结果进攻计时钟显示14秒或更多。

135

50.3 **Stopped and reset to 24 seconds,** with no display visible, when:
- The ball legally enters the basket.
- The ball touches the ring of the opponents' basket and it is controlled by the team that was not in control of the ball before it has touched the ring.
- The team is awarded a backcourt throw-in:
  — As the result of a foul or violation (not for the ball having gone out-of-bounds).
  — As the result of a jump ball situation for the team that previously did not have the control of the ball.
  — The game is stopped because of an action not connected with the team in control of the ball.
  — The game is stopped because of an action not connected with either team, unless the opponents would be placed at a disadvantage.
- The team is awarded free throw(s).

50.4 **Stopped and reset to 14 seconds,** with 14 seconds visible, when:
- The same team that previously had control of the ball is awarded a frontcourt throw-in and 13 seconds or less are displayed on the shot clock:
  — As the result of a foul or violation (not for the ball having gone out-of-bounds).
  — The game being stopped because of an action not connected with the team in control of the ball.
  — The game being stopped because of an action not connected with either team, unless the opponents would be placed at a disadvantage.
- The team that previously did not have the control of the ball shall be awarded a frontcourt throw-in as a result of a:
  — Personal foul or violation (including for the ball having gone out-of-bounds),
  — Jump ball situation.
- A team shall be awarded a throw-in from the throw-in line in its frontcourt as a result of an unsportsmanlike or disqualifying foul.
- After the ball has touched the ring on an unsuccessful shot for a field goal (including when the ball lodges between the ring and the backboard), an unsuccessful last free throw, or on a pass, if the team which regains control of the ball is the same team that was in control of the ball before the ball touched the ring.

50.3 **停止进攻计时钟并复位到24秒**并且无显示，当：
- 球合法地进入球篮。
- 球触及对方球篮的篮圈（球夹在篮圈和篮板之间除外）并且球被球触及篮圈前未控制球的球队所控制。
- 某队获得后场掷球入界球权：
    —— 作为一次犯规或违例的结果（球出界除外）。
    —— 作为跳球情况的结果，球队先前没有控制球。
    —— 比赛因与控制球队无关的行为被停止。
    —— 比赛因与双方都无关的行为被停止，除非对方会被置于不利。
- 某队获得罚球。

50.4 **停止进攻计时钟并复位到14秒**，且14秒可见，当：
- 判给原控制球队在前场掷球入界并且进攻计时钟显示13秒或少于13秒：
    —— 作为一次犯规或违例的结果（球出界除外）。
    —— 比赛因与控制球队无关的行为被停止。
    —— 比赛因与双方都无关的行为被停止，除非对方会被置于不利。
- 作为一个结果，之前未控制球的队应在前场掷球入界：
    —— 侵人犯规或违例（包括出界）。
    —— 跳球情况。
- 作为一次违反体育运动精神的犯规或取消比赛资格的犯规的结果，从该队前场掷球入界线处执行掷球入界。
- 在一次不成功投篮（包括球夹在篮圈和篮板之间时）、最后一次不成功的罚球或者一次传球，球接触篮圈后，如果重新控制球的队和球触圈前控制球的队是同一队。

- The game clock shows 2:00 minutes or less in the fourth quarter or in each over-time following a time-out taken by the team that is entitled to the possession of the ball from its backcourt and the head coach decides that the game shall be resumed with a throw-in for his team from the throw-in line in the team's frontcourt and 14 seconds or more are displayed on the shot clock at the time when the game clock was stopped.

50.5 **Switched off,** after the ball becomes dead and the game clock has been stopped in any quarter or overtime when there is a new control of the ball for either team and there are fewer than 14 seconds on the game clock.

The shot clock signal neither stops the game clock or the game, nor causes the ball to become dead, unless a team is in a control of the ball.

- 第 4 节或每一决胜期比赛计时钟显示2:00分钟或更少，后场拥有球权的队请求了一次暂停，主教练决定比赛由该队从其前场掷球入界线处掷球入界重新开始且比赛计时钟停止时进攻计时钟显示14秒或更多。

50.5 在任一节或决胜期中，每当球成死球并且比赛计时钟停止时，任一球队获得新的控制球，并且比赛计时钟少于14秒，应**关闭进攻计时钟**。

进攻计时钟的信号既不停止比赛计时钟或比赛，也不使球成死球（某队正控制球除外）。

A — REFEREES' SIGNALS

A.1   The hand signals illustrated in these rules are the only valid referees' signals.

A.2   While reporting to the scorer's table it is strongly recommended to verbally support the communication (in international games in the English language).

A.3   It is important that the table officials are familiar with these signals.

Game clock signals

STOP THE CLOCK 
1. Open palm

STOP THE CLOCK FOR FOUL 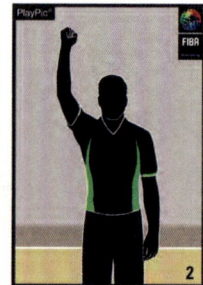
2. One clenched fist

START THE CLOCK 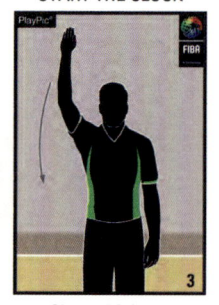
3. Chop with hand

Scoring

1 POINT 
4. 1 finger, 'flag' from wrist

2 POINTS 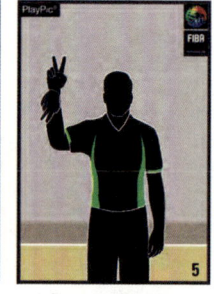
5. 2 fingers, 'flag' from wrist

3 POINTS 
6. 3 fingers extended
One arm: Attempt
Both arms: Successful

A —— 裁判员的手势

A.1　在本规则中阐明的手势是唯一正式认可的手势。

A.2　当向记录台报告时，强烈建议使用口语来支持交流（在国际比赛中应使用英语）。

A.3　记录台人员也要通晓这些手势，这是很重要的。

比赛时钟信号

停止计时钟　　　　**犯规停止计时钟**　　　　**计时开始**

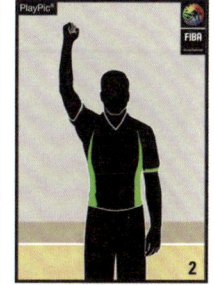

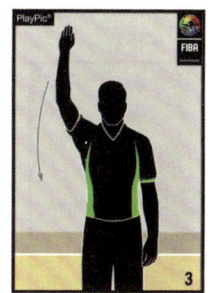

伸开手掌　　　　一拳紧握　　　　用手做砍劈

得　分

1分　　　　　　**2分**　　　　　　**3分**

1指
从腕部下屈

2指
从腕部下屈

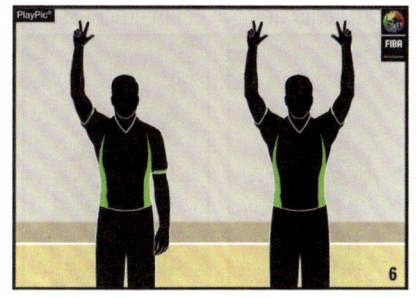

伸展3指
一只胳膊：3分试投
两只胳膊：3分投篮成功

OFFICIAL BASKETBALL RULES 2020

Substitution and Time-out

SUBSTITUTION (7)
Cross forearms

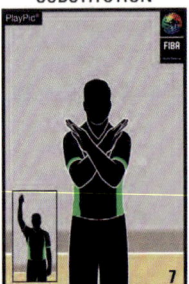

BECKONING-IN (8)
Open palm, wave towards the body

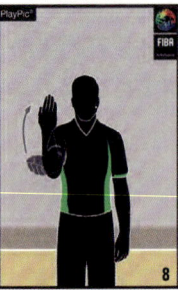

CHARGED TIME-OUT (9)
Form T, show index finger

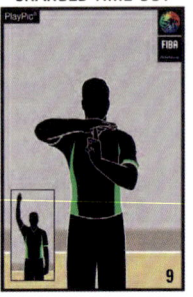

MEDIA TIME-OUT (10)
Open arms with clenched fists

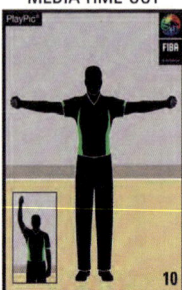

Informative

CANCEL SCORE, CANCEL PLAY (11)
Scissor-like action with arms, once across chest

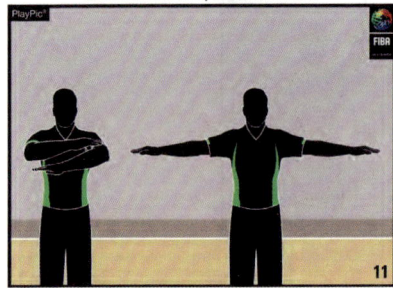

VISIBLE COUNT (12)
Counting while moving the palm

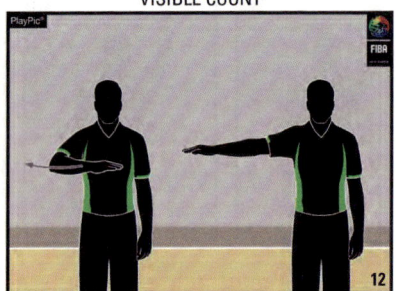

COMMUNICATION (13)
Thumb up

SHOT CLOCK RESET (14)
Rotate hand, extend index finger

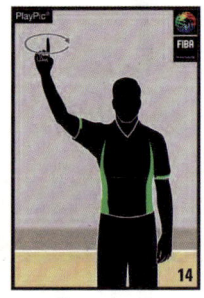

DIRECTION OF PLAY AND/OR OUT-OF-BOUNDS (15)
Point in direction of play, arm parallel to sidelines

HELD BALL/JUMP BALL SITUATION (16)
Thumbs up, then point in direction of play using the alternating possession arrow

篮球规则 2020

替换和暂停

替 换	招呼入场	暂 停	媒体暂停
前臂交叉	伸出手掌 摆向身体	成"T"形 食指示之	张开双臂 紧握拳头

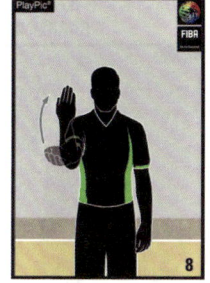

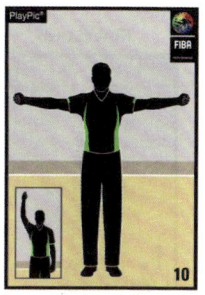

提供信息

取消得分，中止比赛	可见的计数
双臂像剪的动作，胸前交叉一次	移动手掌计数

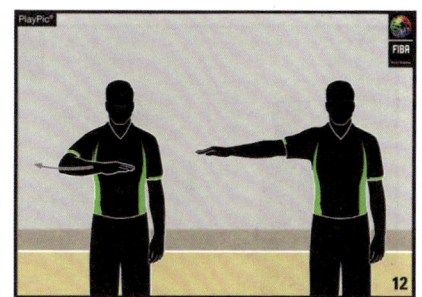

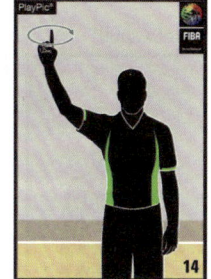

交 流	进攻计时钟复位	比赛方向和/或出界	争球/跳球情况
拇指向上	伸出食指 并转动手	指向比赛方向， 手臂与边线平行	两拇指向上，然后 指向交替拥有箭头 所指的比赛方向

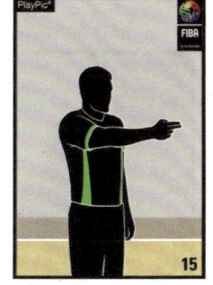

143

OFFICIAL BASKETBALL RULES 2020

Violations

TRAVELLING — 17 — Rotate fists

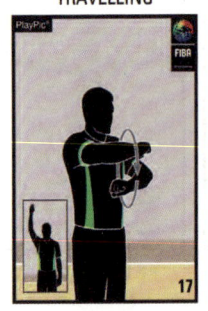

ILLEGAL DRIBBLE: DOUBLE DRIBBLING — 18 — Patting motion with palm

ILLEGAL DRIBBLE: CARRYING THE BALL — 19 — Half rotation with palm

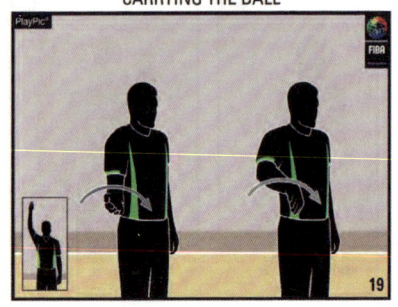

3 SECONDS — 20 — Arm extended, show 3 fingers

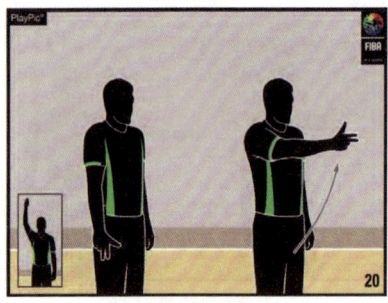

5 SECONDS — 21 — Show 5 fingers

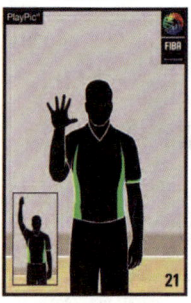

8 SECONDS — 22 — Show 8 fingers

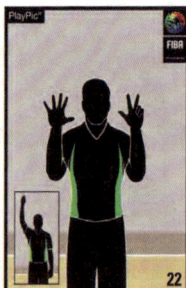

24 SECONDS — 23 — Fingers touch shoulder

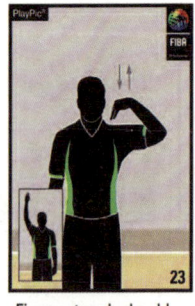

BALL RETURNED TO BACKCOURT — 24 — Wave arm front of body

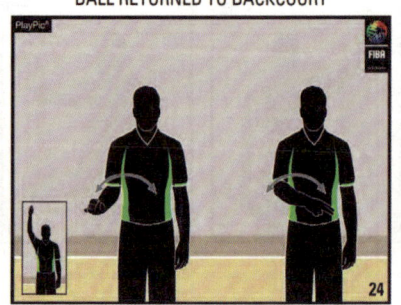

DELIBERATE KICK OR BLOCK OF THE BALL — 25 — Point to the foot

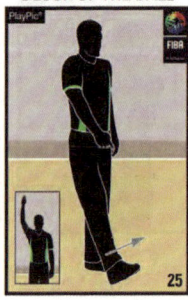

144

篮球规则 2020

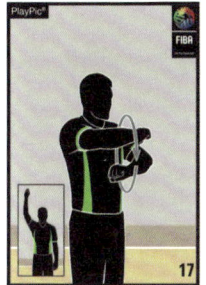

违 例

带球走	非法运球：两次运球	非法运球：携带球
17 转动双拳	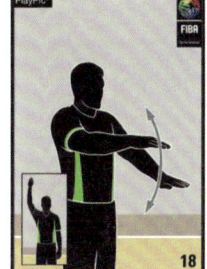 18 用手掌做轻拍动作	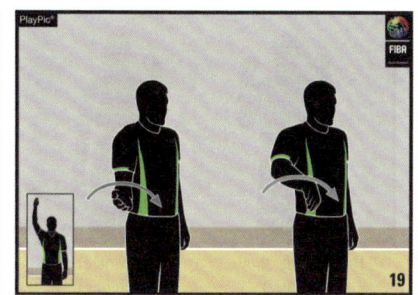 19 半转手掌

3 秒钟	5 秒钟	8 秒钟
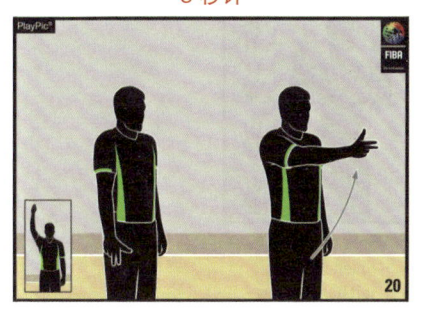 20 伸出手臂示3指	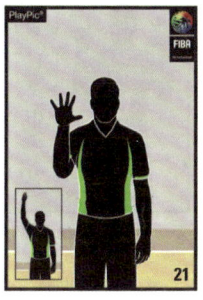 21 示5指	 22 示8指

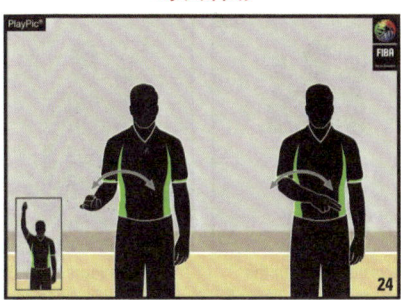

24 秒钟	球回后场	故意脚踢或拦阻球
23 手指触肩	24 身前摆动手臂	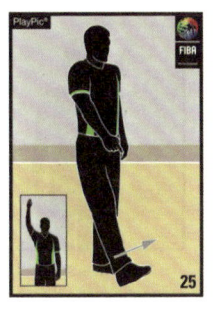 25 手指指脚

145

OFFICIAL BASKETBALL RULES *2020*

Number of Players

No. 00 and 0

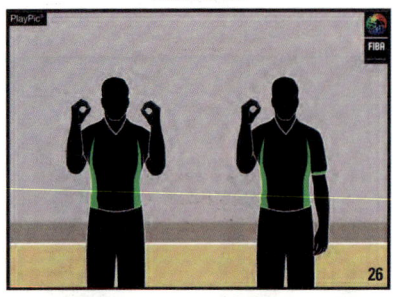

Both hands show number 0

Right hand shows number 0

No. 1 - 5

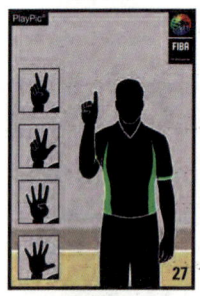

Right hand shows number 1 to 5

No. 6 - 10

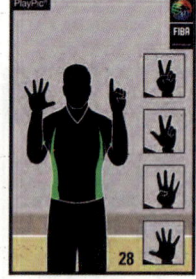

Right hand shows number 5, left hand shows number 1 to 5

No. 11 - 15

Right hand shows clenched fist, left hand shows number 1 to 5

No. 16

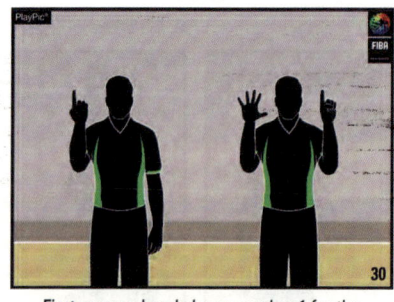

First reverse hand shows number 1 for the decade digit - then open hands show number 6 for the units digit

No. 24

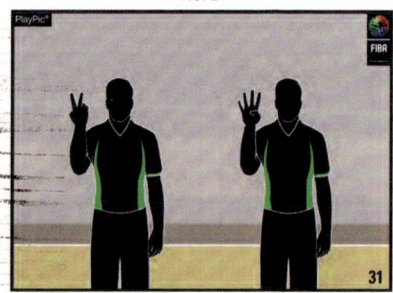

First reverse hand shows number 2 for the decade digit - then open hand shows number 4 for the units digit

篮球规则 2020

队员的号码

No.00 和 No.0

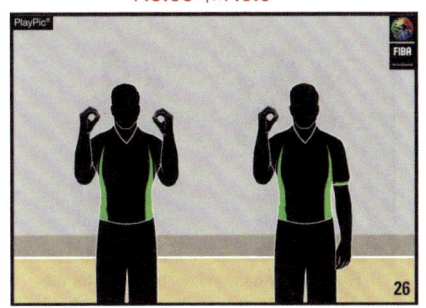

双手示0号　　右手示0号

No.1-5　　No.6-10　　No.11-15

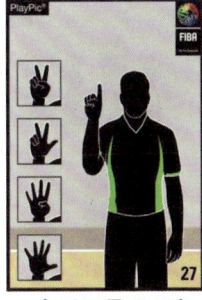

右手示号码1到5　　右手示5号，左手示号码1到5　　右手示握紧的拳头，左手示号码1到5

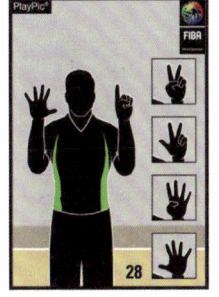

No.16　　No.24

首先手背朝外示1号代表十位数，然后手掌朝外示6号代表个位数　　首先手背朝外示2号代表十位数，然后手掌朝外示4号代表个位数

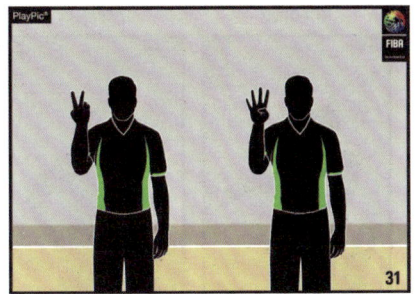

147

OFFICIAL BASKETBALL RULES *2020*

No. 40

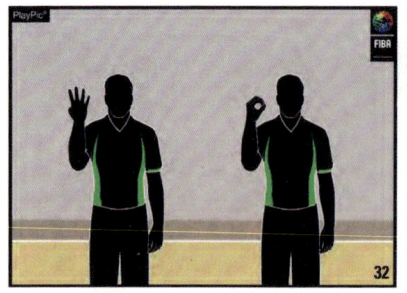

First reverse hand shows number 4 for the decade digit - then open hand shows 0 for the units digit

No. 62

First reverse hands show number 6 for the decade digit - then open hand shows 2 for the units digit

No. 78

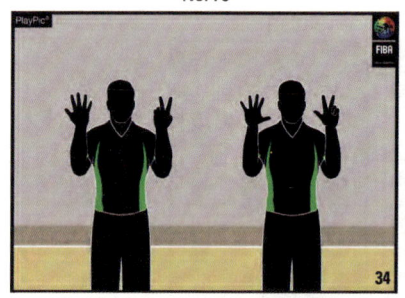

First reverse hands show number 7 for the decade digit - then open hands show number 8 for the units digit

No. 99

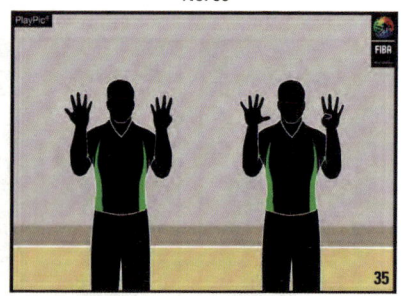

First reverse hands show number 9 for the decade digit - then open hands show number 9 for the units digit

Type of Fouls

HOLDING 
Grasp wrist downward

BLOCKING (DEFENSE), ILLEGAL SCREEN (OFFENSE) 
Both hands on hips

PUSHING OR CHARGING WITHOUT THE BALL 
Imitate push

HANDCHECKING 
Grab palm and forward motion

篮球规则 2020

No.40　　　　　　　　　　　　No.62

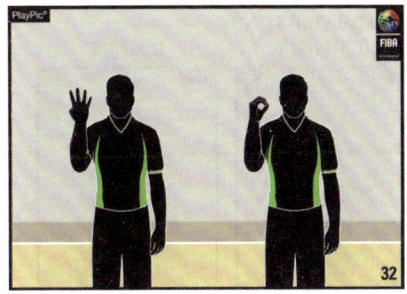

首先手背朝外示4号代表十位数，
然后手掌朝外示0号代表个位数

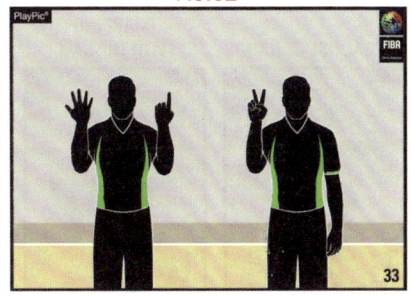

首先手背朝外示6号代表十位数，
然后手掌朝外示2号代表个位数

No.78　　　　　　　　　　　　No.99

首先手背朝外示7号代表十位数，
然后手掌朝外示8号代表个位数

首先手背朝外示9号代表十位数，
然后手掌朝外示9号代表个位数

犯规的类型

拉　人	阻挡（防守）非法掩护（进攻）	推人或不带球撞人	用手推挡
向下抓住手腕	双手置髋部	模仿推	抓住手掌向前移动

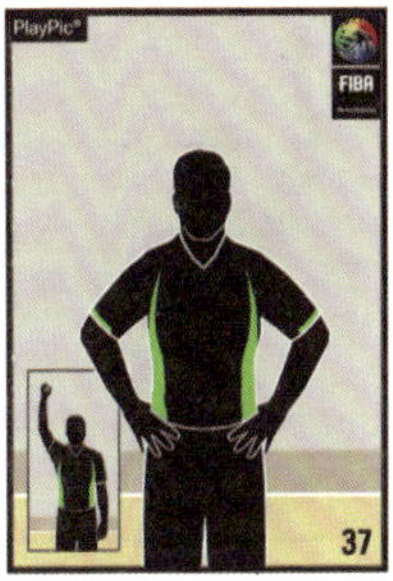

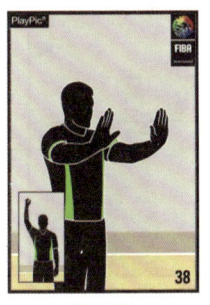

149

FIBA OFFICIAL BASKETBALL RULES 2020

40 — ILLEGAL USE OF HANDS 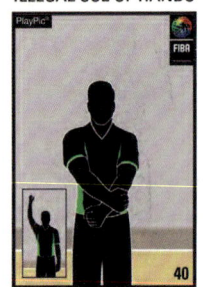
Strike wrist

41 — CHARGING WITH THE BALL 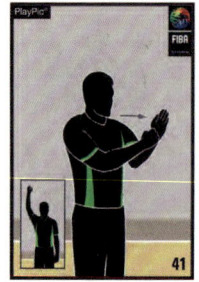
Clenched fist strike open palm

42 — ILLEGAL CONTACT TO THE HAND 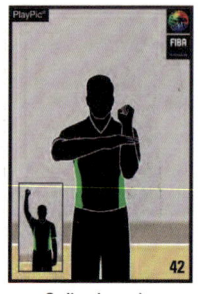
Strike the palm towards the other forearm

43 — HOOKING 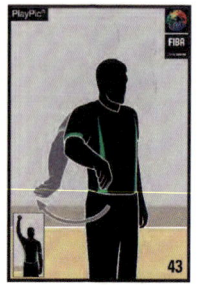
Move lower arm backwards

44 — EXCESSIVE SWINGING OF ELBOW 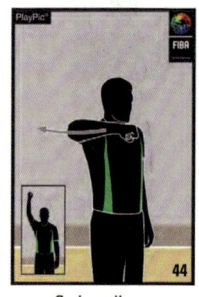
Swing elbow backwards

45 — HIT TO THE HEAD 
Imitate the contact to the head

46 — FOUL BY TEAM IN CONTROL OF THE BALL 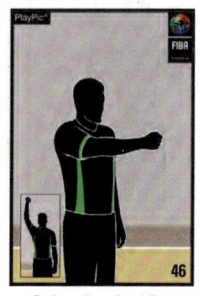
Point clenched fist towards basket of offending team

47 — FOUL ON THE ACT OF SHOOTING 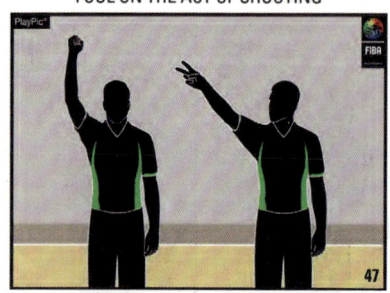
One arm with clenched fist, followed by indication of the number of free throws

48 — FOUL NOT ON THE ACT OF SHOOTING 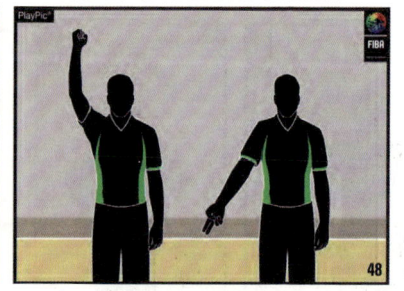
One arm with clenched fist, followed by pointing to the floor

篮球规则 2020

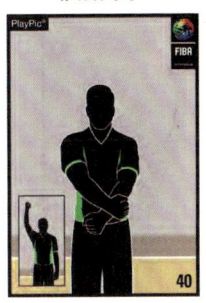

非法用手	带球撞人	对手的非法接触	勾人犯规
击 腕	握拳击掌	掌击另一只前臂	向后移动前臂

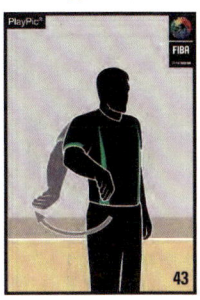

过分挥肘	击 头	控制球队的犯规
向后摆肘	模仿拍击头部	握拳指向犯规队的球篮

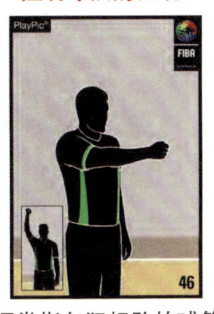

对投篮动作的犯规	对非投篮动作的犯规
单臂握拳举起，随后指示罚球次数	单臂握拳举起，随后指向地面

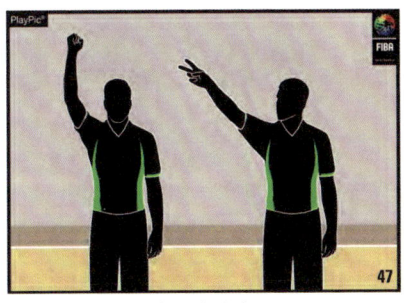

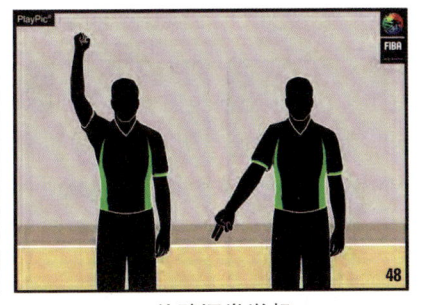

151

OFFICIAL BASKETBALL RULES *2020*

Special Fouls

DOUBLE FOUL (49)
Wave clenched fists on both hands

TECHNICAL FOUL (50)
Form T, showing palms

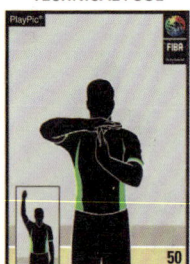

UNSPORTSMANLIKE FOUL (51)
Grasp wrist upward

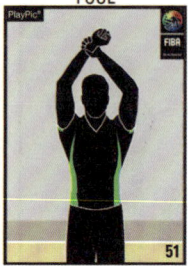

DISQUALIFYING FOUL (52)
Clenched fists on both hands

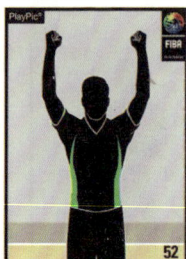

FAKE A FOUL (53)
Raise the lower arm twice

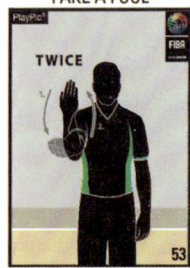

ILLEGAL BOUNDARY LINE CROSSING ON A THROW-IN (54)
Wave arm parallel to boundary line (in last 2 minutes of the fourth quarter and overtime)

IRS REVIEW (55)
Rotate hand with horizontal extended index finger

Foul Penalty Administration Reporting to Table

AFTER FOUL WITHOUT FREE THROW(S) (56)
Point in direction of play, arm parallel to sidelines

AFTER FOUL BY TEAM IN CONTROL OF THE BALL (57)
Clenched fist in direction of play, arm parallel to sidelines

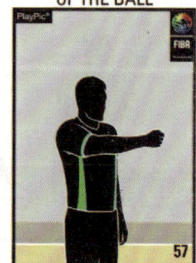

篮球规则 2020

特殊犯规

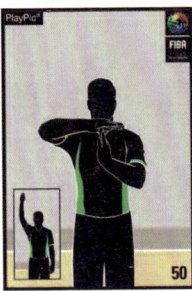

双方犯规	技术犯规	违反体育运动精神的犯规	取消比赛资格的犯规
49	50	51	52
挥动握紧的双拳	成"T"形手掌示之	向上抓住手腕	紧握双拳

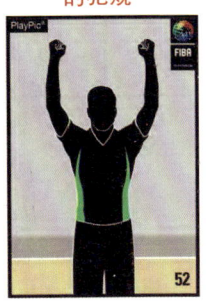

骗取犯规	掷球入界非法越线	调用即时回放系统
53	54	55
前臂上抬两次（从高处做起）	平行于界线摆动手臂（第4节和决胜期最后2:00分钟）	水平伸直食指转动手

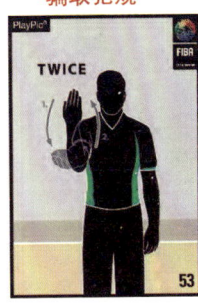

向记录台报告罚则

没有罚球的犯规后	控制球队犯规后
56	57
指向比赛方向，手臂与边线平行	握拳指向比赛方向手臂与边线平行

153

OFFICIAL BASKETBALL RULES 2020

1 FREE THROW	2 FREE THROWS	3 FREE THROWS
Hold up 1 finger	Hold up 2 fingers	Hold up 3 fingers

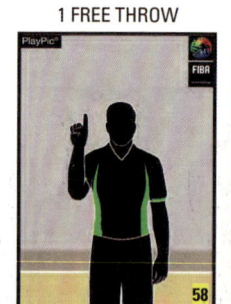

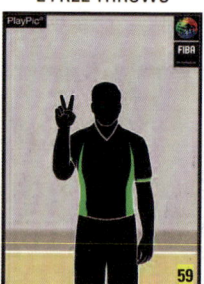

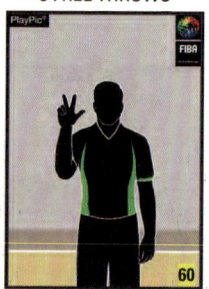

Administrating Free Throws — Active Referee (Lead)

1 FREE THROW	2 FREE THROWS	3 FREE THROWS
1 finger horizontal	2 fingers horizontal	3 fingers horizontal

Administrating Free Throws - Passive Referee (Trail in 2PO & Centre in 3PO)

1 FREE THROW	2 FREE THROWS	3 FREE THROWS
Index finger	Fingers together on both hands	3 fingers extended on both hands

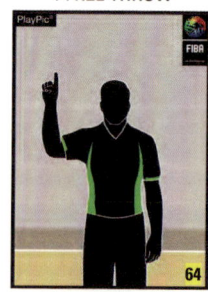

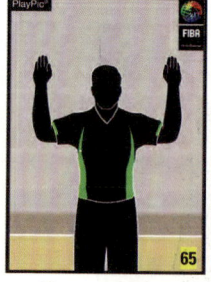

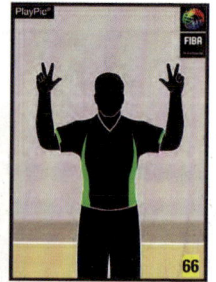

Diagram 7   Officials' signals

篮球规则 2020

1 次罚球	2 次罚球	3 次罚球
举起1指	举起2指	举起3指

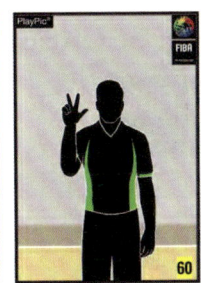

罚球管理 —— 执行裁判（前导裁判）

1 次罚球	2 次罚球	3 次罚球
水平伸1指	水平伸2指	水平伸3指

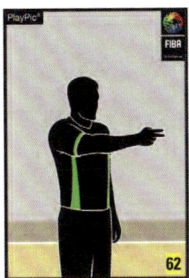

罚球管理 —— 非执行裁判（2人执裁之追踪裁判 & 3人执裁之中央裁判）

1 次罚球	2 次罚球	3 次罚球
伸食指	双手手指并拢	双手伸展3指

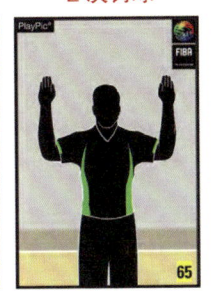

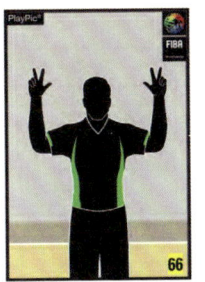

图7 裁判员的手势

155

B — THE SCORESHEET

Diagram 8   Scoresheet

B —— 记录表

图8 记录表

OFFICIAL BASKETBALL RULES 2020

B.1 The scoresheet shown in Diagram 8 is the one approved by the **FIBA** Technical Commission.

B.2 It consists of 1 original and 3 copies, each to be of different coloured paper. The original, on white paper, is for **FIBA**. The first copy, on blue paper, is for the organising body of the competition, the second copy, on pink paper, is for the winning team, and the last copy, on yellow paper, is for the losing team.

> **Note:** 1. The scorer shall use 2 different coloured pens, RED for the first and third quarter and BLUE or BLACK for the second and fourth quarter. For all overtimes, all entries shall be made in BLUE or BLACK (same colour as for the second and fourth quarter).
> 2. The scoresheet may be prepared and completed electronically.

B.3 **At least 40 minutes before the game is scheduled to begin,** the scorer shall prepare the scoresheet in the following manner:

B.3.1 He shall enter the names of the 2 teams in the space at the top of the scoresheet. The **team 'A'** shall always be the local (home) team or for tournaments or games on a neutral playing court, the first team named in the schedule. The other team shall be **team 'B'**.

FEDERATION INTERNATIONALE DE BASKETBALL
INTERNATIONAL BASKETBALL FEDERATION
SCORESHEET

Team A HOOPERS   Team B POINTERS
Competition WCM   Date 20. 11. 2014 Time 20:00   Referee WALTON, M.
Game No. 5   Place GENEVA   Umpire 1 CHANG, Y.   Umpire 2 BARTOK, K.

Diagram 9   Top of the scoresheet

B.3.2 He shall then enter:
- The name of the competition.
- The number of the game.
- The date, the time and the place of the game.
- The names of the crew chief and the umpire(s) and their nationality (IOC code).

B.3.3 Team 'A' shall occupy the upper part of the scoresheet, team 'B' the lower part.

B.3.3.1 In the first column, the scorer shall enter the licence number (last 3 digits) of each player, head coach and first assistant coach. For tournaments, the number of the licences shall only be entered for the first game played by the teams.

B.1 图8中所示的记录表是经过**国际篮球联合会**技术委员会批准的。

B.2 它由1张正页和3张副页组成，每一张颜色均不同。正页是白色，交**国际篮联**。第一张副页是蓝色，交给竞赛的组织部门；第二张副页是粉红色，交给胜队；最后一张副页是黄色，交给负队。

注：1. 记录员必须使用两种不同颜色的笔，第1节和第3节用红色笔，第2节和第4节用蓝色笔或黑色笔。所有决胜期必须使用蓝色笔或黑色笔记录（与第2节和第4节相同）。

2. 记录表可以用电子的方式准备和完成。

B.3 **至少在预定的比赛开始前40分钟**，记录员要按下列样式准备记录表：

B.3.1 在记录表顶部的空格内登录两队的名称。"A"队应总是当地（主）队或者在联赛中或在中立球场的竞赛日程表中列前的队。另一队应是"B"队。（图9）

国际篮球联合会记录表

A队			B队		
竞赛名称：	WCM	日期：20.11.2014 时间： 20:00	主裁判员：	WALTON, M.	
比赛序号：	5	地点： GENEVA	副裁判员1：	CHANG, Y.	副裁判员2： BARTOK, K.

图9 记录表的顶部

B.3.2 然后，他应填入：
- 竞赛的名称。
- 比赛的序号。
- 比赛的日期、时间和地点。
- 主裁判员和副裁判员的姓名和他们的国籍（IOC代码）。

B.3.3 "A"队应占据记录表的上部，"B"队占据下部。

B.3.3.1 在第一栏内，记录员应登录每位队员、主教练和第一助理教练的证件号码（最后3位数字）。对于联赛，证件号码只应在该队首场比赛时填写。

B.3.3.2 In the second column, the scorer shall enter each player's name and initials in the order of the shirt numbers, all in BLOCK CAPITAL letters, using the list of team members as provided by the head coach or his representative. The captain of the team shall be entered with a (CAP) immediately after his name.

B.3.3.3 If a team presents fewer than 12 players, the scorer shall draw a line through the spaces for the player's licence number, name, number, player in, in the line below the last entered player. If there are less than 11 players, the horizontal line shall be drawn horizontally until reaching the player fouls section and continue diagonally down to the bottom.

Licence no.	Players	No.	Player in	Fouls 1 2 3 4 5
001	MAYER, F.	5		
002	JONES, M.	8		
003	SMITH, E.	9		
004	FRANK, Y.	12		
010	NANCE, L.	18		
012	KING, H. (CAP)	22		
014	WONG, P.	24		
015	RUSH, S.	25		
021	MARTINEZ, M.	33		
022	SANCHES, N.	42		
Coach	LOOR, A.			
Assistant Coach	MONTA, B.			

Diagram 10   Teams on the scoresheet (before the game)

B.3.4 At the bottom of each team's section, the scorer shall enter (in BLOCK CAPITAL letters) the names of the team's head coach and first assistant coach.

B.3.5 At the bottom of the scoresheet the scorer shall enter (in BLOCK CAPITAL letters) the names of himself, assistant scorer, timer and shot clock operator.

B.4 **At least 10 minutes before the game is scheduled to begin each head coach shall:**

B.4.1 Confirm his agreement with the names and the corresponding numbers of his team members.

B.4.2 Confirm the names of the head coach and first assistant coach. If there is no head coach and no first assistant coach, the captain shall act as player coach and shall be entered with a (CAP) behind his name.

Coach	KING, H. (CAP)		
Assistant Coach			

B.3.3.2 在第二栏内，记录员应使用由主教练或他的代表提供的成员名单按照球衣号码的顺序填入每名队员的姓和名字的首字母，都用印刷体大写字母。球队的队长在他的姓名后面登录CAP。

B.3.3.3 如果一个球队出场少于12名队员，记录员应用直线画掉最下方一行球员的参赛证号码、姓名、号码、上场队员空白栏。如果少于11名球员，用直线水平画到队员犯规部分，然后用斜线画到底部。

证件号码	队员	号码	上场队员	犯规 1	2	3	4	5
001	MAYER, F.	5						
002	JONES, M.	8						
003	SMITH, E.	9						
004	FRANK, Y.	12						
010	NANCE, L.	18						
012	KING, H. (CAP)	22						
014	WONG, P.	24						
015	RUSH, S.	25						
021	MARTINEZ, M.	33						
022	SANCHES, N.	42						

主教练	LOOR, A.
第一助理教练	MONTA, B.

图 10 记录表中的球队（比赛开始前）

B.3.4 在每队表格的底部，记录员应登录（用印刷体大写字母）该队主教练和第一助理教练的姓名。

B.3.5 在记录表的底部，记录员应登录（用印刷体大写字母）他自己、助理记录员、计时员和进攻计时员的姓名。

B.4 至少在预定的比赛前10分钟，双方主教练应：

B.4.1 确认他们的名单，包括球队成员的姓名和相应的号码。

B.4.2 确认主教练和第一助理教练的姓名。如果没有主教练和第一助理教练，队长将担任队员兼教练，在他的姓名后登录（CAP）。

主教练	KING, H. (CAP)
第一助理教练	

OFFICIAL BASKETBALL RULES 2020

B.4.3 Enter a small 'x' beside the player's number in the 'Player in' column for the 5 players to begin the game.

B.4.4 Sign the scoresheet.
The head coach of team 'A' shall be the first to provide the above information.

B.5 **At the beginning of the game,** the scorer shall circle the small 'x' of the 5 players in the 'Player in' column in each team to begin the game.

B.6 **During the game,** the scorer shall draw a small 'x' (not circled) when the substitute enters the game for the first time as a player.

B.7 Time-outs

B.7.1 Time-outs granted shall be entered on the scoresheet by entering the minute of the playing time of the quarter or overtime in the appropriate boxes below the team's name.

B.7.2 At the end of each half and overtime, unused boxes shall be marked with 2 horizontal parallel lines. Should the team not be granted its first time-out before the game clock shows 2:00 minutes in the fourth quarter, the scorer shall mark 2 horizontal lines in the first box for the team's second half.

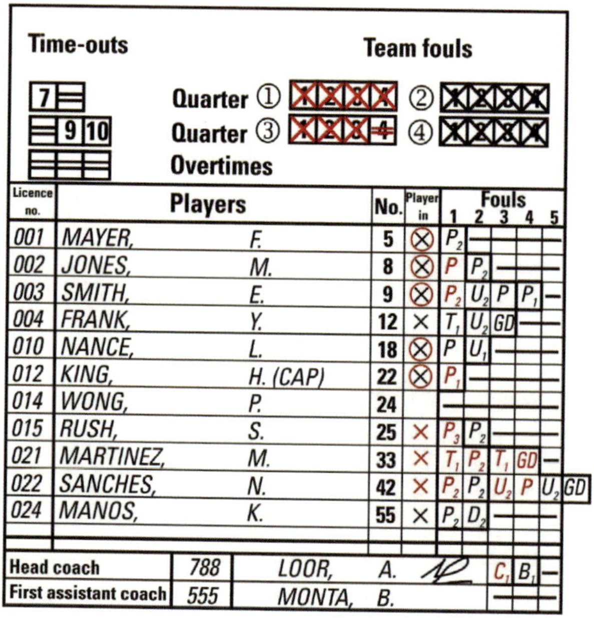

Diagram 11 Teams on the scoresheet (after the game)

162

B.4.3 指明比赛开始时上场的5名队员,并在队员号码旁边的"上场队员"栏内画一小"x"。

B.4.4 在记录表上签字。

"A"队主教练应首先提供上述资料。

B.5 在比赛开始时,记录员应在每一队比赛首发队员的小"x"上圈上圆圈。

B.6 在比赛期间,当替补队员第一次作为队员进入比赛时,记录员应在队员号码旁边的"上场队员"栏内画一小"x"(不套圆圈)。

B.7 暂 停

B.7.1 被准予的暂停应被登记在记录表上,登记时须在球队名称下适当空格内填入每节或决胜期此时的比赛时间(分钟)。

B.7.2 在每半时和决胜期结束时,未用过的空格用两条平行的横线标示。如果球队在第4节比赛计时钟显示2:00分钟之前未登记其第一次暂停,记录员应在球队下半时暂停的第1格内画两条平行的横线。

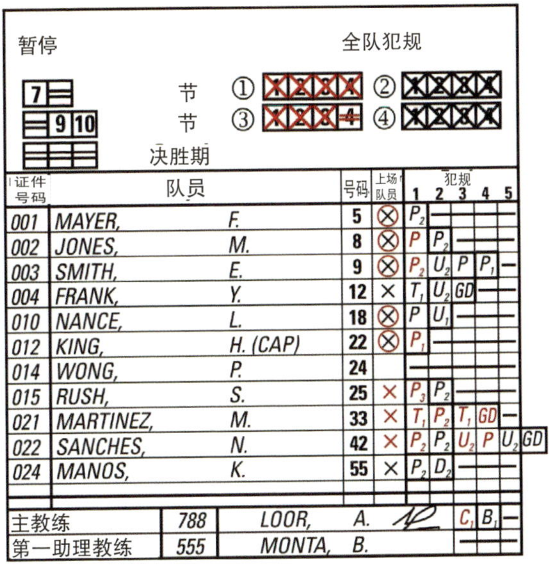

暂停			全队犯规		
7	节	① ✗✗✗✗	② ✗✗✗✗
9 10	节	③ ✗✗✗✗	④ ✗✗✗✗
	决胜期		

证件号码	队员		号码	上场队员	犯规 1 2 3 4 5
001	MAYER,	F.	5	⊗	P₂
002	JONES,	M.	8	⊗	P P₂
003	SMITH,	E.	9	⊗	P₂ U₂ P₁
004	FRANK,	Y.	12	×	T₁ U₂ GD
010	NANCE,	L.	18	⊗	P U₁
012	KING,	H. (CAP)	22	⊗	P₁
014	WONG,	P.	24		
015	RUSH,	S.	25	×	P₃ P₂
021	MARTINEZ	M.	33	×	T₁ P₂ T₁ GD
022	SANCHES,	N.	42	×	P₂ U₂ P U₂ GD
024	MANOS,	K.	55	×	P₂ D₂

| 主教练 | 788 | LOOR, | A. | | C B₁ |
| 第一助理教练 | 555 | MONTA, | B. | | |

图11 记录表中的球队(比赛结束后)

163

B.8 Fouls

B.8.1 Player fouls may be personal, technical, unsportsmanlike or disqualifying and shall be entered to the player.

B.8.2 Fouls committed by head coach, first assistant coach, substitutes, excluded players and accompanying delegation members may be technical or disqualifying and shall be entered to the head coach. In addition, disqualifying fouls committed by persons entered on the scoresheet in a fight shall be entered to these persons.

B.8.3 All fouls shall be entered as follows:

B.8.3.1 A personal foul shall be entered with a 'P'.

B.8.3.2 A technical foul on a player shall be entered with a 'T'. A second technical foul shall also be entered with a 'T', followed by a 'GD' for the game disqualification in the following space.

B.8.3.3 A technical foul on the head coach for his personal unsportsmanlike behaviour shall be entered with a 'C'. A second similar technical foul shall also be entered with a 'C', followed by a 'GD' in the following space.

B.8.3.4 A technical foul on the head coach for any other reason shall be entered with a 'B'. A third technical foul (one of them could be a 'C') shall be entered with a 'B' or 'C', followed by a 'GD' in the following space.

B.8.3.5 An unsportsmanlike foul on a player shall be entered with an 'U'. A second unsports-manlike foul shall also be entered with an 'U', followed by a 'GD' in the next following space.

B.8.3.6 A technical foul on a player with an earlier unsportsmanlike foul or an unsports-manlike foul on a player with an earlier technical foul shall also be entered with an 'U' or 'T' followed by a 'GD' in the next following space.

B.8.3.7 A disqualifying foul shall be entered with a 'D'.

B.8.3.8 Any foul involving a free throw(s) shall be entered with adding the corresponding number of free throws (1, 2 or 3) beside the 'P', 'T', 'C', 'B', 'U' or 'D'.

B.8 犯 规

B.8.1 队员犯规可能是侵人的、技术的、违反体育运动精神的或取消比赛资格的，应登记在该队员的名下。

B.8.2 主教练、第一助理教练、替补队员、出局的队员和随队人员的犯规可能是技术的或取消比赛资格的，应登记在主教练的名下。另外，在一起打架中，记录表上已登录人员的取消比赛资格犯规应登入他们自己的一栏中。

B.8.3 所有的犯规应按下述方式登记：

B.8.3.1 侵人犯规应登录"P"来表示。

B.8.3.2 队员的技术犯规应登录"T"来表示。第2次技术犯规也应登录"T"来表示，随后在接着的空格内登录"GD"来表示取消比赛资格。

B.8.3.3 主教练因他自身违反体育运动精神的行为的技术犯规应登录"C"来表示。第2次技术犯规也应登录"C"来表示，随后在接着的空格内登录"GD"。

B.8.3.4 主教练因任何其他原因的技术犯规应登录"B"来表示。第三次技术犯规（三个中的一个可能是"C"）应登录"B"或"C"来表示，随后在接着的空格内登录"GD"。

B.8.3.5 违反体育运动精神的犯规应登录"U"来表示。第2次违反体育运动精神的犯规也应登录"U"来表示，随后在接着的空格内登录"GD"来表示。

B.8.3.6 一名队员之前已经登记一次违反体育运动精神的犯规，随后又被宣判了一次技术犯规，或者已经登记了一次技术犯规，随后又被宣判了一次违反体育运动精神的犯规，也应登记一个"U"或"T"，并在随后的空格内登录一个"GD"。

B.8.3.7 取消比赛资格的犯规应登录"D"来表示。

B.8.3.8 包含罚球的任何犯规，应在"P""T""C""B""U"或者"D"的旁边加上相应的罚球次数（1、2或者3）来表示。

B.8.3.9 All fouls on both teams involving equal penalties shall be cancelled according to Art. 42 and entered by adding a small 'c' beside the 'P', 'T', 'C', 'B', 'U' or 'D'.

B.8.3.10 A disqualifying foul on an first assistant coach, substitute, excluded player or an accompanying delegation member, including for leaving the team bench area in a fight, shall be entered as a technical foul on the head coach by entering a 'B$_2$'.

B.8.3.11 An 'F' shall be entered, after the 'D2' or 'D', in all remaining spaces of the disqualified head coach, first assistant coach, substitute or excluded player in a fight.

B.8.3.12 Examples of disqualifying fouls on a head coach, first assistant coach, substitute, excluded player or accompanying delegation member:

A disqualifying foul on a head coach shall be entered as follows:

Head coach	788	LOOR, A.	D$_2$	
First assistant coach	555	MONTA, B.		

A disqualifying foul on a first assistant coach shall be entered as follows:

Head coach	788	LOOR, A.	B$_2$	
First assistant coach	555	MONTA, B.	D	

A disqualifying foul on a substitute shall be entered as follows:

| 001 | MAYER, F. | | 5 | ⊗ | D | | | |

and

Head coach	788	LOOR, A.	B$_2$	
First assistant coach	555	MONTA, B.		

A disqualifying foul on an excluded player after his fifth foul shall be entered as follows:

| 015 | RUSH, S. | | 25 | × | T$_1$ | P$_3$ | P$_2$ | P$_1$ | P$_2$ | D |

and

Head coach	788	LOOR, A.	B$_2$	
First assistant coach	555	MONTA, B.		

A disqualifying foul on an accompanying delegation member shall be entered as follows:

Head coach	788	LOOR, A.	B$_2$	
First assistant coach	555	MONTA, B.		

B.8.3.9 对双方球队包含相等罚则并按第42条（特殊情况）被抵消的所有规则，应在"P""T""C""B""U"或"D"的旁边登录一个小"c"来表示。

B.8.3.10 一名第一助理教练、替补队员、出局的队员或者随队人员被判罚取消比赛的资格犯规，包括因为在打架情况中离开球队席，应登记一次主教练的技术犯规，登记为"B$_2$"。

B.8.3.11 在一起打架中，被取消比赛资格的主教练、第一助理教练、替补队员或出局的队员应在登录的"D$_2$"或"D"之后的所有空格内登入"F"。

B.8.3.12 **主教练、第一助理教练、替补队员、出局的队员或随队人员取消比赛资格的犯规举例：**

判罚一名主教练取消比赛资格的犯规，应按如下记录：

主教练	788	LOOR, A.	D$_2$	
第一助理教练	555	MONTA, B.		

判罚一名第一助理教练取消比赛资格的犯规，应按如下记录：

主教练	788	LOOR, A.	B$_2$	
第一助理教练	555	MONTA, B.	D	

判罚一名替补队员取消比赛资格的犯规，应按如下记录：

001	MAYER, F.		5	⊗	D	

和

主教练	788	LOOR, A.	B$_2$	
第一助理教练	555	MONTA, B.		

对一名第5次犯规以后被判出局的队员的取消比赛资格的犯规，应按如下记录：

| 015 | RUSH, S. | | 25 | × | T$_1$ | P$_3$ | P$_2$ | P$_1$ | P$_2$ | D |

和

主教练	788	LOOR, A.	B$_2$	
第一助理教练	555	MONTA, B.		

对随队人员的取消比赛资格的犯规，应按如下记录：

主教练	788	LOOR, A.	B$_2$	
第一助理教练	555	MONTA, B.		

B.8.3.13 Examples of disqualifying fouls for leaving the team bench area in the fight on a head coach, first assistant coach, substitute, excluded player or accompanying delegation member:

Irrespective of the number of persons disqualified for leaving the team bench area, a single technical foul 'B_2' or 'D_2' shall be charged on the head coach.

A disqualifying foul on a **head coach** and a **first assistant coach** shall be entered as follows:

If only the head coach is disqualified:

| Head coach | 788 | LOOR, | A. | D_2 | F | F |
| First assistant coach | 555 | MONTA, | B. | | | |

If only the first assistant coach is disqualified:

| Head coach | 788 | LOOR, | A. | B_2 | | |
| First assistant coach | 555 | MONTA, | B. | D | F | F |

If both the head coach and the first assistant coach are disqualified:

| Head coach | 788 | LOOR, | A. | D_2 | F | F |
| First assistant coach | 555 | MONTA, | B. | D | F | F |

A disqualifying foul on a substitute shall be entered as follows:

If the substitute has fewer than 4 fouls, then a 'D' shall be entered, followed by an 'F' in all remaining foul spaces:

| 003 | SMITH, | E. | | 9 | ⊗ | P_2 | P_2 | D | F | F |

and

| Head coach | 788 | LOOR, | A. | B_2 | | |
| First assistant coach | 555 | MONTA, | B. | | | |

If it is the substitute's fifth foul, then a 'D' shall be entered, followed by an 'F' in the column behind the last foul space:

| 002 | JONES, | M. | | 8 | ⊗ | T_1 | P_3 | P_1 | P_2 | D | F |

and

| Head coach | 788 | LOOR, | A. | B_2 | | |
| First assistant coach | 555 | MONTA, | B. | | | |

B.8.3.13 主教练、第一助理教练、替补队员、出局的队员或随队人员在一起打架中因离开球队席区域被判取消比赛资格犯规的举例:

无论离开球队席区域被取消比赛资格的人的数量,应登录主教练一个单一的技术犯规("B_2"或"D_2")。

判罚**主教练**或**第一助理教练**取消比赛资格的犯规,应按如下记录:

如果只有主教练被取消比赛资格:

主教练	788	LOOR, A.	D_2	F	F
第一助理教练	555	MONTA, B.			

如果只有第一助理教练被取消比赛资格:

主教练	788	LOOR, A.	B_2		
第一助理教练	555	MONTA, B.	D	F	F

如果主教练和第一助理教练都被取消比赛资格:

主教练	788	LOOR, A.	D_2	F	F
第一助理教练	555	MONTA, B.	D	F	F

判罚一名替补队员取消比赛资格的犯规,应按如下登录:

如果该替补队员少于4次犯规,则先登录"D",然后在所有剩余的犯规空格内应登录"F"。

003	SMITH, E.	9	⊗	P_2	P_2	D	F	F

和

主教练	788	LOOR, A.	B_2		
第一助理教练	555	MONTA, B.			

如果这是替补队员的第5次犯规,则先登录"D",然后在最后的犯规空格后登录"F"。

002	JONES, M.	8	⊗	T_1	P_3	P_1	P_2	D	F

和

主教练	788	LOOR, A.	B_2		
第一助理教练	555	MONTA, B.			

A disqualifying foul on an **excluded player** shall be entered as follows:
As an excluded player has no more foul spaces, then a 'D' shall be entered, followed by an 'F', both in the column behind the last foul:

| 015 | RUSH, | S. | 25 | × | T_1 | P_3 | P_2 | P_1 | P_2 | DF |

and

| Head coach | 788 | LOOR, | A. | B_2 | | | |
| First assistant coach | 555 | MONTA, | B. | | | | |

A disqualifying foul on an **accompanying delegation member** shall be charged on the head coach and entered as follows:

| Head coach | 788 | LOOR, | A. | B_2 | (B) | | |
| First assistant coach | 555 | MONTA, | B. | | | | |

Each disqualification of an accompanying delegation member shall be charged on the head coach, entered as Ⓑ, but shall not count to the three technical fouls for his game disqualification.

B.8.3.14 Examples of disqualifying fouls for his active involvement in the fight on a head coach, first assistant coach, substitute, excluded player or accompanying delegation member:

Irrespective of the number of persons disqualified for leaving the team bench area, a single technical foul 'B_2' or 'D_2' shall be charged on the head coach. If the head coach is actively involved in the fight, he shall be charged with one 'D_2' foul only. A disqualifying foul on a head coach and a first assistant coach shall be entered as follows:

If only the head coach is disqualified:

| Head coach | 788 | LOOR, | A. | D_2 | F | F |
| First assistant coach | 555 | MONTA, | B. | | | |

If only the first assistant coach is disqualified:

| Head coach | 788 | LOOR, | A. | B_2 | | |
| First assistant coach | 555 | MONTA, | B. | D_2 | F | F |

If both the head coach and the first assistant coach are disqualified:

判罚一名**出局的队员**取消比赛资格的犯规，应按如下登录：
因为该出局的队员没有多余的犯规空格，则先登录"D"，再登录"F"，都应在最后的犯规栏后：

| 015 | RUSH, | S. | 25 | × | T₁ | P₃ | P₂ | P₁ | P₂ | DF |

和

| 主教练 | 788 | LOOR, A. | B₂ | | |
| 第一助理教练 | 555 | MONTA, B. | | | |

判罚**随队人员**取消比赛资格的犯规，应按如下登录在主教练上：

| 主教练 | 788 | LOOR, A. | B₂ | Ⓑ |
| 第一助理教练 | 555 | MONTA, B. | | |

每个随队人员取消比赛资格都应登记在主教练上，记录为Ⓑ，但不累计为主教练被取消比赛资格的3次技术犯规。

B.8.3.14 主教练、第一助理教练、替补队员、出局的队员和随队人员在一起打架中积极参与打架被判取消比赛资格犯规的举例：

无论离开球队席区域被取消比赛资格的人的数量，应登记主教练一个单一的技术犯规（"B₂"或"D₂"）。如果主教练积极参与了打架，他只应被登记一个"D₂"。判罚主教练和第一助理教练取消比赛资格的犯规，应按如下记录：

如果只有主教练被取消比赛资格：

| 主教练 | 788 | LOOR, A. | D₂ | F | F |
| 第一助理教练 | 555 | MONTA, B. | | | |

如果只有第一助理教练被取消比赛资格：

| 主教练 | 788 | LOOR, A. | B₂ | | |
| 第一助理教练 | 555 | MONTA, B. | D₂ | F | F |

如果主教练和第一助理教练都被取消比赛资格：

OFFICIAL BASKETBALL RULES 2020

Head coach	788	LOOR,	A.	D₂	F	F
First assistant coach	555	MONTA,	B.	D₂	F	F

A disqualifying foul on a substitute shall be entered as follows:

If the substitute has fewer than 4 fouls, then a 'D₂' shall be entered, followed by an 'F' in all remaining foul spaces:

| 001 | MAYER, | F. | | 5 | ⊗ | P₂ | P₂ | D₂ | F | F |

and

Head coach	788	LOOR,	A.	B₂		
First assistant coach	555	MONTA,	B.			

If it is the substitute's fifth foul, then a 'D₂' shall be entered, followed by an 'F' in the column behind the last foul space:

| 002 | JONES, | M. | | 8 | ⊗ | T₁ | P₃ | P₁ | P₂ | D₂ | F |

and

Head coach	788	LOOR,	A.	B₂		
First assistant coach	555	MONTA,	B.			

A disqualifying foul on an **excluded player** be entered as follows:

As an excluded player has no more foul spaces, then a 'D₂' shall be entered, followed by an 'F', both in the column behind the last foul:

| 015 | RUSH, | S. | | 25 | × | T₁ | P₃ | P₂ | P₁ | P₂ | D₂F |

and

Head coach	788	LOOR,	A.	B₂		
First assistant coach	555	MONTA,	B.			

A disqualifying foul on an **accompanying delegation members** shall be charged on the head coach and entered as follows:

Head coach	788	LOOR,	A.	B₂	Ⓑ₂	
First assistant coach	555	MONTA,	B.			

A disqualifying foul on two **accompanying delegation members** shall be charged on the head coach and entered as follows:

Head coach	788	LOOR,	A.	B₂	Ⓑ₂	Ⓑ₂
First assistant coach	555	MONTA,	B.			

| 主教练 | 788 | LOOR, A. | D₂ | F | F |
| 第一助理教练 | 555 | MONTA, B. | D₂ | F | F |

判罚一名替补队员取消比赛资格犯规，应按如下登录：

如果该替补队员少于4次犯规，则先登录"D₂"，然后在随后的犯规空格内登录"F"。

| 001 | MAYER, F. | 5 | ⊗ | P₂ | P₂ | D₂ | F | F |

和

| 主教练 | 788 | LOOR, A. | B₂ | | |
| 第一助理教练 | 555 | MONTA, B. | | | |

如果这是替补队员的第5次犯规，则先登录"D₂"，然后在最后的犯规空格后登录"F"。

| 002 | JONES, M. | 8 | ⊗ | T₁ | P₃ | P₁ | P₂ | D₂ | F |

和

| 主教练 | 788 | LOOR, A. | B₂ | | |
| 第一助理教练 | 555 | MONTA, B. | | | |

判罚一名**出局的队员**取消比赛资格的犯规，应按如下登录：

因为该出局的队员没有多余的犯规空格，则先登录"D₂"，再登录"F"，都在最后的犯规栏后。

| 015 | RUSH, S. | 25 | × | T₁ | P₃ | P₂ | P₁ | P₂ | D₂F |

和

| 主教练 | 788 | LOOR, A. | B₂ | | |
| 第一助理教练 | 555 | MONTA, B. | | | |

判罚一名**随队人员**取消比赛资格的犯规，应按如下登录在主教练上：

| 主教练 | 788 | LOOR, A. | B₂ | Ⓑ₂ | |
| 第一助理教练 | 555 | MONTA, B. | | | |

判罚两名**随队人员**取消比赛资格的犯规，应按如下登录在主教练上：

| 主教练 | 788 | LOOR, A. | B₂ | Ⓑ₂ | B₂ |
| 第一助理教练 | 555 | MONTA, B. | | | |

Each disqualification of an accompanying delegation member shall be charged on the head coach, entered as Ⓑ, but shall not count to the three technical fouls for his game disqualification.

Note: Technical or disqualifying fouls according to Art. 39 shall not count as team fouls.

B.8.4 At the end of the second quarter and at the end of the game, the scorer shall draw a thick line between the spaces that have been used and those that have not been used.

At the end of the game, the scorer shall obliterate the remaining spaces with a thick horizontal line.

B.9 Team fouls

B.9.1 For each quarter, 4 spaces are provided on the scoresheet (immediately below the team's name and above the players' names) to enter the team fouls.

B.9.2 Whenever a player commits a personal, technical, unsportsmanlike or disqualify –ing foul, the scorer shall enter the foul on the team of that player by marking a large 'X' in the designated spaces in turn.

B.9.3 At the end of each quarter, the scorer shall obliterate the remaining spaces with 2 horizontal parallel lines.

B.10 The running score

B.10.1 The scorer shall keep a chronological running summary of the points scored by each team.

B.10.2 There are 4 main columns on the scoresheet for running score.

B.10.3 Each main column is divided into 4 columns. The 2 on the left are for team 'A' and the 2 on the right for team 'B'. The centre columns are for the running score (160 points) for each team.

The scorer shall:
- **First,** draw a diagonal line (/ for right-handed or \ for left-handed) for any valid field goal scored and a filled circle (●) for any valid free throw scored, over the **new total** number of points as accumulated by the team that has just scored.
- **Then,** in the blank space on the same side of the new total number of points (beside the new / or \ or ●), enter the number of the player who scored the field goal or the free throw.

每个随队人员取消比赛资格都应登记在主教练上，记录为Ⓑ，但不累计为主教练被取消比赛资格的3次技术犯规。

注：按照第39条的规定，技术犯规或取消比赛资格的犯规不应记入全队犯规之中。

B.8.4 在第2节结束和全场比赛结束时，记录员应在已经被用过的和那些还未被用过的方格之间画一粗线。

在比赛时间结束时，记录员应用一粗横线将剩余的空格划掉。

B.9 全队犯规

B.9.1 在记录表中，每一节有4个空格（紧靠球队的名称下面，队员的姓名上面）供登录全队犯规用。

B.9.2 每当一名队员发生了一起侵人的、技术的、违反体育运动精神的或取消比赛资格的犯规，记录员应使用一个大"X"依次在指定的空格内标示，对那名队员的球队记录犯规。

B.9.3 在每一节结束时，记录员应用两条平行线划掉剩余的空格。

B.10 累积分

B.10.1 记录员应记录两队按时间顺序得分的累积分表。

B.10.2 记录表上有4个累积分主栏。

B.10.3 每一主栏再被分成4列。左边的两列给"A"队，右边的两列给"B"队。中间列是给每个球队的累积分（160分）。

记录员应：

- **首先**，在刚得分队所累积的**新的得分总数**上对任一有效的投篮得分画一斜线（右手画"/"，左手画"\"），以及对任一有效的罚球得分涂一实圆（●）。

- 然后，在新的得分总数同一侧的空格内（在新的"/"或"\"或"●"旁）登录投篮或罚球得分的队员号码。

OFFICIAL BASKETBALL RULES 2020

B.11 The running score: Additional instructions

B.11.1 A 3-point field goal scored by a player shall be entered by drawing a circle around the player's number.

B.11.2 A field goal accidentally scored by a player in his own basket shall be entered as having been scored by the captain of the oppo-nents' team on the playing court.

B.11.3 Points scored when the ball does not enter the basket (Art. 31) shall be entered as having been scored by the player who attemp-ted the shot.

B.11.4 At the end of each quarter or overtimes, the scorer shall draw a thick circle (**O**) around the latest number of points scored by each team, followed by a thick horizontal line under those points and under the number of each player who scored those last points.

B.11.5 At the beginning of each quarter or overtimes the scorer shall continue to keep a chronological running summary of the points scored from the point of interruption.

B.11.6 Whenever possible, the scorer should check his running score with the visual scoreboard. If there is a discrepancy, and his score is correct, he shall immediately take steps to have the scoreboard corrected. If in doubt or if one of the teams raises an objection to the correction, he shall inform the crew chief as soon as the ball becomes dead and the game clock is stopped.

B.11.7 The referees may correct any error in scorekeeping involving the score, number of fouls or number of time-outs under the provisions of the rules. The crew chief shall sign the corrections. Extensive corrections shall be documented on the reverse side of the scoresheet.

B.12 The running score: Summing up

B.12.1 At the end of each quarter and last overtime, the scorer shallenter the score of that quarter and of all overtimes in the proper section in the lower part of the scoresheet.

B.12.2 Immediately at the end of the game, the scorer shall enter the time in the 'Game ended at (hh:mm)' column.

B.12.3 At the end of the game, the scorer shall draw 2 thick horizontal lines under the final number of points scored

Diagram 12
Running score

B.11 累积分：附加说明

B.11.1 队员的3分投篮得分应通过画一圆圈套住该队员的号码来记录。

B.11.2 队员无意地投入本方球篮的得分应作为对方队的场上队长得分来记录。

B.11.3 当球没有进入球篮的得分（第31条：干涉得分和干扰得分）应作为试投队员的得分来记录。

B.11.4 每节或每个决胜期比赛结束时，应分别画一粗体圆圈"○"套在每一队的最后得分数上，随后在这些分数下面，以及得这些最后分数的每一队号码下面画一粗横线。

B.11.5 在每节或每个决胜期开始时，记录员应从得分中断处继续按时间顺序记录累积分。

B.11.6 每当可能，记录员应与公开的记录屏核对他的累积分。如果有不一致，并且他的记录是正确的，他应立即采取措施去改正记录屏。如果有疑问或其中一队对改正有异议，当球成死球且比赛计时钟停止时立即通知主裁判员。

B.11.7 裁判员可以按规则的规定纠正记录表上涉及得分、犯规次数和暂停次数中出现的任何错误。主裁判员须签字确认这些修改。如果出现大量的修改，应在记录表的背面做出说明。

B.12 累积分：总结

B.12.1 在每节和最后一个决胜期结束时，记录员应在记录表下端的适当空格内登录该节和所有决胜期的比分。

B.12.2 在比赛结束后，记录员应在"比赛结束时间"栏内填入比赛结束时间，格式为：时:分。

B.12.3 在比赛结束时，记录员应在每一球队的最终得

图12 累积分

by each team and the numbers of the players who scored those last points. He shall also draw a diagonal line to the bottom of the column in order to obliterate the remaining numbers (running score) for each team.

B.12.4 At the end of the game, the scorer shall enter the final score and the name of the winning team.

B.12.5 All table officials shall then sign the scoresheet next to their names.

B.12.6 The crew chief, after signed by the umpire(s), shall be the last to approve and sign the scoresheet. This act terminates the referees' administration and connection with the game.

> **Note:** Should the captain (CAP) sign the scoresheet under protest (using the 'Captain's signature in case of protest' column), the table officials and the umpire(s) shall remain at the disposal of the crew chief until he gives them the permission to leave.

Diagram 13 Summing up

Scorer	MAIER, N.	Scores	Quarter ①	A 15	B 18
Assistant scorer	SABAY, O.		Quarter ②	A 19	B 10
Timer	LEBLANC, R.		Quarter ③	A 26	B 19
Shot clock operator	AUSTIN, K.		Quarter ④	A 26	B 25
			Overtimes	A /	B /
Crew chief M. Walton		Final Score	Team A 76	Team B 72
Umpire 1 Y. Chang Umpire 2 K. Bartok		Name of winning team	HOOPERS	
Captain's signature in case of protest		Game ended at (hh:mm)	21:50	

Diagram 14 Bottom of the scoresheet

分数下面，以及得这些最后分数的每一队员号码下面画两条粗横线。而且，为了划掉每一队的剩余数字（累积得分），他应画一斜线到该栏的底部。（图13）

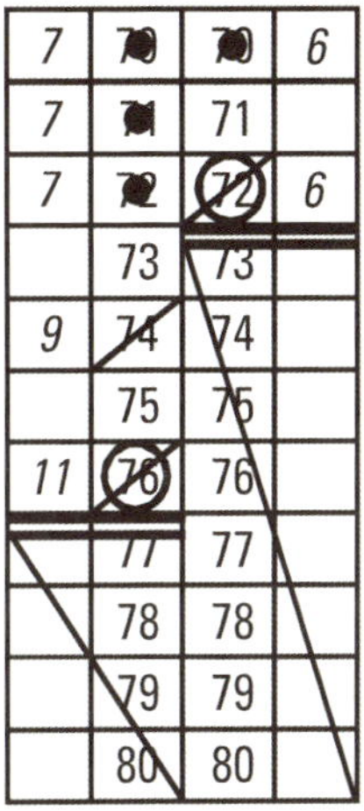

B.12.4　比赛结束时，记录员应登录最后比分和胜队的名称。

B.12.5　所有记录台人员应在他们姓名旁边签字。

B.12.6　在副裁判员（们）签字后，主裁判员应最后批准并在记录表上签字。这个举动结束了裁判员对比赛的管理和联系。（图14）

注：如果某队长（CAP）在记录表申诉格内签字（标示"球队申诉队长签名"的栏内），记录台人员和副裁判员应在主裁判员的处理过程中留下，直到他允许大家离开。

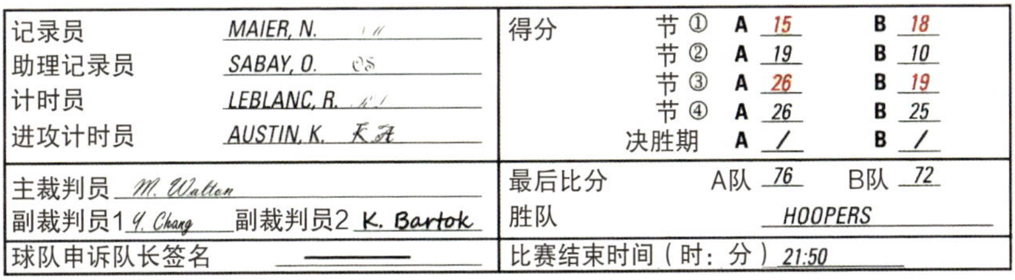

图13　总结

记录员	MAIER, N.		得分	节①	A 15	B 18
助理记录员	SABAY, O.			节②	A 19	B 10
计时员	LEBLANC, R.			节③	A 26	B 19
进攻计时员	AUSTIN, K.			节④	A 26	B 25
				决胜期	A /	B /
主裁判员	M. Walton		最后比分		A队 76	B队 72
副裁判员1 Y. Chang	副裁判员2 K. Bartok		胜队		HOOPERS	
球队申诉队长签名			比赛结束时间（时：分） 21:50			

图14　记录表的底部

C — PROTEST PROCEDURE

C.1 A team may file a protest if its interests have been adversely affected by:

    a) An error in scorekeeping, timekeeping or shot clock operations, which was not corrected by the referees.
    b) A decision to forfeit, cancel, postpone, not resume or not play the game.
    c) A violation of the applicable eligibility rules.

C.2 In order to be admissible, a protest shall comply with the following procedure:

    a) The captain (CAP) of that team shall, no later than 15 minutes following the end of the game, inform the crew chief that his team is protesting against the result of the game and sign the scoresheet in the 'Captain's signature in case of protest' column.
    b) The team shall submit the protest reasons to the crew chief in writing no later than 1 hour following the end of the game.
    c) A fee of CHF 1,500 shall be applied to each protest and shall be paid in case the protest is rejected.

C.3 The crew chief (or commissioner, if present) shall, following receipt of the protest reasons, report in writing the incident which leads to the protest, to the **FIBA** representative or to the competent body.

C.4 The competent body shall issue any procedural requests which it deems appropriate and shall decide on the protest as soon as possible, and in any event no later than 24 hours following the end of the game. The competent body shall use any reliable evidence and can take any appropriate decision, including without limitation partial or full replay of the game. The competent body may not decide to change the result of the game unless there is clear and conclusive evidence that, had it not been for the error that gave rise to the protest, the new result would have certainly materialised.

C.5 The decision of the competent body is also considered as a field of play rule decision and is not subject to further review or appeal. Exceptionally, decisions on eligibility may be appealed as provided for in the applicable regulations.

C —— 申诉程序

C.1 如果某球队认为下列情况已对该队造成不利，可以提出申诉：
 a）记录、计时或进攻计时钟出现错误，且没有被裁判员纠正。
 b）弃权、取消、延期、不恢复或不进行比赛的决定。
 c）违反所适用的球员资格规定的行为。

C.2 为了使该申诉被接受，应遵从下列程序：
 a）该队队长（CAP）应在比赛结束后15分钟内告知主裁判员：他的球队对比赛的结果提出申诉，并在记录表上标示"球队申诉队长签名"的栏内签字。
 b）该队应在比赛结束后1小时内提交申诉原因的书面文件给主裁判员。
 c）每次申诉应支付1 500瑞士法郎的费用，如申诉被拒绝，该费用将不予退回。

C.3 主裁判员（或到场的技术代表）在收到申诉原因的文件后，应用书面报告向**国际篮联**的代表或主管机构陈述导致该申诉的事件情况。

C.4 主管机构应启动那种它认为恰当的受诉程序，并且尽可能快地对该申诉做出裁决；无论如何，该裁决的做出时间不应超过该场比赛结束后的24小时。主管机构应使用一切可靠的证据，包括并不限于使用部分或全部的比赛重放，来做出恰当的裁决。除非有清晰确凿的证据证明申诉文件所述的原因定会导致比赛结果的不同，主管机构不会裁决更改比赛的结果。

C.5 主管机构的裁决也被认为是该赛事仲裁的最终决定，不接受进一步的审查或上诉。例外：对有关资格问题的裁决可根据适用的条例规定提出上诉。

C.6 Special rules for **FIBA** competitions or competitions which do not provide otherwise in their regulations:
   a) In case the competition is in tournament format, the competent body for all protests shall be the Technical Committee (see **FIBA** Internal Regulations, Book 2).
   b) In case of home and away games, the competent body for protests relating to eligibility issues shall be the FIBA Disciplinary Panel. For all other issues giving rise to a protest, the competent body shall be **FIBA** acting through one or more persons with expertise on the implementation and interpretation of the Official Basketball Rules (see **FIBA** Internal Regulations, Book 2).

C.6 **国际篮联**的比赛或其规程中未做其他规定的比赛的特别规则：
a）如果是锦标赛形式的比赛，则接受所有申诉的主管机构应是技术委员会（见**国际篮联**的内部章程，第2册）。
b）如果是主客场赛制的比赛，接受与资格问题有关的申诉的主管机构应是国际篮联纪律委员会。对于所有其他引起申诉的问题，主管机构应由**国际篮联**组织一名或多名对**国际篮联**篮球规则的实践和解释有专长的人士组成（见**国际篮联**的内部章程，第2册）。

D — CLASSIFICATION OF TEAMS

D.1 Procedure

D.1.1 Teams shall be classified according to their win-loss record, namely 2 classification points for each game won, 1 classification point for each game lost (including lost by default) and 0 classification point for a game lost by forfeit.

D.1.2 The procedure is to be applied for all competitions with a round-robin system.

D.1.3 If 2 or more teams have the same win-loss record of all games in the group, the game(s) between these 2 or more teams shall decide on the classification. If these 2 or more teams have the same win-loss record of the games between them, further criteria shall be applied in the following order:
- Higher game points difference of the games between them.
- Higher number of game points scored in the games between them.
- Higher game points difference of all games in the group.
- Higher number of game points scored in all games in the group.

If still tied before all games have been played in the group, tied teams shall share the same ranking. If these criteria still cannot decide at the end of the group phase, a draw shall decide on the final classification.

D.1.4 If at any level of these criteria one or more team(s) are already classified, the procedure of D.1.3 shall be repeated from the beginning for all the remaining teams not classified yet.

D.2 Examples

D.2.1 Example 1

A vs. B	100 – 55	B vs. C	100 – 95
A vs. C	90 – 85	B vs. D	80 – 75
A vs. D	75 – 80	C vs. D	60 – 55

D —— 球队的名次排列

D.1 程 序

D.1.1 球队应按他们的胜负记录来排列名次，胜1场得2分，负1场（包括比赛因缺少队员告负）得1分，比赛因弃权告负得0分。

D.1.2 此程序适用于所有采用循环赛制的比赛。

D.1.3 如果组内2支或多于2支球队在所有比赛后有相同的胜负记录，这2支或这些球队之间的比赛将决定他们的名次排列。如果这2支或多于2支球队之间的比赛有相同的胜负记录，将按照下列原则依顺序进行排列：

- 他们之间比赛净胜分的多少。
- 他们之间比赛得分的多少。
- 组内所有比赛净胜分的多少。
- 组内所有比赛得分的多少。

如果在该组所有比赛打完之前仍然是相同的，则相同的队并列名次。如果在小组赛结束后采用这些原则仍无法决定，将用抽签进行最终名次排列。

D.1.4 如果在这些原则的任何阶段，1支或多于1支球队已经能被排列出来，则将从开始重复D.1.3的程序以排列出剩余的球队。

D.2 示 例

D.2.1 示例1

A vs. B	100 – 55	B vs. C	100 – 95
A vs. C	90 – 85	B vs. D	80 – 75
A vs. D	75 – 80	C vs. D	60 – 55

OFFICIAL BASKETBALL RULES *2020*

Team	Games played	Wins	Losses	Classification points	Game points	Game points difference
A	3	2	1	5	265 : 220	+45
B	3	2	1	5	235 : 270	−35
C	3	1	2	4	240 : 245	−5
D	3	1	2	4	210 : 215	−5

Therefore: 1st A — winner against B
 2nd B
 3rd C — winner against D
 4th D

D.2.2 Example 2

A vs. B 100 − 55 B vs. C 100 − 85
A vs. C 90 − 85 B vs. D 75 − 80
A vs. D 120 − 75 C vs. D 65 − 55

Team	Games played	Wins	Losses	Classification points	Game points	Game points difference
A	3	3	0	6	310 : 215	+95
B	3	1	2	4	230 : 265	−35
C	3	1	2	4	235 : 245	−10
D	3	1	2	4	210 : 260	−50

Therefore: 1st A

Classification of the games between B, C, D:

Team	Games played	Wins	Losses	Classification points	Game points	Game points difference
B	2	1	1	3	175 : 165	+10
C	2	1	1	3	150 : 155	−5
D	2	1	1	3	135 : 140	−5

Therefore: 2nd B
 3rd C — winner against D
 4th D

球队	场数	胜	负	积分	得失分	净胜分
A	3	2	1	5	265∶220	+45
B	3	2	1	5	235∶270	−35
C	3	1	2	4	240∶245	−5
D	3	1	2	4	210∶215	−5

因此：第一名 A （胜B）

第二名 B

第三名 C （胜D）

第四名 D

D.2.2 示例2

A vs. B　100 − 55　　B vs. C　100 − 85

A vs. C　 90 − 85　　B vs. D　 75 − 80

A vs. D　120 − 75　　C vs. D　 65 − 55

球队	场数	胜	负	积分	得失分	净胜分
A	3	3	0	6	310∶215	+95
B	3	1	2	4	230∶265	−35
C	3	1	2	4	235∶245	−10
D	3	1	2	4	210∶260	−50

因此：第一名 A

B、C、D之间比赛的排序：

球队	场数	胜	负	积分	得失分	净胜分
B	2	1	1	3	175∶165	+10
C	2	1	1	3	150∶155	−5
D	2	1	1	3	135∶140	−5

所以：第二名 B

第三名 C（胜D）

第四名 D

OFFICIAL BASKETBALL RULES 2020

D.2.3 Example 3

A vs. B	85 – 90	B vs. C	100 – 95
A vs. C	55 – 100	B vs. D	75 – 85
A vs. D	75 – 120	C vs. D	65 – 55

Team	Games played	Wins	Losses	Classification points	Game points	Game points difference
A	3	0	3	3	215 : 310	−95
B	3	2	1	5	265 : 265	0
C	3	2	1	5	260 : 210	+50
D	3	2	1	5	260 : 215	+45

Therefore: 4th   A

Classification of the games between B, C, D:

Team	Games played	Wins	Losses	Classification points	Game points	Game points difference
B	2	1	1	3	175 : 180	−5
C	2	1	1	3	160 : 155	+5
D	2	1	1	3	140 : 140	0

Therefore: 1st   C
              2nd   D
              3rd   B

D.2.4 Example 4

A vs. B	85 – 90	B vs. C	100 – 90
A vs. C	55 – 100	B vs. D	75 – 85
A vs. D	75 – 120	C vs. D	65 – 55

D.2.3 示例3

A vs. B	85 – 90	B vs. C	100 – 95
A vs. C	55 – 100	B vs. D	75 – 85
A vs. D	75 – 120	C vs. D	65 – 55

球队	场数	胜	负	积分	得失分	净胜分
A	3	0	3	3	215 : 310	-95
B	3	2	1	5	265 : 265	0
C	3	2	1	5	260 : 210	+50
D	3	2	1	5	260 : 215	+45

因此：第四名 A

B、C、D之间比赛的排序：

球队	场数	胜	负	积分	得失分	净胜分
B	2	1	1	3	175 : 180	-5
C	2	1	1	3	160 : 155	+5
D	2	1	1	3	140 : 140	0

所以：第一名 C

第二名 D

第三名 B

D.2.4 示例4

A vs. B	85 – 90	B vs. C	100 – 90
A vs. C	55 – 100	B vs. D	75 – 85
A vs. D	75 – 120	C vs. D	65 – 55

OFFICIAL BASKETBALL RULES *2020*

Team	Games played	Wins	Losses	Classification points	Game points	Game points difference
A	3	0	3	3	215 : 310	−95
B	3	2	1	5	265 : 260	+5
C	3	2	1	5	255 : 210	+45
D	3	2	1	5	260 : 215	+45

Therefore: 4th A

Classification of the games between B, C, D:

Team	Games played	Wins	Losses	Classification points	Game points	Game points difference
B	2	1	1	3	175 : 175	0
C	2	1	1	3	155 : 155	0
D	2	1	1	3	140 : 140	0

Therefore: 1st B
2nd C
3rd D

D.2.5 Example 5

A vs. B	100 – 55		B vs. F	110 – 90
A vs. C	85 – 90		C vs. D	55 – 60
A vs. D	120 – 75		C vs. E	90 – 75
A vs. E	80 – 100		C vs. F	105 – 75
A vs. F	85 – 80		D vs. E	70 – 45
B vs. C	100 – 95		D vs. F	65 – 60
B vs. D	80 – 75		E vs. F	75 – 80
B vs. E	75 – 80			

球队	场数	胜	负	积分	得失分	净胜分
A	3	0	3	3	215：310	-95
B	3	2	1	5	265：260	+5
C	3	2	1	5	255：210	+45
D	3	2	1	5	260：215	+45

因此：第四名 A

B、C、D之间比赛的排序：

球队	场数	胜	负	积分	得失分	净胜分
B	2	1	1	3	175：175	0
C	2	1	1	3	155：155	0
D	2	1	1	3	140：140	0

所以：第一名 B

第二名 C

第三名 D

D.2.5 示例 5

A vs. B　100 – 55　　B vs. F　110 – 90

A vs. C　85 – 90　　C vs. D　55 – 60

A vs. D　120 – 75　　C vs. E　90 – 75

A vs. E　80 – 100　　C vs. F　105 – 75

A vs. F　85 – 80　　D vs. E　70 – 45

B vs. C　100 – 95　　D vs. F　65 – 60

B vs. D　80 – 75　　E vs. F　75 – 80

B vs. E　75 – 80

OFFICIAL BASKETBALL RULES 2020

Team	Games played	Wins	Losses	Classification points	Game points	Game points difference
A	5	3	2	8	470 : 400	+70
B	5	3	2	8	420 : 440	−20
C	5	3	2	8	435 : 395	+40
D	5	3	2	8	345 : 360	−15
E	5	2	3	7	375 : 395	−20
F	5	1	4	6	385 : 440	−55

Therefore: 5th E
6th F

Classification of the games between A, B, C, D:

Team	Games played	Wins	Losses	Classification points	Game points	Game points difference
A	3	2	1	5	305 : 220	+85
B	3	2	1	5	235 : 270	−35
C	3	1	2	4	240 : 245	−5
D	3	1	2	4	210 : 255	−45

Therefore: 1st A — winner against B
2nd B
3rd D — winner against C
4th C

D.2.6 Example 6

A vs. B	71 – 65	B vs. F	95 – 90
A vs. C	85 – 86	C vs. D	95 – 100
A vs. D	77 – 75	C vs. E	82 – 75
A vs. E	80 – 86	C vs. F	105 – 75
A vs. F	85 – 80	D vs. E	68 – 67
B vs. C	88 – 87	D vs. F	65 – 60
B vs. D	80 – 75	E vs. F	80 – 75
B vs. E	75 – 76		

球队	场数	胜	负	积分	得失分	净胜分
A	5	3	2	8	470∶400	+70
B	5	3	2	8	420∶440	−20
C	5	3	2	8	435∶395	+40
D	5	3	2	8	345∶360	−15
E	5	2	3	7	375∶395	−20
F	5	1	4	6	385∶440	−55

因此：第五名 E
第六名 F

A、B、C、D之间比赛的排序：

球队	场数	胜	负	积分	得失分	净胜分
A	3	2	1	5	305∶220	+85
B	3	2	1	5	235∶270	−35
C	3	1	2	4	240∶245	−5
D	3	1	2	4	210∶255	−45

所以：第一名 A（胜B）
第二名 B
第三名 D（胜C）
第四名 C

D.2.6 示例 6

A vs. B	71 − 65	B vs. F	95 − 90
A vs. C	85 − 86	C vs. D	95 − 100
A vs. D	77 − 75	C vs. E	82 − 75
A vs. E	80 − 86	C vs. F	105 − 75
A vs. F	85 − 80	D vs. E	68 − 67
B vs. C	88 − 87	D vs. F	65 − 60
B vs. D	80 − 75	E vs. F	80 − 75
B vs. E	75 − 76		

OFFICIAL BASKETBALL RULES 2020

Team	Games played	Wins	Losses	Classification points	Game points	Game points difference
A	5	3	2	8	398 : 392	+6
B	5	3	2	8	403 : 399	+4
C	5	3	2	8	455 : 423	+32
D	5	3	2	8	383 : 379	+4
E	5	3	2	8	384 : 380	+4
F	5	0	5	5	380 : 430	−50

Therefore: 6th   F

Classification of the games between A, B, C, D, E:

Team	Games played	Wins	Losses	Classification points	Game points	Game points difference
A	4	2	2	6	313 : 312	+1
B	4	2	2	6	308 : 309	−1
C	4	2	2	6	350 : 348	+2
D	4	2	2	6	318 : 319	−1
E	4	2	2	6	304 : 305	−1

Therefore: 1st   C
             2nd   A

Classification of the games between B, D, E:

Team	Games played	Wins	Losses	Classification points	Game points	Game points difference
B	2	1	1	3	155 : 151	+4
D	2	1	1	3	143 : 147	−4
E	2	1	1	3	143 : 143	0

Therefore: 3rd   B
             4th   E
             5th   D

球队	场数	胜	负	积分	得失分	净胜分
A	5	3	2	8	398∶392	+6
B	5	3	2	8	403∶399	+4
C	5	3	2	8	455∶423	+32
D	5	3	2	8	383∶379	+4
E	5	3	2	8	384∶380	+4
F	5	0	5	5	380∶430	−50

因此：第六名 F

A、B、C、D、E之间比赛的排序：

球队	场数	胜	负	积分	得失分	净胜分
A	4	2	2	6	313∶312	+1
B	4	2	2	6	308∶309	−1
C	4	2	2	6	350∶348	+2
D	4	2	2	6	318∶319	−1
E	4	2	2	6	304∶305	−1

所以：第一名 C
　　　第二名 A

B、D、E 之间比赛的排序：

球队	场数	胜	负	积分	得失分	净胜分
B	2	1	1	3	155∶151	+4
D	2	1	1	3	143∶147	−4
E	2	1	1	3	143∶143	0

所以：第三名 B
　　　第四名 E
　　　第五名 D

D.2.7 Example 7

A vs. B	73 – 71	B vs. F	95 – 90
A vs. C	85 – 86	C vs. D	95 – 96
A vs. D	77 – 75	C vs. E	82 – 75
A vs. E	90 – 96	C vs. F	105 – 75
A vs. F	85 – 80	D vs. E	68 – 67
B vs. C	88 – 87	D vs. F	80 – 75
B vs. D	80 – 79	E vs. F	80 – 75
B vs. E	79 – 80		

Team	Games played	Wins	Losses	Classification points	Game points	Game points difference
A	5	3	2	8	410 : 408	+2
B	5	3	2	8	413 : 409	+4
C	5	3	2	8	455 : 419	+36
D	5	3	2	8	398 : 394	+4
E	5	3	2	8	398 : 394	+4
F	5	0	5	5	395 : 445	−50

Therefore: 6th F

Classification of the games between A, B, C, D, E:

Team	Games played	Wins	Losses	Classification points	Game points	Game points difference
A	4	2	2	6	325 : 328	−3
B	4	2	2	6	318 : 319	−1
C	4	2	2	6	350 : 344	+6
D	4	2	2	6	318 : 319	−1
E	4	2	2	6	318 : 319	−1

Therefore: 1st C
5th A

D.2.7 示例 7

A vs. B	73 – 71	B vs. F	95 – 90
A vs. C	85 – 86	C vs. D	95 – 96
A vs. D	77 – 75	C vs. E	82 – 75
A vs. E	90 – 96	C vs. F	105 – 75
A vs. F	85 – 80	D vs. E	68 – 67
B vs. C	88 – 87	D vs. F	80 – 75
B vs. D	80 – 79	E vs. F	80 – 75
B vs. E	79 – 80		

球队	场数	胜	负	积分	得失分	净胜分
A	5	3	2	8	410 : 408	+2
B	5	3	2	8	413 : 409	+4
C	5	3	2	8	455 : 419	+36
D	5	3	2	8	398 : 394	+4
E	5	3	2	8	398 : 394	+4
F	5	0	5	5	395 : 445	-50

因此：第六名 F

A、B、C、D、E之间比赛的排序：

球队	场数	胜	负	积分	得失分	净胜分
A	4	2	2	6	325 : 328	-3
B	4	2	2	6	318 : 319	-1
C	4	2	2	6	350 : 344	+6
D	4	2	2	6	318 : 319	-1
E	4	2	2	6	318 : 319	-1

所以：第一名 C
第五名 A

Classification of the games between B, D, E:

Team	Games played	Wins	Losses	Classification points	Game points	Game points difference
B	2	1	1	3	159 : 159	0
D	2	1	1	3	147 : 147	0
E	2	1	1	3	147 : 147	0

Therefore: 2nd B
3rd D — winner against E,
4th E

D.3 Forfeit

D.3.1 A team which without valid reason, fails to show up for a scheduled game or withdraws from the playing court before the end of the game, shall lose the game by forfeit and receive 0 classification point.

D.3.2 If the team forfeits for a second time, the results of all games played by this team shall be nullified.

D.3.3 If the team forfeits for a second time in a competition played in groups, and the best placed team(s) from each group shall qualify for the next round of the competition, the results of all games played by the last placed team in the cross-over group shall also be nullified.

Example
Team 4A in group A forfeits twice, therefore all its games shall be nullified.
Final standings:

Group A	Wins	Losses	Classification points
Team 1A	4	0	8
Team 2A	2	2	6
Team 3A	0	4	4
Team 4A			

Group B	Wins	Losses	Classification points
Team 1B	6	0	12
Team 2B	4	2	10
Team 3B	1	5	7
Team 4B	0	5	7

Results of the games played between teams 3B and 4B:
3B vs 4B   88 – 71
4B vs 3B   76 – 75
Therefore: 3rd 3B
4th 4B

B、D、E 之间比赛的排序：

球队	场数	胜	负	积分	得失分	净胜分
B	2	1	1	3	159：159	0
D	2	1	1	3	147：147	0
E	2	1	1	3	147：147	0

所以：第二名 B

第三名 D（胜 E）

第四名 E

D.3 弃 权

D.3.1 某队无正当理由不出席预定的比赛或在比赛结束前从球场上撤离，应由于弃权使比赛告负并在名次排列中计0分。

D.3.2 如果某队第2次弃权，该队所有比赛结果应无效。

D.3.3 如果一支队伍在小组赛中第2次因弃权使比赛告负，且各组中排名靠前的一支或几支球队有资格参加下一轮比赛，则交叉组中排名最后的球队所进行的所有比赛的结果也将视为无效。

举 例

A 组中的4A 两次因弃权使比赛告负，因此他所有的比赛无效。

A 队	胜	负	积分
1A 队	4	0	8
2A 队	2	2	6
3A 队	0	4	4
4A 队			

B 队	胜	负	积分
1B 队	6	0	12
2B 队	4	2	10
3B 队	1	5	7
4B 队	0	5	7

最终排名：

3B 与 4B 的比赛结果：

3B vs. 4B   88 - 71

4B vs. 3B   76 - 75

所以：第三名 3B

第四名 4B

Revised final standings in Group B:

Group B	Wins	Losses	Classification points
Team 1B	4	0	8
Team 2B	2	2	6
Team 3B	0	4	4

D.3.4 If the team forfeits for a second time in a competition played in groups, and for the final group classification all the teams in all groups must have the same number of games played, the results of all games played by the last placed teams in all groups shall also be nullified.

Example

Team 6B in group B forfeits twice, therefore all its games shall be nullified. Final standings:

Group A	Wins	Losses	Classification points
Team 1A	10	0	20
Team 2A	8	2	18
Team 3A	6	4	16
Team 4A	4	6	14
Team 5A	2	8	12
Team 6A	0	10	10

Group B	Wins	Losses	Classification points
Team 1B	8	0	16
Team 2B	6	2	14
Team 3B	4	4	12
Team 4B	2	6	10
Team 5B	0	8	8
Team 6B			

Group C	Wins	Losses	Classification points
Team 1C	10	0	20
Team 2C	8	2	18
Team 3C	5	5	15
Team 4C	5	5	15
Team 5C	2	8	12
Team 6C	0	10	10

Group D	Wins	Losses	Classification points
Team 1D	9	1	19
Team 2D	9	1	19
Team 3D	6	4	16
Team 4D	4	6	14
Team 5D	1	9	11
Team 6D	1	9	11

篮球规则 2020

修订后B组的最终排名：

B队	胜	负	积分
1B队	4	0	8
2B队	2	2	6
3B队	0	4	4

D.3.4 如果一支队伍在小组赛中第2次因弃权使比赛告负，且所有组的所有队伍打了相同的比赛场次，所有小组排名最后球队的所有比赛结果也将被视为无效。

举 例

B组中的6B 两次因弃权使比赛告负，因此他所有的比赛无效。最终排名：

A队	胜	负	积分
1A队	10	0	20
2A队	8	2	18
3A队	6	4	16
4A队	4	6	14
5A队	2	8	12
6A队	0	10	10

B队	胜	负	积分
1B队	8	0	16
2B队	6	2	14
3B队	4	4	12
4B队	2	6	10
5B队	0	8	8
6B队			

C队	胜	负	积分
1C队	10	0	20
2C队	8	2	18
3C队	5	5	15
4C队	5	5	15
5C队	2	8	12
6C队	0	10	10

D队	胜	负	积分
1D队	9	1	19
2D队	9	1	19
3D队	6	4	16
4D队	4	6	14
5D队	1	9	11
6D队	1	9	11

Results of the games played between teams 5D and 6D:

5D vs 6D   83 – 81
6D vs 5D   92 – 91
Therefore: 5th   5D
               6th   6D

Revised final standings in Groups A, C and D:

Group A	Wins	Losses	Classification points
Team 1A	8	0	16
Team 2A	6	2	14
Team 3A	4	4	12
Team 4A	2	6	10
Team 5A	0	8	8

Group C	Wins	Losses	Classification points
Team 1C	8	0	16
Team 2C	6	2	14
Team 3C	3	5	11
Team 4C	3	5	11
Team 5C	0	8	8

Group D	Wins	Losses	Classification points
Team 1D	7	1	15
Team 2D	7	1	15
Team 3D	4	4	12
Team 4D	2	6	10
Team 5D	0	8	8

Note:

Should the comparative ranking need to be established between the teams placed on the same position in the groups, one group of all teams in questions shall be established. The criteria shall be applied in the following order:

- Better win-loss record of all games played in their revised final group standings.
- Higher game points difference of all games in their revised final group standings.
- Higher number of the game points scored in all games in their revised final group standings.
- If these criteria still cannot decide, a draw shall decide on the final classification.

5D 和 6D 之间的比赛结果：
5D vs. 6D　　83 – 81
6D vs. 5D　　92 – 91
因此：第五名 5D
　　　第六名 6D

修订后 A、C 和 D 组的最终排名：

A队	胜	负	积分
1A 队	8	0	16
2A 队	6	2	14
3A 队	4	4	12
4A 队	2	6	10
5A 队	0	8	8

C队	胜	负	积分
1C 队	8	0	16
2C 队	6	2	14
3C 队	3	5	11
4C 队	3	5	11
5C 队	0	8	8

D队	胜	负	积分
1D 队	7	1	15
2D 队	7	1	15
3D 队	4	4	12
4D 队	2	6	10
5D 队	0	8	8

注意：

如果不同小组中处于相同位置的队伍之间要建立比较排名，应对涉及的队伍建立统一的小组标准。然后根据如下顺序排定排名：

- 修订后的最终的小组排名中的更好的胜负关系。
- 修订后的最终的小组排名中的更高的净胜分。
- 修订后的最终的小组排名中的更高的所有的比赛得分。
- 如果仍无法决定，将用抽签进行最终名次排列。

Example for the teams placed second in the revised final group standings.

Group X	Wins	Losses	Game points	Classification points	Game points difference
Team 2D	7	1	628 : 521	15	
Team 2B	6	2	551 : 488	14	+63
Team 2A	6	2	531 : 506	14	+25
Team 2C	6	2	525 : 500	14	+25

Therefore
1st Team 2D   Best win-loss record
2nd Team 2B   Higher game points difference as teams 2A and 2C
3rd Team 2A   Same game points difference as team 2C but higher number of game points scored
4th Team 2C   Same game points difference as team 2A but lower number of game points scored

D.4 Home and away games (aggregate score)

D.4.1 For a 2-games home and away total points series (aggregated score) competition system, the 2 games shall be considered as 1 game of 80 minutes duration.

D.4.2 If the score is tied at the end of the first game, no overtime shall be played.

D.4.3 If the aggregated score of both games is tied, the second game shall continue with as many overtimes of 5 minutes as necessary to break the tie.

D.4.4 The winner of the series shall be the team that:
- Is the winner of both games.
- Has scored the greater number of the aggregated game points at the end of the second game, if both teams have won 1 game.

D.5 Examples

D.5.1 Example 1
A vs B   80 - 75
B vs A   72 - 73
Team A is the winner of series (winner of both games).

D.5.2 Example 2
A vs B   80 - 75
B vs A   73 - 72
Team A is the winner of series (aggregate score A 152 - B 148).

最终小组排名第2的队伍举例：

X 组	胜	负	得失分	积分	净胜分
2D 队	7	1	628：521	15	
2B 队	6	2	551：488	14	+63
2A 队	6	2	531：506	14	+25
2C 队	6	2	525：500	14	+25

因此：

第一名2D　　最好的胜负关系。

第二名2B　　比2A 和2C 更高的净胜分。

第三名2A　　与2C 净胜分相同，但比2C 的比赛得分高。

第四名2C　　与2A 净胜分相同，但比2A 的比赛得分低。

D.4 主客场比赛（总比分）

D.4.1 对于2场比赛（主和客）总分定胜负的一组比赛，可以把2场比赛视为1场持续80分钟比赛。

D.4.2 如果第一场比赛结束时比分相同，没有必要进行决胜期。

D.4.3 如果在第2场比赛结束时，两队两场比赛得分的总和相等，比赛有必要再继续一个或几个5分钟的决胜期来打破平局。

D.4.4 主客场比赛的优胜队是：

- 同时赢得两场比赛的一方。
- 在第二场比赛结束后，如果两队各胜了1场，总得分高的一方。

D.5 示　例

D.5.1 示例1

　　　　A vs. B　　80 - 75

　　　　B vs. A　　72 - 73

　　　　A队是比赛的优胜队（同时赢得两场比赛）。

D.5.2 示例2

　　　　A vs. B　　80 - 75

　　　　B vs. A　　73 - 72

　　　　A队是比赛的优胜队（总得分A队152：B队148）。

D.5.3 Example 3

A vs B   80 – 80
B vs A   92 – 85
Team B is the winner of series (aggregate score A 165 – B 172).
No overtime for the first game.

D.5.4 Example 4

A vs B   80 – 85
B vs A   75 – 75
Team B is the winner of series (aggregate score A 155 – B 160).
No overtime for the second game.

D.5.5 Example 5

A vs B   83 – 81
B vs A   79 – 77
Aggregate score A 160 – B 160.
After overtime(s) of the second game:

B vs A   95 – 88
Team B is the winner of series (aggregate score A 171 – B 176).

D.5.6 Example 6

A vs B   76 – 76
B vs A   84 – 84
Aggregate score A 160 – B 160.
After overtime(s) of the second game:

B vs A   94 – 91
Team B is the winner of series (aggregate score A 167 – B 170).

D.5.3 示例3

A vs. B　　80 – 80

B vs. A　　92 – 85

B队是比赛的优胜队（总得分A队165：B队172）。

第一场比赛没有决胜期。

D.5.4 示例4

A vs. B　　80 – 85

B vs. A　　75 – 75

B队是比赛的优胜队（总得分A队155：B队160）。

第2场比赛没有决胜期。

D.5.5 示例5

A vs. B　　83 – 81

B vs. A　　79 – 77

总得分A队160：B队160。

在第2场比赛的决胜期后：

B vs. A　　95 – 88

B队是比赛的优胜队（总得分A队171：B队176）。

D.5.6 示例6

A vs. B　　76 – 76

B vs. A　　84 – 84

总得分A队 160：B队 160。

第二场比赛决胜期后：

B vs. A　　94 – 91

B 队是系列赛的胜者（总得分A 队167：B队 170）。

E — MEDIA TIME-OUTS

E.1 Definition
The organising body of the competition may decide for itself whether Media time-outs shall be used and, if so, of what duration (60, 75, 90 or 100 seconds).

E.2 Rule

E.2.1 In each quarter 1 Media time-out is permitted, in addition to the regular team time-outs. Media time-outs in an overtime are not permitted.

E.2.2 The first time-out in each quarter (team or Media) shall be 60, 75, 90 or 100 seconds in duration.

E.2.3 The duration of all other time-outs in a quarter shall be 60 seconds.

E.2.4 Both teams shall be entitled to 2 time-outs during the first half and 3 timeouts during the second half.

These time-outs may be requested at any time during the game and their duration may be:

- If considered to be a Media time-out 60, 75, 90 or 100 seconds, i.e. the first in a quarter, or

- If not considered to be a Media time-out 60 seconds, i.e. requested by either team, after the Media time-out has been granted.

E.3 Procedure

E.3.1 Ideally, the Media time-out shall be taken before the 5:00 minutes remaining in the quarter. However, there is no guarantee that this shall be the case.

E.3.2 If neither team has requested a time-out before the 5:00 minutes remaining in the quarter then a Media time-out shall be granted at the first opportunity when the ball is dead and the game clock is stopped. This time-out shall not be charged on either team.

E.3.3 If either team is granted a time-out before the 5:00 minutes remaining in the quarter, that time-out shall be used as a Media time-out.

E —— 媒体暂停

E.1 定 义
竞赛组织部门可自行决定是否运用媒体暂停，如运用，须决定何种持续时间（60秒、75秒、90秒或100秒）。

E.2 规 定

E.2.1 在每一节中，在正规的暂停之外加一次球队暂停是可允许的；在决胜期中，媒体暂停是不可允许的。

E.2.2 每一节的第一次暂停（球队或媒体）应是60秒、75秒、90秒或100秒的持续时间。

E.2.3 在一节中，所有其他暂停的持续时间应是60秒。

E.2.4 在上半时中，双方球队各有权请求2次暂停。在下半时中，各有权请求3次暂停。

这些暂停可在比赛中的任何时间请求，并且他们的持续时间可能是：
- 60秒、75秒、90秒或者100秒，如果被认为是一次媒体暂停，也就是一节中的第一次暂停；或
- 60秒，如果不被认为是一次媒体暂停，也就是在准予了媒体暂停之后由任一队请求的暂停。

E.3 程 序

E.3.1 理想的媒体暂停应发生在该节中剩余时间为5分钟之前。然而，这种情况没有保证。

E.3.2 如果在该节剩余的5分钟之前，任一球队都未请求一次暂停，当球成死球且比赛计时钟停止的第一次机会中，应准予一次媒体暂停。这次暂停将不对任一球队进行登记。

E.3.3 如果在该节剩余的5分钟之前任一球队被准予一次暂停，此暂停应作为媒体暂停来使用。

This time-out shall count as both a Media time-out and a team time-out for the team requesting it.

E.3.4 According to this procedure, there would be a minimum of 1 time-out in each quarter and a maximum of 6 time-outs in the first half and a maximum of 8 time-outs in the second half.

F — INSTANT REPLAY SYSTEM

F.1 Definition

The Instant Replay System (IRS) review is the working method used by the referees to verify their decisions by watching the game situations on the screen of the approved video technology.

F.2 Procedure

F.2.1 The referees are authorised to use the IRS until they sign the scoresheet after the game, within the limits provided in this Appendix.

F.2.2 For the use of the IRS the following procedure shall apply:

- The crew chief shall approve the IRS equipment before the game, if available.
- The crew chief makes the decision whether the IRS review shall be used or not.
- If a decision of the referees is subject to the IRS review, the initial decision must be shown by the referees on the playing court.
- After gathering all information from other referees, table officials, commissioner, the review shall start as fast as possible.
- The crew chief and minimum 1 umpire (who made the call) shall take part at the review. If the crew chief made the call, he shall choose one of the umpire to accompany him for the review.
- During the IRS review the crew chief shall ensure that no unauthorised persons have access to the IRS monitor.

这次暂停应同时记作一次媒体暂停和一次由该队请求的球队暂停。

E.3.4 依照这个程序，在每一节中最少将有一次暂停，在上半时中最多将有6次暂停，在下半时中最多将有8次暂停。

F —— 即时回放系统

F.1 定 义
即时回放系统（The Instant Replay System，IRS）复审是一种通过在批准的视频技术设备上观看比赛的情况验证判罚的裁判工作方法。

F.2 程 序

F.2.1 在比赛结束后他们在记录表上签字之前，裁判员有权在附录的规定的限定范围内使用即时回放系统。

F.2.2 在使用即时回放系统时，应该遵守以下程序：
- 如果提供即时回放系统，主裁判应该在比赛之前批准即时回放系统设备。
- 是否使用即时回放系统由主裁判做出决定。
- 如果决定使用即时回放系统，那么裁判员必须先在比赛场地上做出最初的宣判。
- 在从其他裁判员、记录台人员、技术代表那里获得信息后，回放复审应该尽快开始。
- 主裁判和至少一名裁判（谁做出的判罚）应该参与到这个回放复审。如果是主裁判做出的判罚，他应该选择其中一名裁判员陪同进行回放复审。
- 在使用即时回放过程中，主裁判应该确保没有无授权人员在即时回放的屏幕前。

- The review shall take place before time-outs or substitutions are administered and before the game is resumed.
- After the review the referee who made the call shall report the final decision and the game shall be resumed accordingly.
- The initial decision of the referee(s) can be corrected only if the IRS review provides the referees with clear and conclusive visual evidence for the correction.
- After the crew chief has signed the scoresheet, an IRS review can no longer be performed.

F.3 Rule

The following game situations may be reviewed:

F.3.1 At the end of the quarter or overtime,

- whether a shot for a successful field goal was released before the game clock signal sounded for the end of the quarter or overtime.
- whether and how much time shall be displayed on the game clock, if:
  — An out-of-bounds violation of the shooter occurred.
  — A shot clock violation occurred.
  — An 8-second violation occurred.
  — A foul was committed before the end of the quarter or overtime.

F.3.2 When the game clock shows 2:00 minutes or less in the fourth quarter and in each overtime,

- whether a shot for a successful field goal was released before the shot clock signal sounded.
- whether a foul away from a shooting situation was committed. In this case
  — whether the game or shot clock has expired,
  — whether the act of shooting has started,
  — whether the ball was still in the hand(s) of the shooter.
- whether a goaltending or basket interference violation was called correctly.
- to identify the player who has caused the ball to go out-of-bounds.

- 回放复审应该在暂停或者换人前和比赛重新开始前执行。
- 回放复审结束后，原宣判的裁判应报告最终决定，并依此重新开始比赛。
- 裁判最初的判罚只有在即时回放系统为其提供清晰和确凿的影像证据时，才能予以更正。
- 在主裁判在记录表上签字后，即时回放系统就不能再被使用。

F.3 规 定

以下比赛情况可使用即时回放系统复审：

F.3.1 在每节或决胜期的最后时刻：

- 一次成功的投篮是否在结束该节或决胜期的比赛计时钟信号响之前球离手。
- 如果出现宣判了下述情况时，在比赛计时钟上是否还显示剩余时间，以及剩余多少时间：
    —— 投篮队员出界违例。
    —— 进攻时间违例。
    —— 8 秒违例。
    —— 在某节或某决胜期比赛结束之前宣判一起犯规。

F.3.2 当第4节和每一决胜期比赛计时钟显示2:00分钟或更少时：

- 一次成功的投篮是否在进攻计时钟响之前离手。
- 宣判一起远离投篮的犯规。在这种情况下：
    —— 比赛计时钟或进攻计时钟是否已经终了，
    —— 投篮的连续动作是否已经开始，
    —— 球是否还在投篮队员手中。
- 是否正确地宣判了一起干涉得分或干扰得分违例。
- 辨认是哪名队员使球出界。

F.3.3 During any time of the game,

- whether the successful field goal shall count for 2 or 3 points.
- whether 2 or 3 free throws shall be awarded, after a foul was called on a shooter for an unsuccessful field goal.
- whether a personal, unsportsmanlike or disqualifying foul met the criteria for such a foul or shall be upgraded or downgraded or shall be considered as a technical foul.
- after a malfunction of the game clock or the shot clock occurs, on how much time the clock(s) shall be corrected.
- to identify the correct free-throw shooter.
- to identify the involvement of team members, head coaches, first assistant coaches and accompanying delegation members during any act of violence.

END OF RULES AND GAME PROCEDURES

F3.3　在比赛的任何时间：
- 成功的投篮是计2分还是3分。
- 宣判了一起对投篮队员的犯规后，球未中篮，是判给2次还是3次罚球。
- 一起侵人犯规、违反体育运动精神的犯规或取消比赛资格的犯规是否符合相应标准或是否应升级还是降级或是否应被视为一起技术犯规。
- 在比赛计时钟或进攻计时钟发生故障后，应该修正多少时间。
- 辨认正确的罚球队员。
- 辨认一起暴力行为涉及的球员、主教练、第一助理教练和随队人员。

规则和比赛程序结束

第二部分
篮球器材 2020
Basketball Equipment 2020

前　言

《篮球规则 2020》的篮球器材部分，详细说明了比赛中需要的所有篮球器材。一级比赛的参考手册注明器材规格对于该级别的比赛是绝对必要的和必不可少的，并推荐在二级比赛中使用这些器材。二级比赛的参考手册注明器材规格对于该级别的比赛也是绝对必要的和必不可少的。

与比赛有直接关联的所有参与者以及篮球设备制造商、当地的组织者和国际篮联为它的设备批准说明书，以及制定国家和国际的标准均应使用这个附录。

对于制造商和国际篮联批准的测试机构，所有对于国际篮联批准的器材开展的测试都应该遵守国际篮联器材和场馆中心颁布的《测试方法和要求手册》中详细说明的程序。这一文件可以从国际篮联器材和场馆中心获取。

篮球比赛分为2个水平：

- **一级比赛**：国际篮联国家队和俱乐部比赛，以及其他精英级别的国家和国际顶级俱乐部和国家队比赛。

国家级的俱乐部比赛可能会受到国家管理机构颁布的附加规则的约束。"国际篮联国家队和俱乐部比赛"的定义在管辖国际篮联比赛的国际篮联内部规章第二本中有解释。这些比赛的所有设备必须经国际篮联批准适合一级比赛，并且可以按照国际篮联批准的布局显示批准的器材标识或者以国际篮联批准的形式来引用批准标识。

- **二级比赛**：不包括一级比赛在内的任何其他比赛。

对于二级比赛，所有篮球器材的技术规格必须被遵守，强烈推荐使用国际篮联批准的器材。

说明：
1. 本附录着重于要求和规格，不描述测试程序。测试程序和测量公差可在《测试方法和要求手册》中找到，该手册可从国际篮联器材和场馆中心获得(equipmentandvenue@fiba.basketball)。
2. 以下设备类别：篮球架、记录屏/视频显示屏、比赛地板、场地照明、即时回放系统、哨音计时控制系统和观众坐席，这些国际篮联批准的器材设备对应其相关的比赛水平在购买之后的8年内有效。8年有效期之后，任何不再被国际篮联批准的设备都必须更换。

1　篮球架

有两个篮球架（图1或图2），分别放置在比赛场地的两端，每一个篮球架包括下列部分：

- 1块篮板。
- 1个带有固定篮圈钢板的篮圈。
- 1个篮网。
- 1个篮球支撑构架。
- 包扎物。

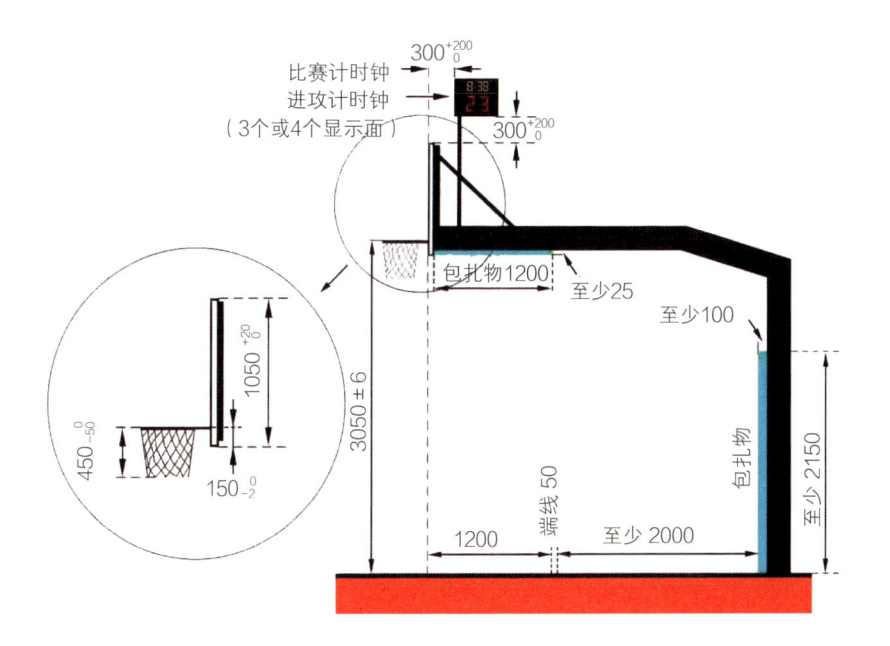

图1　一级比赛篮球架（进攻计时钟方式一）

（注：除特别说明外，本部分图示的单位都是毫米。）

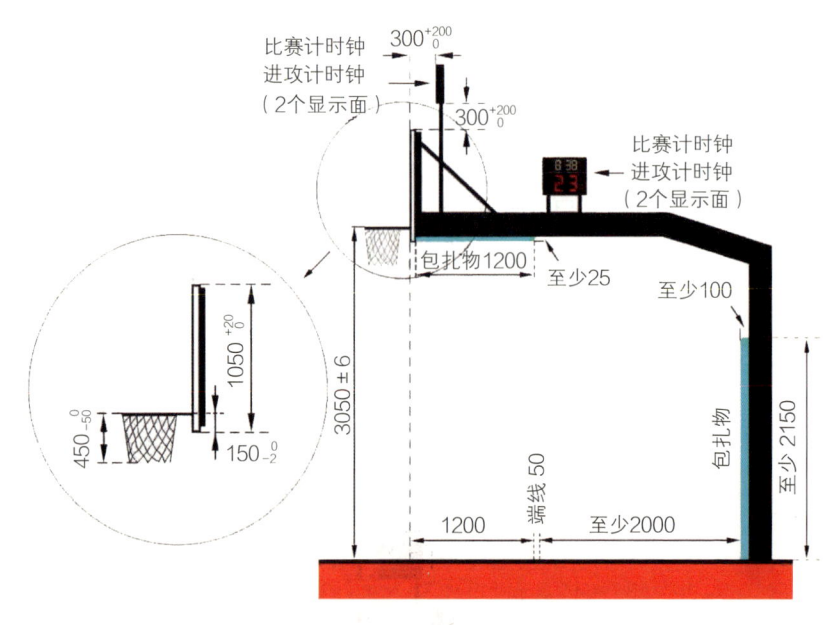

图2 一级比赛篮球架（进攻计时钟方式二）

1.1 篮 板

1.1.1 对于一级比赛，篮板应用不反光的夹层安全玻璃或钢化玻璃支撑，厚度介于11.8毫米与13.5毫米之间，前表面平整，并且：
- 围绕在篮板支撑构架的外沿应有保护性的框架。
- 篮板应制造成这样：如果损坏，玻璃碎片不飞出或造成任何受伤的风险。

1.1.2 对于二级比赛，篮板可以是下列任意材质：
- 夹层玻璃/钢化玻璃（和一级比赛相同）。
- 透明的丙烯酸或聚碳酸材料。
- 木材、玻璃纤维、钢或铝合金，漆成白色。

1.1.3 篮板（包括框架），横宽1800毫米（最大多出30毫米），竖高1050毫米（最大多出20毫米）

1.1.4 篮板上的所有线条：
- 如果篮板是透明的，应是白色的。
- 如果篮板漆成白色，应是黑色的（只对于二级比赛）。

- 线宽应为50毫米。

1.1.5 篮板的四周边应画上边线（图3），并按下列要求在篮圈后面画一个附加的长方形：
- 外沿的尺寸宽590毫米（最大多出20毫米），高450毫米（最大多出8毫米）。

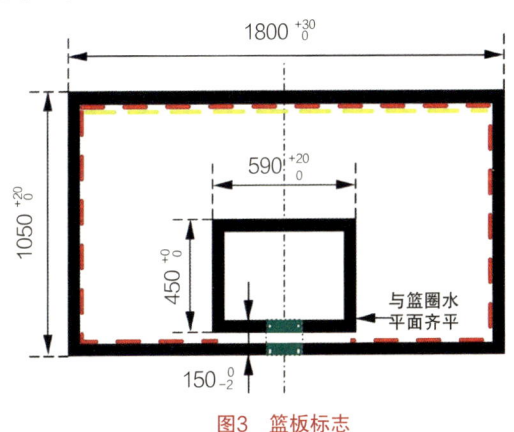

图3　篮板标志

- 长方形底线的上沿与篮圈的上沿齐平，距篮板的下沿150毫米（最多减少2毫米）。

1.1.6 对于一级比赛，每块篮板的四周边应配备闪光带，安装在篮板边沿里面，当结束一节或一个决胜期比赛的比赛计时钟信号响起时，亮起红光。闪光带应至少宽10毫米，并至少沿篮板玻璃区域边缘覆盖90%。

1.1.7 对于一级比赛，每块篮板上沿顶部应配备闪光带，安装在篮板边沿里面，仅当进攻时钟信号响起时，亮起黄光。闪光带置应至少宽10毫米并直接安装在比赛计时钟的红色灯下面。

1.1.8 篮板应牢固地安置在比赛场地两端的篮板支撑架上，与比赛地板成直角，平行于端线（图1或图2）。篮板前表面的中央垂直线延伸至比赛地板，与比赛地板的接触点落在与端线成直角的假想线上，此点距离端线内沿中心1200毫米。

1.1.9 对于一级比赛，当一个篮球从1.8米处落在篮板上时，应最少有50%的反弹高度。

1.2 篮 圈

1.2.1 篮圈用实心钢材制成并应：
- 其内沿直径最小为450毫米，最大为459毫米。
- 漆成橙色，此橙色在下列自然颜色体系（NCS）或经典色卡谱（RAL）：

NCS：
S0580-Y70R (CMYK: 0, 63, 79, 4)
S0585-Y70R (CMYK: 0, 70, 92, 5)
S1080-Y70R (CMYK: 0, 65, 85, 13)

RAL：
RAL 2004 (CMYK: 0, 65, 87, 0)
RAL 2008 (CMYK: 0, 70, 90, 0)
RAL 2010 (CMYK: 0, 78, 100, 0)

- 圈材直径最小为16毫米，最大为20毫米。

1.2.2 篮网应系在每个篮圈的12个位置上，系篮网的附件不应：
- 有任何尖棱或缺口。
- 有大于8毫米的空隙，以防止手指进入。（图4、图5）
- 对于一级比赛，不设计成挂钩。

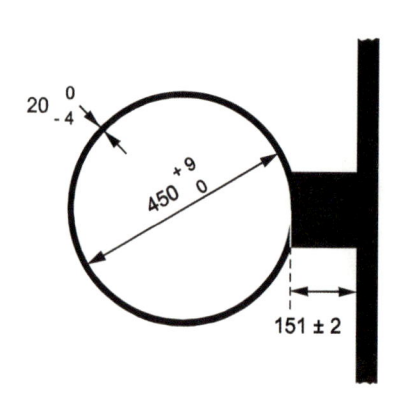

图4 篮圈尺寸

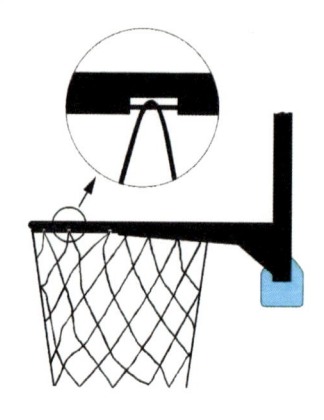

图5 篮网的安装（例）

1.2.3 篮圈应固定在支撑篮板的构架上，这样，任何施加在篮圈上的力不能被传递到篮板上。因此，在固定篮圈的钢板和篮板之间不应有直接的接触。

1.2.4 每个篮圈的顶沿应水平放置，距地面3050毫米（最多±6毫米），与篮板的两条竖边等距离。

1.2.5 从最靠近篮板的篮圈内周上的点到篮板面的距离是151毫米（最多±2毫米）。（图6）

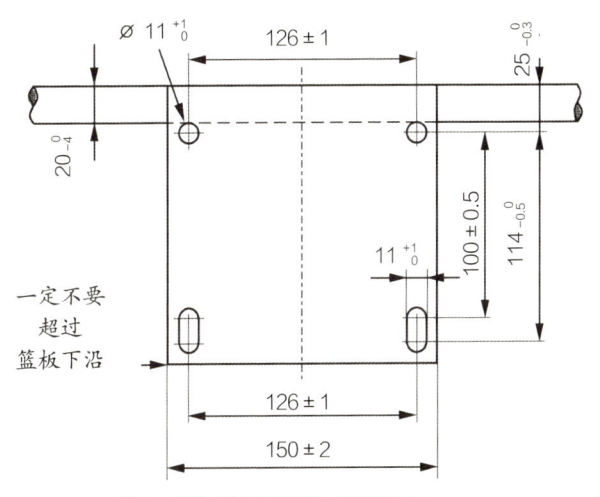

图6 固定篮圈的钢板（示例尺寸）

1.2.6 对于现存的球篮支撑结构，建议按照图7给出的尺寸，把固定篮圈的钢板安装在构架上。

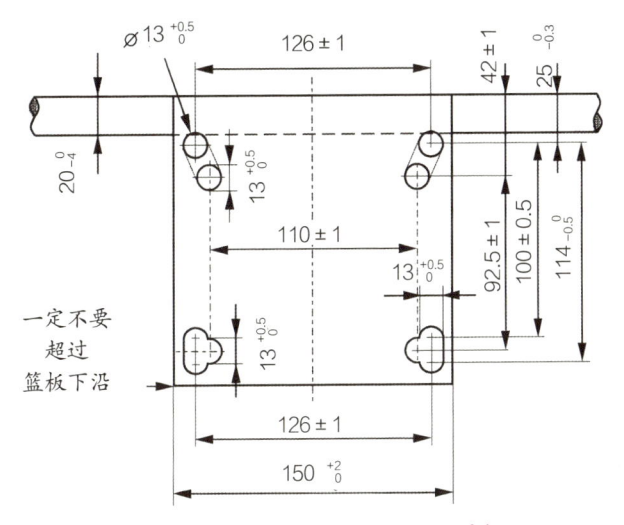

图7 现存球篮的固定篮圈的钢板（示例尺寸）

1.2.7 符合下列规格的抗压篮圈应在一级比赛中使用,并且也适用于申请国际篮联批准的二级比赛:
- 抗压篮圈的反弹性能与固定篮圈的反弹性能应接近。压力释放装置不应对篮圈或篮板造成任何损坏。篮圈的设计及其建造应确保队员的安全。
- 在最少82千克、最多105千克的静荷载被垂直地施加在离篮板最远点的篮圈顶部之前,带有"正锁定"机械装置的抗压篮圈不应松开。
- 当压力释放装置放开时,篮圈的前部或边沿应转动到原先的水平位置之下,角度不大于30度,也不小于10度。
- 在放开之后,并且不再施加荷载时,篮圈应自动地立即返回到原先的位置。不能看到篮圈有裂缝和永久的变形。
- 篮圈和支撑系统的弹力/弹性应是吸收能量占总冲击能量的35%～50%,两个互为对方的篮圈之间的差别应小于5%。

1.3 篮 网

1.3.1 篮网应用白色细线绳制成,并且:
- 悬挂在篮圈上。
- 制成的篮网要使球穿过球篮时稍受阻碍。
- 长度不短于400毫米,也不长于450毫米。
- 制成的篮网有12个环孔,以便系在篮圈上。

1.3.2 篮网的上部应是半硬式的,以防止:
- 篮网反弹向上穿过篮圈或者翻到篮圈以上,造成可能的缠挂。
- 球停留在篮网中或被弹出。

1.4 篮板支撑构架

1.4.1 对于一级比赛,只可使用活动的或固定在地面上的篮板支撑构架。对于二级比赛,除了使用活动的或固定在地面上的篮板支撑构架以外,还可以使用吊装在天花板上或安装在墙上的篮板支撑构架。吊装在天花板上的篮板,不应使用在天花板高度超过10000毫米的场馆内,以避免支架的过度震动。

1.4.2 篮板支撑构架应：

- 对于一级比赛，距端线外沿测量到篮球架包扎物前沿至少2000毫米（图1或图2）。
- 对于二级比赛，距端线外沿测量到篮球架包扎物前沿至少1000毫米。对于安装在墙上的或吊装在天花板上的单位，测量应从端线外沿到墙面或距离最近的障碍物。
- 与背景相比颜色鲜明，以便队员清晰看见。
- 牢牢地固定在比赛地板上，以防止任何移动。如果不可能固定在比赛地板上，为防止任何移动，必须在支撑球篮的底座上使用足够的镇重物。
- 被校准到从篮圈顶部至地面的高度是3050毫米，这个高度不得改变。
- 带有篮圈的篮板支撑构架的刚性应达到ENI 1270 标准的要求。
- 扣篮后篮板支撑单元超过5毫米的明显颤动应持续少于4秒钟。

1.5 包扎物

1.5.1 篮板和篮板支撑构架必须包扎。
1.5.2 包扎物应为单一的纯色，与两块篮板以及支撑构架颜色应相同。
1.5.3 包扎物距离篮板的前、后和侧面应有20～27毫米厚，距离篮板的底沿应有48～55毫米厚。（图8）

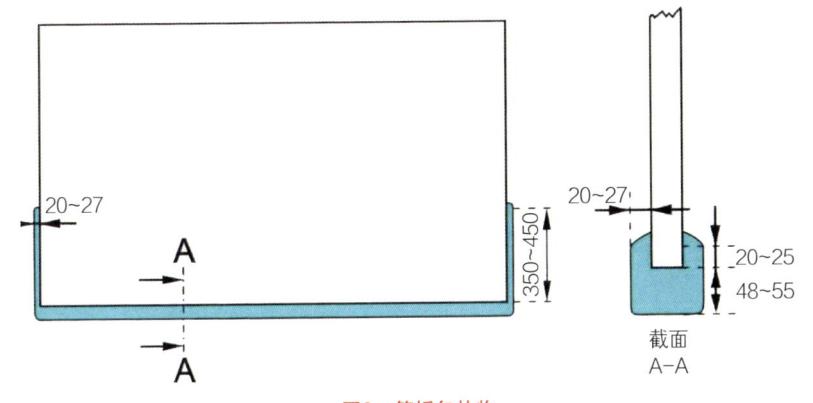

图8 篮板包扎物

1.5.4 包扎物应覆盖每一篮板的底表面,侧表面距底沿高度应为350~450毫米。前后表面应距每一篮板的底部至少覆盖20～25毫米高。

1.5.5 **篮板支撑构架的包扎物应覆盖:**
- 每侧的垂直边沿,从比赛地板向上的最低高度是2150毫米,最小厚度是100毫米(图1或图2)。
- 篮板支撑臂的底部和侧表面,从篮板背面起沿臂包扎,超过1200毫米的最小长度,最小厚度是25毫米。

1.5.6 **为在撞击中保护队员,所有包扎物应:**
- 能防止肢体陷入。
- 具有最大50%的压痕系数。这意味着当外力突然施加在包扎物上时,包扎物的凹陷不超过原先厚度的50%。(图1或图2)
- 峰值减速度值为500 m/s^2 或更小。

2　篮球

2.1　对于一级比赛,球的外壳应由皮革或人造的 / 复合的 / 合成的皮革制成。对于二级比赛,除了皮革或人造的 / 复合的 / 合成的皮革以外,球的外壳还可用橡胶制成。

2.2　球的外壳应完全遵守相关的当地和国家法规,包括遵守有关使用有毒物质和可能引起过敏反应的物质(包括AZO染料、可溶性重金属、邻苯二甲酸脂和多环芳烃)的任何适用安全指令。球类制造商有责任根据适用的规定对球进行测试。

2.3　篮球的外壳应在整个球体上提供适当的抓力。

2.4　**球应:**
- 是圆形的,最多有12条接缝,宽度不应超过6.35毫米;是单一暗橙色的,或是国际篮联批准的结合色。
- 充气到使球从大约1800毫米的高度(从球的底部量起)落到比赛地板上,反弹起来的高度应在960~1160毫米之间(从球的底部量起)。

- 标注有建议的充气压力或压力范围。
- 标明各自的尺寸号码。
- 在表1列出的周长和重量公差之内。对于所有男子比赛，都应使用7号球；在所有女子比赛中，都应使用6号球；对于所有迷你篮球，都应使用5号或5号轻量球（Lightweight 5）。

表1 篮球的周长与重量

球的尺寸	7	6	5	5号轻量球
周长（毫米）	750~770	715~730	685~700	685~700
重量（克）	580~620	510~550	465~495	360~390

2.5 除核对上面列出的规格外，应符合下列要求：
- 耐久性测试。
- 压力损失测试。
- 充气压力测试（只对于一级比赛）。
- 热贮藏量测试（只对于一级比赛）。

3 记录屏/视频显示屏

3.1 对于一级比赛，两块大记录屏或视频显示屏应：
- 各设置在比赛场地的每一端。
- 如果比赛场地中央的上方设置了一块记录屏（立方形的），那么只需要在球队席的对面放置一块两队均清晰可见的副记录屏即可。
- 让与比赛有关的（包括观众在内）的每一个人都能清楚地看到。如果使用了视频显示器，在比赛的过程中（包括比赛休息期间）完整的必需的比赛信息必须随时可见。被显示信息的可读性与数字计分板的信息应完全一致。

3.2 应给计时员提供一个比赛计时钟控制板，并给助理记录员提供一个单独的记录屏控制板。计算机键盘板可以用来输入记录屏上的数据，然而，必须使用专用控制板来操作设备。这个专用控制板应能够容易地改正任何不正确的数据，并且具有贮藏最少30分钟所有比赛数据的多个储存器支持。

3.3 记录屏应包括和/或指明：

- 数字倒计时比赛计时钟。比赛剩余时间应以分和秒（mm:ss）显示，除了在每节或决胜期的最后一分钟时，应以秒和1/10秒显示（ss:f）。
- 每队的得分；对于一级比赛，每个队员的累积得分。
- 对于一级比赛，每个队员的号码（按照00，0，1，2，3，4，5，6，7，8，9，10及11—99的顺序），还有他们相应的姓。应不少于12位字母来显示每个队员的姓。
- 双方队的队名。应不少于3位字母来显示队名。
- 对于一级比赛，球队中每个队员从第1次犯规到第5次犯规的次数。第5次犯规应用红色或橙色指明。犯规次数可用5个指示器或一个最低高度为135毫米的数字显示来指明。另外，第5次犯规可用一个5秒的慢闪光显示（~1赫兹）来指明。应可以在记录屏上从队员犯规次数中独立出来显示球队的犯规次数。
- 1~4次的全队犯规次数，和在4次全队犯规次数后球再次成为活球时显示红色方格（图9）。红色方格应为正方形，它的边应为球队犯规数字宽度的介于80%到120%。

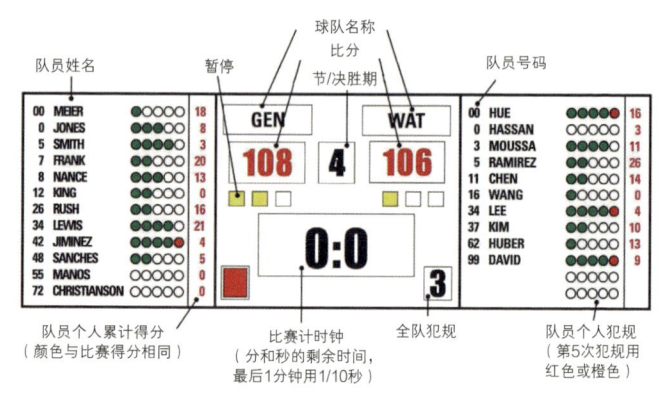

队员姓名	暂停	球队名称 比分 节/决胜期	队员号码
00 MEIER ●●●○○ 18 0 JONES ●●●○○ 8 5 SMITH ●●●○○ 20 8 FRANK ●●●○○ 13 8 NANCE ●●●○○ 13 12 KING ●●●○○ 0 26 RUSH ●●●●● 16 34 LEWIS ●●●●○ 21 42 JIMINEZ ●●●○○ 4 48 SANCHES ●●●○○ 6 55 MANOS ○○○○○ 0 72 CHRISTIANSON ○○○○○ 0		GEN WAT 108 4 106 0:0 3	00 HUE ●●●●● 16 0 HASSAN ●●●○○ 3 3 MOUSSA ●●●●○ 11 5 RAMIREZ ●●●●● 26 11 CHEN ●●●●○ 14 16 WANG ●●●○○ 8 34 LEE ●●●●● 4 37 KIM ●●●○○ 10 62 HUBER ●●●○○ 13 99 DAVID ●●●●○ 7
队员个人累计得分 （颜色与比赛得分相同）		比赛计时钟 （分和秒的剩余时间， 最后1分钟用1/10秒）	全队犯规	队员个人犯规 （第5次犯规用 红色或橙色）

图9　一级篮球比赛的记录屏（样例）

228

- 1~4的节数，0指示决胜期。
- 每半时0~3的暂停次数。第4节当比赛计时钟剩余2:00分钟或更少时，球队应只能使用2次暂停。其余的暂停应显示已使用。
- 暂停计时钟（可选择的），比赛计时钟不得用于暂停。

3.4 对于一级（必须的）和二级（推荐的）：

- 记录屏上显示的颜色对比度应是鲜明的。
- 显示的背景应是不刺眼的。
- 记录屏上的比赛计时钟、比赛得分和进攻计时钟应有最小130度的观察角度。
- 记录屏的数字和字母应符合表2的尺寸要求。

表2 记录屏数字和字母要求

	一级比赛必须	二级比赛推荐（对申请国际篮联批准的二级比赛器材为必须）
比赛计时钟、比分	高度 ≥300毫米 宽度 ≥150毫米	高度 ≥250毫米 宽度 ≥125毫米
比赛节数、全队犯规	高度 ≥250毫米 宽度 ≥125毫米	高度 ≥200毫米 宽度 ≥100毫米
球队名称	高度 ≥150毫米 最少3位字母	高度 ≥100毫米 最少3位字母
暂停次数	3个指示亮点	3个指示亮点
队员名字	高度 ≥150毫米 最少12位字母	不适用
队员号码	高度 ≥150毫米	不适用
队员犯规次数	5个指示亮点 或高度 ≥135毫米	不适用
队员个人得分	高度≥150毫米	不适用

3.5 记录屏应：

- 没有任何尖棱或毛边。
- 被牢固地安装。
- 符合DIN 18032-3标准，能够经受得住任何球的剧烈碰撞。
- 如有必要，具有特定的不损伤记录屏清晰度的防护物。
- 根据各自国家的法定要求，具有电磁兼容性。

4 比赛计时钟

4.1 对于一级比赛，主比赛计时钟（图9）应：
- 是一个带有显示器，一显示零（00:00.0）就自动发出结束一节或一个决胜期信号的数字倒计时钟。
- 有指示剩余的分、秒以及只在每节或每个决胜期最后1分钟内指示1/10秒时间的功能。
- 放置在与比赛有关的（包括观众在内）的每一个人都能清楚地看到的地方。

4.2 如果主比赛计时钟设置在场地中央的上方，那么只需要在球队席的对面放置一个比赛双方均清晰可见的副比赛计时钟即可。每一个副比赛计时钟应显示整场比赛的比分和剩余的比赛时间。

4.3 裁判员们为停止比赛计时钟，应使用一种与配备在比赛计时钟上的连接器相连的哨音计时控制系统，这个系统被使用在特定竞赛的所有比赛中。裁判员们还应开动比赛计时钟，在同一时间，比赛计时钟也被计时员操作。所有国际篮联批准的一级比赛的记录屏应装备哨音计时控制系统接口。

5 进攻计时钟

5.1 进攻计时钟应有：
- 一个提供给进攻计时员的单独的控制器，带有非常响亮的自动信号，以便指明进攻周期结束。
- 一个带有数字倒计时的显示器，指示秒的时间。

5.2 对于一级比赛，进攻计时钟应：
- 用秒数指明剩余时间，在进攻周期的最后5秒以1/10秒来指明。

5.3 进攻计时钟应有下列功能：
- 从24秒开始。
- 从14秒开始。
- 比赛停止时显示器指示剩余的秒数。

- 从停止的时间处重新开动。
- 如有必要，显示器无显示。

5.4 对于一级比赛，进攻计时钟应与比赛计时钟相连接，以便当：
- 比赛计时钟停止时，该装置也停止。
- 比赛计时钟开动时，手工开动该装置是可能的。
- 装置停止并发出声响时，比赛计时钟继续计时；如有必要，可被手工停止。

5.5 对于一级比赛，进攻计时钟显示器（图10）和一个副比赛计时钟在一起，应：

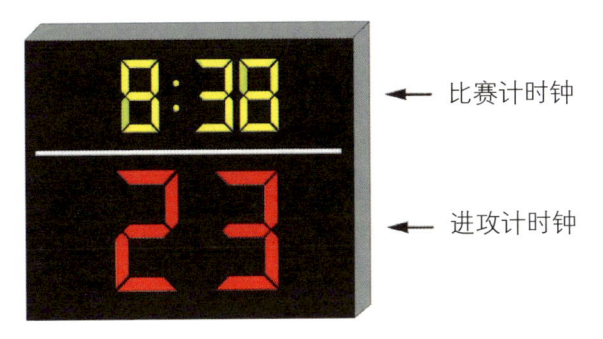

图10 用于一级比赛和二级比赛的进攻计时钟、副比赛计时钟（布置样例）

- 安装在每个篮板支撑构架上，在篮板上方及后面最少300毫米处（图1或图2）或悬挂在天花板上。
- 进攻计时钟的数字为红色，副比赛计时钟的数字为黄色。
- 进攻计时钟显示的数字最少高230毫米，并且比副比赛计时钟的数字大。
- 每个显示器有3个或4个显示面，或者2个双面的显示器（建议二级比赛使用），要保证与比赛有关的（包括观众在内）的每一个人都能清楚地看到。
- 包括支撑架构，重量不超过60千克。
- 在其四周安装闪光带（可选择），仅当结束一节或决胜期的比赛计时钟信号响起时亮起红光。

- 沿其上部的边安装闪光带（可选择），仅当进攻计时钟信号响起时亮起黄光，并直接安装在比赛计时钟的红色闪光带下面。
- 通过进攻计时钟耐久性测试，可以承受来自篮球的直接撞击。
- 根据各自国家的法定要求，具有电磁兼容性。

6　信号

6.1　应至少有2种单独的声响信号，带有截然不同的非常响亮的声音：
- 一种提供给记录员，应自动地响起以指明每节或每个决胜期比赛时间结束。当在适当的时候要引起裁判员的注意时，记录员应能够手动发出信号。
- 一种提供给进攻计时员，应自动地响起以指明24秒结束。

6.2　两种信号应当足够强，在最不利或者嘈杂的情况下也能容易听到。音量应是可调整的，根据体育馆的大小和人群的喧闹声，音量可调到120分贝的最大声压水平（距声源1米处测量）。强烈建议与体育馆的公共信息系统相连接。

7　队员犯规标示牌

为计时员提供的5块队员犯规标示牌应是：
- 白色的。
- 数字最小长200毫米，宽100毫米。
- 两面都印有数字，从1~5（1~4的数字为黑色，5为红色）。

8　全队犯规标示牌

为计时员提供的两块全队犯规标示牌应是：
- 红色的。
- 最小高350毫米、宽200毫米。
- 放置于记录台的两边位置上，让与比赛有关的每一个人（包括观众在内）都能够清楚地看到。

篮球器材 *2020*

- 用以指示从1~4的全队犯规次数，和在4次全队犯规次数后球再次成为活球时显示红色，表明该队达到全队犯规处罚状态。
- 可以使用电动或电子的装置，但必须符合上述规格。

9　交替拥有指示器

为记录员提供一台交替拥有指示器（图11），应：

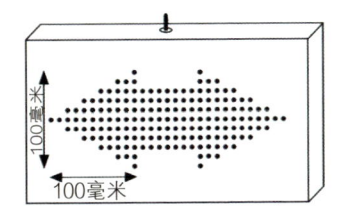

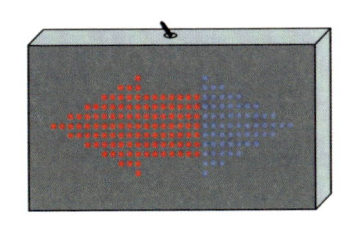

图11　交替拥有指示器（样例）

- 有一个最少长100毫米和高100毫米的箭头。
- 在前面显示一个箭头，打开开关时，明亮的红色箭头指明交替拥有的方向。
- 放置于记录台的中央位置上，让与比赛有关的每一个人（包括观众在内）都能够清楚地看到。

10　比赛地板

10.1 比赛地板表面应由：
- 永久的木制室内地面材料制成（一级和二级）。
- 活动的木制室内地面材料制成（一级和二级）。
- 永久的人造室内地面材料制成（二级）。
- 活动的人造室内地面材料制成（二级）。

10.2 比赛地板应：
- 最小长32000毫米，最小宽19000毫米。
- 有一个不耀眼的表面。

10.3 地板必须遵守以下运动功能要求（表3、表4）：

表3 木质地板要求（一级和二级）

表现属性	一级 永久的地板	一级 活动的地板	二级 永久和活动的地板
减力， 参照EN14808	≥ 50 % ~ ≤ 75 %		≥ 40 % ~ ≤ 75 %
	统一（绝对值）：（相对于平均值 ± 5 %）		
垂直变形， 参照EN14809	≥ 2.3 毫米 ~ ≤ 5.0 毫米	≥ 1.5 毫米 ~ ≤ 5.0 毫米	≥ 1.5 毫米 ~ ≤ 5.0 毫米
	统一（相对于平均值 ± 0.7 毫米）		
球的反弹， 参照EN12235	≥ 93 %	≥ 93 %	≥ 90 %
	统一（绝对值）：（相对于平均值 ± 3%）		
防滑性， 参照EN13036	平均值：≥ 80 ~ ≤ 110		
耐磨性， 参照EN5470	≤ 80 毫克		≤ 100 毫克
高光反射（%）	≤ 45 % *		不适用
	统一（方差≤10）		
滚动负荷， 参照EN1569	永久压痕≤0.5 毫米		

* 推荐值，可最大程度地减少球员视线和电视节目的比赛场地眩光。当放置照明时，可以使用高光泽度替代品，以避免不必要的比赛场地眩光（请参阅12 照明）。

表4 合成材料地板要求（二级）

表现属性	一级 永久的地板	一级 活动的地板	二级 永久和活动的地板
减力， 参照EN14808	点弹性：25 % ~ 75 %		统一（绝对值）相对于平均值 ± 5 %
	混合弹性：45 % ~ 75 %		
	区域弹性：40 % ~ 75 %		
	组合弹性：45 % ~ 75 %		
垂直变形， 参照EN14809	点弹性：≤ 3.5 毫米		统一相对于平均值 ± 0.7 %
	混合弹性：≤ 3.5 毫米		
	区域弹性：1.5 毫米 ~ 5.0 毫米		
	组合弹性：1.5 毫米 ~ 5.0 毫米		
球的反弹， 参照EN12235	≥ 90 %		
	统一（绝对值）相对于平均值 ± 3%		

续表

表现属性	一级 永久的地板	一级 活动的地板	二级 永久和活动的地板
防滑性， 参照EN13036	平均值：≥ 80 - ≤ 110		
耐磨性， 参照EN5470	≤ 100 毫克		
高光反射（%）	不适用		
滚动负荷， 参照EN1569	永久压痕≤0.5 毫米		

注：在每个系统测试点都必须满足上述属性的要求。

10.4 制造商和地板安装公司应被责成为每一客户提供至少包括以下内容的文件：样品测试结果、安装程序的说明、由批准的检验人员进行的现有安装的检验和认可的结果。

10.5 比赛地板必须能够支撑可移动或固定的篮板支撑结构，并且不降低篮板支撑结构的功效。相反，活动的篮板支撑架应按照自重能分布到一个更大的接触面来构建，这样在比赛位置和在比赛场地上运输过程中都消除了对地板损伤的风险。

10.6 当将贴纸或喷漆在比赛场地表面上而不用额外的饰面涂层覆盖时，它们必须遵守与表3和表4中规定的正常比赛地面区域相同的防滑性和高光反射标准。

11 比赛场地

11.1 比赛场地应：
- 按照篮球竞赛规则，用50毫米宽的线标出。（图12）
- 由最少宽2000毫米的带有明显反差颜色的外层界线标出。

11.2 记录台最少长6000毫米、高800毫米，必须安放在一个最少高200毫米的平台上。

11.3 所有观众必须就座于距比赛场地的界线外沿最少2000毫米处。

11.4 天花板的高度或比赛场地上空最低障碍物的高度至少应为7米。

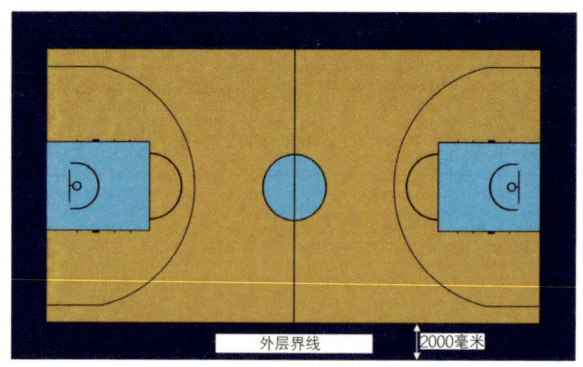

OFFICIAL BASKETBALL RULES 2020

图12 比赛场地

12 照明

12.1 垂直照度（EC——对主摄像机的照度和EV——移动摄像机的照度）是图像质量的一个关键参数。如果在球场上的不同位置的垂直照度不同，那么当摄像机倾斜时可能会造成影响。因此，整个球场的垂直照度分布（即垂直照度的均匀性）是完全一致的。

垂直照度应尽可能保持恒定，面对球场的四个主要方向的两侧通常是放置摄像机的位置。

水平照度（EH）是球场上落下的光的数量。因为被照明的球场是摄像机的视野的主要部分，所以水平照度应尽可能均匀，平均水平照度和平均垂直照度对主摄像头之间的比例应保持在一个水平，确保高质量的图片反差。

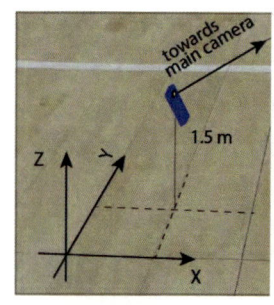

对主摄像机的照度EC 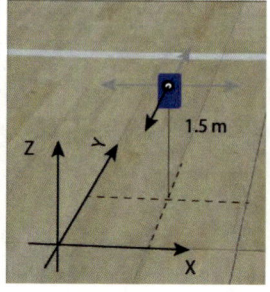　　移动摄像机的照度EV 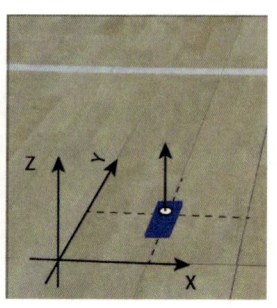　　水平照度EH

12.2 照明要求和建议

场馆照明必须为电视直播而设计，同时尽量减小运动员和裁判员的眩光。

12.2.1 照度水平

- 比赛场地应被均匀和充分地照亮。以上描述的照明标准必须被计算并应符合表5的规定值。
- 原则上的比赛区域也就是比赛场地，包括边线和所有的比赛区域（19米×32米），以及全部的比赛区域，包括球场周围1.5米宽的场地包括队员席（22米×35米），应加以区分。
- 美拍摄像机不需要计算。

表5 照度要求

	EC：主摄像机照度			EV：垂直照度（所有方向）				EH：水平照度		
	平均（勒克斯）	最小/最大	最小/平均	平均（勒克斯）	最小/最大	最小/平均	最小/最大 4个方向	平均（勒克斯）	最小/最大	最小/平均
PPA	2000	0.7	0.8	1700	0.7	0.8	0.6	1500~3000	0.7	0.8
TPA	2000	0.6	0.7	1700	0.6	0.7	0.6	1500~3000	0.6	0.7

12.2.2 朝向主摄像机的强光

明亮的光源在球场上的反射会引起亮点，这会影响摄像机图像，如下图所示。必须避免高强度光从反光的球场表面向主摄像机方向反射而引起的眩光，尤其是在球场中的线上。

仔细注意和简单必要的几何图形通常会消除这些不需要的反射光（附件2）。

12.2.3 眩光

最主要的是，篮球运动员在比赛时不能看到任何影响他们视野的眩光。照明位置和方向的确定应考虑到运动员的视野（附件2）。光源的强度必须与安装高度相适应。

12.2.4 观众区域

前15排座位的主摄像机平均照度应在球场平均照度的10%~25%之间，前15排的照度应均匀减小。

12.2.5 光源

闪烁系数，显色指数和色温如下所述。TPA的每个点均应满足表6中所述的要求：

表6 光源要求

闪烁系数	显色指数（CRI）	色温（K）	
≤ 1 %	≥ Ra 80	4000 ~ 6000	相对于平均值 ± 500 K

- 术语"闪烁系数"是指整个周期内给定平面上的亮度调制。它表示一段时间（整个周期）内某个点的最大和最小照度之间的关系，并以百分比表示。灯光的这种闪烁可能会对广播图像的质量产生负面影响，尤其是在使用慢动作的情况下。如果以50赫兹或60赫兹的电源供应电磁齿轮，那么放电灯的强度（一般用于体育照明）就会波动。
- 光源的显色指数（CRI）是一个定量值，用于测量与理想或自然光源相比，其显示对象颜色的能力。CRI值对于广播质量以及场馆观众是非常重要的因素。
- 色温以光显示的暖色（红色）或冷色（蓝色）的方式描述了照明系统的输出。电视广播公司需要恒定的色温。

所有球场照明应在比赛开始前至少90分钟打开，并符合赛前热身和比赛规定的要求。比赛结束后至少30分钟应保持充分照明。

只有当照明系统即时重燃能力不改变光源的颜色特性时，聚光灯才可以用于介绍团队或特殊的仪式和娱乐。

12.2.6 目视检查

应目视检查、评价照明装置。

当站在主相机位置时，反射光不可见。由于电视摄像机比人眼更敏感，所以可以用数码相机拍照检查。应当注意尽可能位于泛光照度。不应该让球员感到眼花缭乱，特别是当他们看着篮筐的时候。

附件1：计算网格点和通常摄像机位置

附件2：照明位置的建议

泛光灯的位置要符合照明要求。它必须确保照明的要求可以实现，同时不干扰运动员的可见度，也不会对主摄像机产生任何眩光。应让照明设计师自由地摆放泛光灯以提供最好的技术解决方案。当主摄像机的位置已经确定，可以通过避免在禁止区域安装泛光灯来消除眩光，如下图所示。

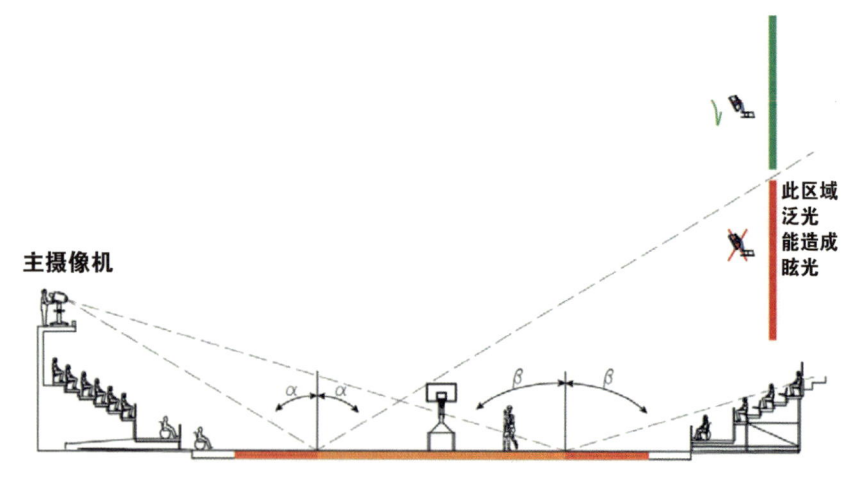

照明装置的禁区，以避免眩光直射主摄像头

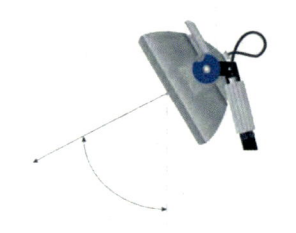

照明瞄准角（从垂直向下测量）应≤60度，以减少对运动员的眩光。

照明瞄准角

应注意根据运动员的目标方向确定泛光灯摆放的位置以不干扰运动员的视野，特别是当他们看着篮筐时。

下面的示例说明了泛光灯位置的关键。在这个例子中，泛光灯位于20度区域不会直接朝向做投篮动作的任何球员。

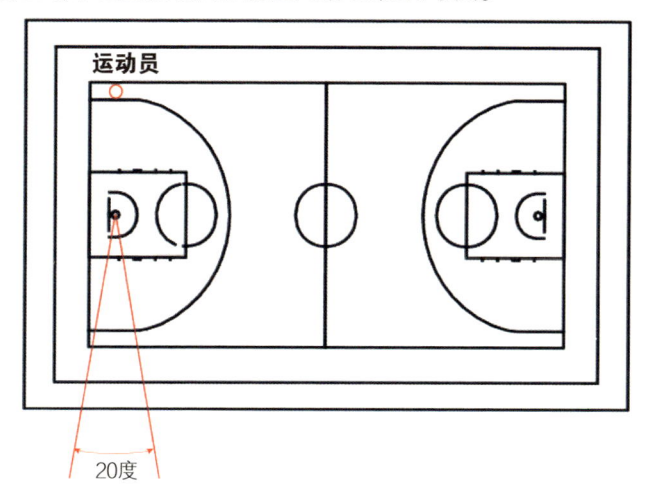

运动员

20度

13 哨音计时控制系统

13.1 裁判员们为停止比赛计时钟，应使用一种与配备在比赛计时钟上的连接器相连的哨音计时控制系统，这个系统被使用在特定竞赛的所有比赛中。裁判员们还应开动比赛计时钟，在同一时间，比赛计时钟也被计时员操作。所有国际篮联批准的一级比赛的记录屏应装备哨音计时控制系统接口。

13.2 裁判吹哨时，哨音计时控制系统应停止比赛时钟，其响应时间为0.1秒或更短。

13.3 覆盖范围：在篮球场上的所有位置，比赛计时钟必须能通过哨音计时控制系统停止和重新启动。

13.4 哨音计时控制系统应仅在裁判员吹哨时停止比赛时钟，并且不会因任何比赛外部的哨声而停止比赛时钟。

14 口哨

14.1 裁判员用的口哨应符合表7所列的分贝和频率要求。

表7 口哨的音量和频率要求

比赛类型	分贝8.3千帕			频率范围8.3千帕		
	初始测试	后期耐久性测试	后期损坏测试	初始测试	后期耐久性测试	后期损坏测试
一级比赛	≥ 105	≥ 105 & 上一次结果 ± 10%		≥ 170	≥ 170赫兹&上一次结果 ± 10%	
二级比赛	≥ 95	≥ 95 & 上一次结果 ± 10%		≥ 150	≥ 150赫兹&上一次结果 ± 10%	

14.2 口哨应该：
- 能够承受高压下的重复使用（耐久性测试）。
- 能够承受反复跌落（损坏测试）。所有数据应在距哨子前面3米处获取。

14.3 口哨应由不会对使用者造成直接伤害的材料制成。因此，除非当地标准允许偏差，否则哨子应符合以下要求：
- EN 71-3+A1:2014玩具安全——第3部分某些元素铝、锑、砷、钡、镉、铬（iii）、铬（vi）、钴、铜、铅、锰、汞、镍、硒、锶、锡和锌的迁移。
- 多环芳烃测试符合REACH建议附录十七——苯并[a]芘（BaP）、苯并[e]芘（BeP）、苯并[a]蒽（BaA）、䓛（CHR）、苯并[b]荧蒽（BbFA）、苯并[k]荧蒽（BkFA）和二苯并[a,h]蒽（DBAha）。
- 邻苯二甲酸酯的测试符合REACH建议附件十七——邻苯二甲酸二-2-乙基己酯（DEHP）、邻苯二甲酸二异壬酯（DINP）、邻苯二甲酸二正丁酯（DBP）、邻苯二甲酸二正辛酯（DNOP）、邻苯二甲酸苄丁酯（BBP）和邻苯二甲酸二异癸酯（DIDP）。

15 广告板

15.1 广告板可设置在比赛场地的四周，并且：
- 应设置在离端线和边线最少2000毫米处。它们可以被设置在环绕球场的任意一边。（图13、图14）

篮球器材 2020

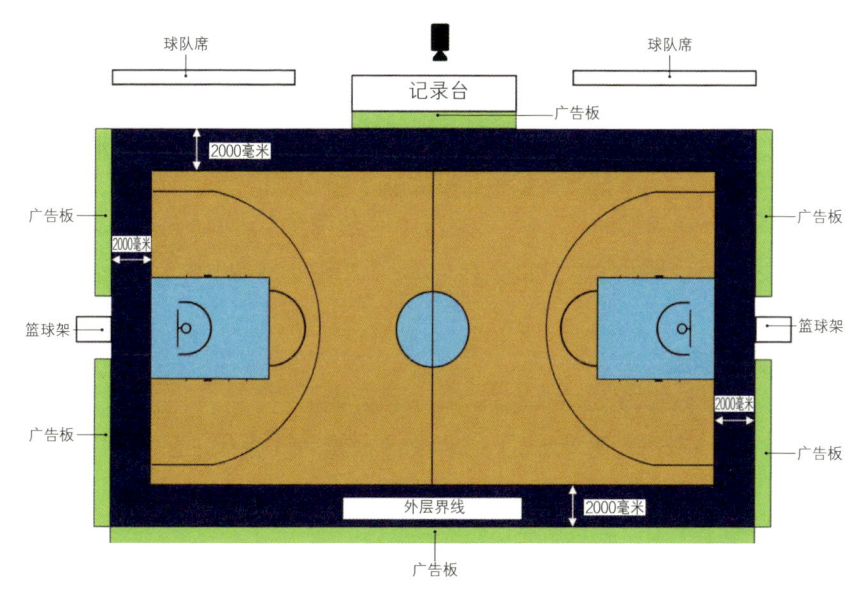

图13　广告板——主摄像机在记录台一侧

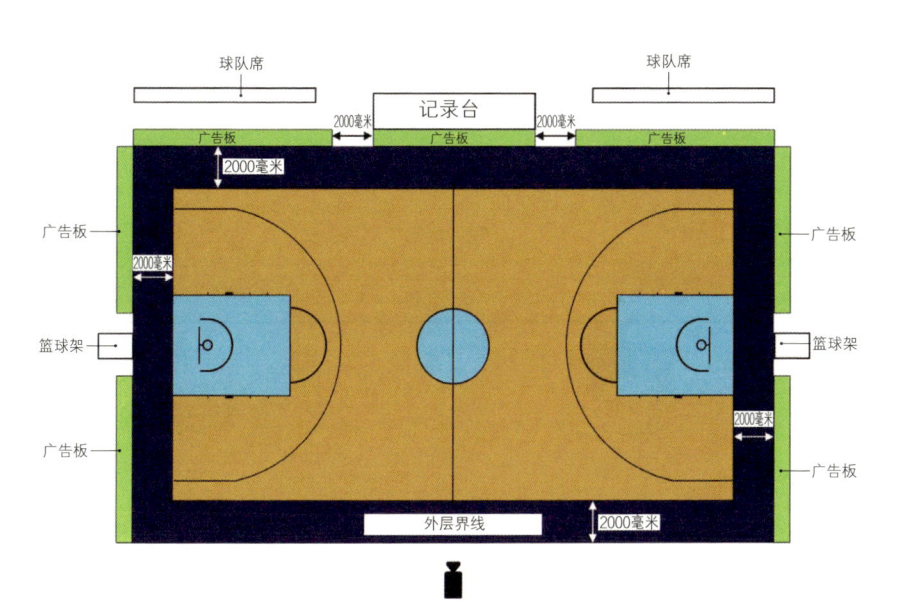

图14　广告板——主摄像机在记录台对侧

243

- 如有必要，沿端线的广告板与活动的篮球架的两边的空隙应最少宽900毫米，以便擦地板人员和手提式电视摄影机能通过，同时还要为队员提供了一条逃生通道。
- 在记录台侧的广告牌与记录台的两边的空隙最少要有2000毫米宽，以允许队员、替补队员通过。（图14）
- 对于电视转播的比赛，边线的广告板应置于主摄像机的对侧。
- 允许被置于记录台正前方，如果它们能正好与记录台水平和垂直对齐。

15.2 广告板应：

- 离比赛场地地面的高度不超过1000毫米。
- 围绕顶部和两侧包扎，侧边最小厚度为20毫米（图15），并应满足1.5.6所述的所有球员安全要求。
- 没有毛口，并且所有边棱应被磨圆。
- 符合各国家或地区的电气设备安全技术规范。
- 对所有发动机从动部分有机械保护。
- 是不易燃的。

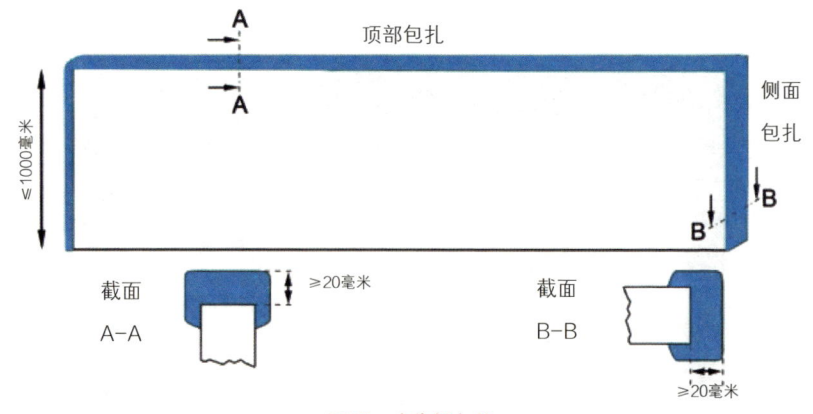

图15 广告板包扎

15.3 出于制作目的，建议广告牌应具有：

- 调暗照度的功能。
- 高于3000赫兹的刷新率。

16 观众区域

以下规格16.2~16.6仅供参考。座椅总成的所有部件均应完全遵守当地和国家的有关法规。

16.1 观众区域应：

- 让公众包括残疾人自由移动。
- 让广大观众能够舒服地观看比赛。
- 从所有的座位上看都有无障碍的视线（图16），除非当地标准允许偏差。
- 对于所有可触及部件的设计不应带有锐利的边缘/角。

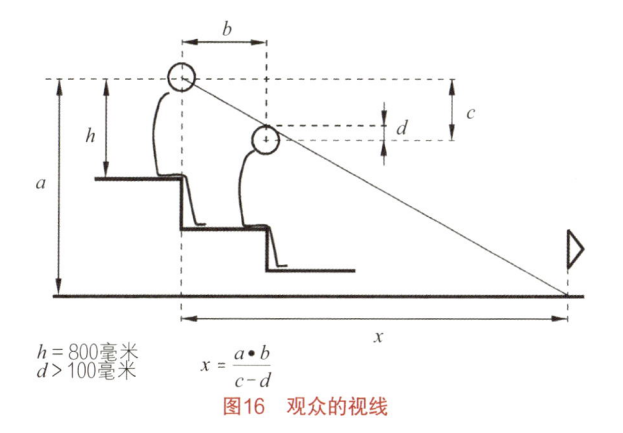

$h = 800$ 毫米
$d > 100$ 毫米

$$x = \frac{a \cdot b}{c - d}$$

图16 观众的视线

16.2 座位的容量限定如下，除非当地标准允许偏差：

- 体育馆的总容量是就座和站立位置数量的总和。
- 就座位置的数量是座位的总数量，或以台阶（或长凳）的总长度（毫米）除以480毫米。
- 站立位置的数量是指定的10平方米可站立35名观众的地面空地。

16.3 除非当地标准允许偏差，否则座椅应符合以下规定：

- 座椅不同部件的材料应符合EN 13200-4：观众设施中所述的要求；座位；产品特性。

- 所有金属部件，包括安装所需的固定件和紧固件，应根据EN ISO 9227：人工大气中的腐蚀试验耐腐蚀；盐雾试验。
- 所有塑料部件均应符合EN ISO 4892-2：塑料的耐大气介质/光稳定性的要求；暴露于实验室光源的方法；氙弧灯。
- 座椅总成的所有部件应完全符合国家有关销售和安装区域消防安全的规定。

16.4 除非当地标准规定偏差，否则建议参考图17进行以下安装：
- F：座深不得小于350毫米。
- Cse：座椅高度不得超过450毫米。
- S：靠背高度（如果适用）应不小于450毫米。

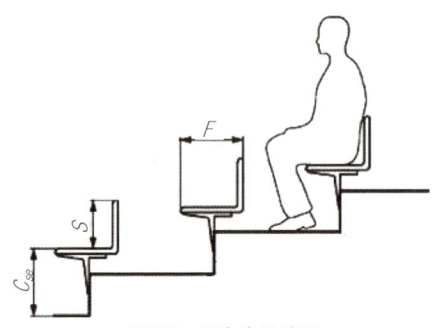

图17 观众座位建议

16.5 建议座椅符合以下测试：
- 参照EN 1728，座椅和靠背静载荷试验。
- 参照EN 1728，座椅前边缘静载荷试验。
- 参照EN 1728，在靠背上进行水平向前静态负载试验。
- 参照EN 1728，背部垂直荷载。
- 参照EN 1728，臂侧静载荷。
- 参照EN 1728，臂向下静载荷。
- 参照EN 1728，座椅和靠背组合耐久性试验。
- 参照EN 1728，座椅前缘耐久性试验。
- 参照EN 12727，向后水平向前耐久性试验。
- 参照EN 1728，进行臂耐久性试验。

- 参照EN 1728，座椅冲击试验。
- 参照EN 1728，臂冲击试验。
- 参照EN 1728，进行背冲击试验。
- 参照EN 1728，倾翻座椅操作试验。

16.6 除非当地标准允许偏差，否则座椅标记应包含以下内容：

- 制造商的名称标识或商标。
- 产品识别方式。
- 批号。
- 生产年份。

17 参考

[1] 国际篮联测试方法和要求手册，国际篮联器材和场馆中心.

[2] SIS标准的国家颜色体系，文档号：SS019102.

[3] RAL颜色标准.

[4] EN 1270：赛场设备、篮球设备功能和安全要求及测试方法.

[5] EN 14808：运动区表面-减震性测定.

[6] EN 14809：运动区表面-垂直变形的测定.

[7] EN 12235：运动区表面-垂直球行为的测定.

[8] EN 13036-4：道路和机场表面特性-试验方法-第4部分：表面防滑/防滑测量方法-摆锤试验.

[9] EN ISO 5470-1：橡胶或塑料涂层织物-耐磨性测定-第1部分：泰伯研磨机.

[10] EN 1569：运动场表面-滚动载荷下性能的测定.

[11] EN 71-3+A1：玩具安全-第3部分：某些元素铝、锑、砷、钡、镉、铬(iii)、铬(vi)、钴、铜、铅、锰、汞、镍、硒、锶、锡和锌的迁移.

[12] REACH建议：多环芳烃测试符合REACH建议附件十七-苯并[a]芘（BaP）、苯并[e]芘（BeP）、苯并[a]蒽（BaA）、䓛（CHR）、苯并[b]荧蒽（BbFA）、苯并[k]荧蒽（BkFA）和二苯并[a, h]蒽并

（DBAha）.

[13] REACH建议：按照REACH建议附件十七-邻苯二甲酸二-2-乙基己酯（DEHP、邻苯二甲酸二异壬酯（DINP）、邻苯二甲酸二丁酯（DBP）、邻苯二甲酸二正辛酯（DNOP）、邻苯二甲酸苄丁酯（BBP）和邻苯二甲酸二异癸酯（DIDP）进行邻苯二甲酸二异辛酯测试.

[14] EN 13200-4：观众设施-座椅-产品特性.

[15] EN ISO 9227：人工大气中的腐蚀试验-盐雾试验.

[16] EN ISO 4892-2：塑料-实验室光源暴露方法-氙弧灯.

[17] EN 1728：家具-座椅-强度和耐久性测定的试验方法.

[18] EN 12727：家具-分级座椅-安全、强度和耐久性要求.